THE OTHER
NINTH
AIR FORCE

THE OTHER NINTH AIR FORCE

NINTH US ARMY LIGHT AIRCRAFT OPERATIONS IN EUROPE, 1944-45

KEN WAKEFIELD

FONTHILL

Learn more about Fonthill Media. Join our mailing list to
find out about our latest titles and special offers at:
www.fonthillmedia.com

Fonthill Media Limited
Fonthill Media LLC
www.fonthillmedia.com
office@fonthillmedia.com

First published in the United Kingdom 2014 and the United States of America 2014

British Library Cataloguing in Publication Data:
A catalogue record for this book is available from the British Library

Typeset in 10pt on 13pt Minion Pro
Printed and bound in England

Connect with us
 facebook.com/fonthillmedia  twitter.com/fonthillmedia

CONTENTS

Introduction

In October 1943, the US Ninth Air Force, previously in the Mediterranean theatre of operations, was re-formed in Britain to provide tactical air support for ground forces in the forthcoming battle to free Europe from German occupation. Like the strategic Eighth Air Force, which had been pounding targets in Germany and occupied territory alongside the Royal Air Force since 1942, the Ninth was to gain wide and worthy recognition, but there was another comparatively unknown 'Ninth Air Force'. Known to some as 'Colonel Leich's Air Force' and to others as the 'Conquer Air Force', this was the fleet of aircraft operated autonomously by the Ninth US Army, but unlike the powerful fighters, medium bombers and troop carriers of the Ninth Air Force proper, this 'other Ninth Air Force' consisted of 200–300 liaison (L-classification) light aircraft, flown and maintained by Field Artillery personnel. They were used primarily as Air Observation Posts (Air OPs), seeking frontline targets and adjusting artillery fire on them, but they also carried out visual reconnaissance, general observation, administrative, photographic and other missions, mainly for the Artillery but also for the Infantry, Armored, Intelligence and other Sections that made up an Army Headquarters. By the end of the war, Ninth US Army (NUSA) light aircraft had flown 45,489 combat missions, of which 9,446 were directing artillery fire.

Light aircraft also equipped Liaison Squadrons of the US Army Air Force, one such squadron being attached to the headquarters of each US Army in Europe. These 'air' units had much in common with the Artillery Air Sections of Army Ground Forces, although their missions were wider ranging. Chief among them were priority mail runs and the transportation of couriers and other personnel between command posts, but other tasks included low-altitude visual and photographic reconnaissance, telephone wire-laying, casualty evacuation, the delivery of maps to fast moving armoured units, and directing fighter-bomber attacks on enemy armour and other targets.

Unlike the First and Third US Armies, comparatively little is known about the Ninth Army, yet its operational life began only a few weeks after D-Day, when it took over from the Third Army the assault on Brest, and ended in May 1945, when ordered to halt its advance when only 53 miles from Berlin. Along the way the Ninth was the first Allied army to reach and cross the River Elbe and in nineteen days advanced 230 miles into Germany, capturing 758,923 enemy troops, freeing 600,000 Allied prisoners of war, and liberating more than a million displaced persons.

The communications codename for Headquarters Ninth US Army was *Conquer*, and no name could have been more appropriate. In nine months and ten days of combat it achieved much, with its light aircraft, their pilots, observers and ground crews playing their part in full.

Sources and Acknowledgements

This book might best be described as an in-depth look at how the Artillery Air Section of a US Army Headquarters functioned during the Second World War. It relates how Air OP aircraft of an American Army were assigned, crewed, operated, serviced and repaired, as recorded by the officer responsible for such matters at an Army headquarters. In this instance the headquarters was that of Ninth US Army, and the officer responsible was the late Brig. Gen. Robert M. 'Bob' Leich. Among his many duties as Army Artillery Air Officer, Lt Col. (as he then was) Leich maintained a daily journal which he retained after the war, and this is the principal source on which this book is based. The result is a 'war diary' of a different kind, revealing in detail events of an operational and administrative nature that took place each day in the Air Section of the Army's headquarters. In addition to covering artillery Air OP operations, the journal well illustrates the close connection that existed between Headquarters Ninth Army and the two USAAF squadrons attached to it, namely the 125th Liaison Squadron, which carried out communications and other duties, and the 50th Mobile Reclamation and Repair Squadron, responsible for the major servicing and repair of Ninth Army aircraft.

The opportunity to make use of the journal is entirely due to Robert M. 'Bob' Leich Jr, son of the former Ninth Army Artillery Air Officer and himself a former US Army officer and Vietnam veteran. Bob inherited his father's journal and other records, including his flying log books and numerous photographs, and unhesitatingly made this unique collection available to me. Without his co-operation this book could not have been written, and my thanks go to Bob for his kind help, unfailing support, generosity, and friendly encouragement.

To present an overall view of the Ninth Army's combat operations, extensive use has also been made of other official documents, including after action reports, station lists, unit histories, orders of battle and other records kindly made available by the library of the US Army Field Artillery School at Fort Sill, Oklahoma. My thanks also go to the US Air Force Historical Research Center at Maxwell Air Force Base, Alabama, for providing copies of records of the two USAAF units attached to Ninth Army, and to the British National Archives, which provided access to Royal Air Force records, including those of Embarkation Units contracted to administer the arrival at British ports of crated American liaison and other aircraft.

Some of the information obtained from these records fulfils a secondary function. Many of the liaison aircraft mentioned in them survived the war and in recent years an increasingly large number of them, mainly Piper L-4s and Stinson L-5s, have been restored to their wartime colours and markings. However, a major problem for restorers has been establishing the unit to which specific aircraft were assigned, and without this knowledge it is impossible to apply the authentic unit or 'squadron code' markings they originally carried. This difficulty arises because aircraft intended for use by Army Ground Forces were procured by the USAAF and their individual aircraft record cards (raised upon acceptance from the manufacturer) show only the Air Force units to which aircraft were assigned. Entries ceased when liaison aircraft were transferred to Army Ground Forces and resumed only when they returned to Air Force control, usually to be salvaged or stored prior to disposal as war surplus equipment. Unfortunately, ground forces did not maintain a similar record card, so details of the units to which their aircraft were assigned cannot readily be traced. Fortunately, this information occasionally comes to light in other documentation, and especially useful in this respect have been the Ninth Army Air Journal and the records of the 50th Mobile Reclamation and Repair Squadron. Accordingly, this book contains many references to specific liaison aircraft by their USAAF serial or 'tail' numbers, and while these will be of minimal interest to some readers, they are included for the benefit of the many owners and restorers of these historic aircraft. In this connection it should be borne in mind that such details are not restricted to aircraft operated only by Ninth Army units. Divisions and non-divisional battalions frequently moved between armies, with the result that many of the Ninth Army aircraft specifically mentioned in this book also served at other times with the First, Third and other US Armies.

Of the other material used in the preparation of this book, much of it, including a number of photographs, came from the late Lt Col. Charles W. 'Chuck' Lefever, the former Artillery Air Officer at Headquarters 12th Army Group. In this capacity Chuck, a very good friend now sadly passed on, was responsible for overseeing the supply of aircraft, pilots and air-related supplies to the armies of 12th Army Group and he provided valuable guidance to me on these matters. I am similarly indebted to the late Colonel William R. 'Randy' Mathews, the former Assistant Artillery Air Officer at Headquarters Ninth Army, whom I had the good fortune to meet in his home in San Antonio, Texas. For anecdotes and other recollections I am most grateful to Andrew T. Kennedy Jr, Joseph F. Gordon, the late William R. 'Bill' Roberts, Edwin D. 'Skeeter' Carlson, Ray E. Davis and Allen H. Knisley. My sincere thanks also go to my son Paul, for producing the maps; to Paul Smith, for his considerable help in compiling Appendix 6; and to Richard Haynes, who kindly supplied a number of photographs relating to the 50th Mobile Reclamation and Repair Squadron. Photographs also came from other private collections, as credited in the captions, and my thanks go to their owners for permission to use them. Some of the photographs are of inferior quality but they are included for their historical interest. The origins of some are also obscure and in some cases it has been impossible to establish their true copyright, but when known such details are given in the caption. Finally, to anyone whose name I have inadvertently failed to mention I can only apologise; to all who made a contribution, no matter how small, I am most grateful.

Ken Wakefield

Prologue

I first became aware of US liaison aircraft in 1943, when I was fifteen years old and living with my parents in Bristol. This was the time of the huge pre D-Day build-up of US forces in Britain, and Bristol, with its docks at Avonmouth, played a significant part in this. Together with much other US war material, Avonmouth received many crated and partly dismantled aircraft, the majority of which continued by road to Filton, the factory airfield of the Bristol Aeroplane Company and also, at that time, the home of IX Base Aircraft Assembly Depot of the US 9th Air Force. When assembled these aircraft – mainly fighter and communications aircraft – were test flown and then delivered to units. Being a keen young aviation enthusiast I welcomed this activity, and I was similarly enthusiastic about the later arrival of US liaison aircraft. These included what was almost certainly the smallest, slowest and quietest operational aircraft of the Second World War – the Piper L-4 Cub.* Although I was unaware of it at the time, the appearance of this type coincided with the arrival of Headquarters First US Army at Clifton College, Bristol. Operated by the Artillery Air Section of that Headquarters, the Cubs flew from the college sports field at nearby Abbots Leigh, and it was this 'off airport' activity that particularly fascinated me. I was similarly drawn to the Stinson L-5 Sentinels that operated from both the Abbots Leigh airstrip and Bristol's Whitchurch Airport, which was close to my home and was the main base of British Overseas Airways Corporation (BOAC) in wartime. It also housed an Air Transport Auxiliary Ferry Pool and a depot of the Bristol Aeroplane Company. With the arrival of D-Day, and the associated departure of First US Army to Normandy, the L-4s and L-5s disappeared from the scene, only to reappear shortly afterwards when HQ Ninth Army took over the vacated Clifton College premises.

Before and during the war I spent much of my free time watching the extensive flying that took place at Whitchurch, and after leaving school in 1944, I was able to get even closer to aeroplanes by obtaining a job there as a junior clerk with BOAC. At lunchtime each day I would wander among the variety of aircraft parked on the airport's north side, but one day in August 1944 my attention was drawn to an L-4 Cub parked some 800 yards distant on the south side. The Cub then started to taxi, and moments later it was airborne, heading

* The official name of the L-4 was the Grasshopper, but it was more widely known as the Cub, the name of the light civil aircraft from which it evolved.

in my direction at a height of no more than a few feet above the grass. The Cub passed over the airport's east-west runway and then landed, slowed down and came to a stop close to a petrol bowser beside which I was standing. The pilot then switched off the Cub's engine and casually climbed out to have a few words with the bowser driver before refuelling his aircraft. I was fascinated by this remarkable demonstration of 'airborne taxiing', and from that day on I was a Cub enthusiast.

Although this was my first close-up encounter with an L-4, I failed to make a note of its serial number, something I often did upon seeing a 'new' type of aircraft at close quarters for the first time. Nor, apart from the fact that he was a US Army officer, do I recall anything about the pilot, and I now regret both omissions for in recent years I have discovered that the pilot was almost certainly Lt Col. Robert M. Leich, the Ninth Army's Artillery Air Officer, whose Air Section's lone L-4 was based at Whitchurch at that time.

Fascinated by that experience, I resolved that one day I would own a Cub and this eventually came about in 1982, shortly after I retired from a long career as an airline pilot. Research into my Cub's history subsequently revealed that it was an L-4H that arrived in the UK at Avonmouth Docks in July 1944, as crated deck cargo on the tanker *Bulklube* and had then been assigned to the Ninth US Army. It was therefore quite an occasion when, in September 2002, I was able to take Bob Leich Jr, son of the former Ninth Army Air Officer, for a flight in one of his late father's wartime Cubs. This took place from a farm airstrip near Bristol, following which I took Bob to see his father's wartime headquarters accommodation in Clifton College. For both Bob and myself, it was a day to remember.

US Army Abbreviations

1/Lt or 1st Lt	First Lieutenant
2/Lt or 2nd Lt	Second Lieutenant
AA	Anti-Aircraft
AAA	Anti-Aircraft Artillery
AADA	Advanced Air Depot Area
AAF	Army Air Forces
Abn	Airborne (Division)
AC	Air Corps
ADA	Air Depot Area
ADG	Air Depot Group
AEF	Allied Expeditionary Force
AF	Air Force
AFSC	Air Force Service Command
AGF	Army Ground Forces
Air OP	Air Observation Post
ALG	Advanced Landing Ground
AOG	Aircraft On Ground (awaiting replacement parts)
Armd	Armored (Division)
Arty	Artillery
ASC	Air Service Command
Asst	Assistant
BAAD	Base Aircraft Assembly Depot
BAD	Base Air Depot
Bgde	Brigade
Bn	Battalion
Brig. Gen.	Brigadier General
Bty	Battery
cal	Calibre
Capt.	Captain
CG	Commanding General
Cmnd	Command
CO	Commanding Officer

Col.	Colonel
Com Z	Communications Zone (formerly Services of Supply)
CP	Command Post
Cpl	Corporal
Det	Detachment
Dsp	Disposal
Div	Division
Engnr	Engineer
ETO	European Theater of Operations
ETOUSA	European Theater of Operations, United States Army
Evac	Evacuation
FA	Field Artillery
FUSA	First US Army
FUSAG	First US Army Group
Gen.	General
GFRC	Ground Forces Reinforcement Center
GI	Government Issue (equipment); also term for a US soldier
Gp	Group
Hosp	Hospital
Inf	Infantry
HQ	Headquarters
LCT	Landing Craft, Tank
LS	Liaison Squadron
LST	Landing Ship, Tank
Lt	Lieutenant
Lt Col.	Lieutenant Colonel
Lt Gen.	Lieutenant General
Maj.	Major
Maj. Gen.	Major General
MIA	Missing in Action
MP	Military Police
MR&RS	Mobile Reclamation and Repair Squadron
M/Sgt	Master Sergeant
NUSA	Ninth US Army
Ops	Operations
Pfc	Private, First Class
PTO	Pacific Theater of Operations
Pvt.	Private
RAF	Royal Air Force
RD	Replacement Depot
Recce	Reconnaissance
RON	Remain overnight
Serv Gp	Service Group

Sgt	Sergeant
SHAEF	Supreme Headquarters, Allied Expeditionary Force
SOS	Services of Supply (later Com Z)
Sq	Squadron
S/L	Squadron Leader
S/Sgt	Staff Sergeant
T/1 (2, 3, 4, 5)	Technician, 1st (2nd, 3rd, 4th, 5th) Grade
TAC	Tactical Air Command
TAD	Tactical Air Depot
TCG	Troop Carrier Group
TD	Tank Destroyer
TO&E	Table of Organization and Equipment
T/Sgt	Technical Sergeant
TUSA	Third US Army
USAAF	United States Army Air Forces
USSTAFE	United States Strategic Air Forces in Europe
WO	Warrant Officer

CHAPTER 1

Wings for Army Ground Forces

In 1942, US Army Ground Forces, dissatisfied with some aspects of the service it was receiving from the US Army Air Corps, won the right to operate its own light aircraft for artillery air observation purposes. In so doing it overcame stiff opposition not only from the Air Corps, shortly to become Army Air Forces (AAF) but also from certain senior officers within Ground Forces. In the hierarchy of both organisations there was resistance to change, but on 6 June 1942, the War Department issued a directive authorising 'organic' aviation for Army Ground Forces (AGF). Implementing the new policy, the War Department approved the allocation of two light Observation O-class (later redesignated Liaison or L-class) aircraft to each Field Artillery Battalion, with two more going to the Artillery Headquarters at Army, Corps, Division, Brigade and Group levels. Accordingly, each infantry and airborne division received ten light aircraft, two being allocated to the Division Artillery Headquarters (Div Arty HQ) and two to each of its four Field Artillery (FA) battalions. In armoured divisions, which normally possessed three armoured FA battalions and a Div Arty HQ, the allocation was eight aircraft. Similar numbers were allocated to separate non-divisional battalions, but the number in an FA Brigade or FA Group varied with the number of separate battalions attached to them. Cumulative totals for higher formations were sixty-seventy aircraft in a Corps, with something like 250-300 in an Army. It follows that an Army Group, consisting perhaps of four Armies, might well have 1,000–1,200 Air Observation Post (Air OP) aircraft, as they were termed, an establishment guaranteed to produce many problems with regard to logistics, maintenance, and operational support. Accordingly, the War Department decreed that the AAF was to retain certain responsibilities in support of AGF aviation, including the procurement of aircraft and the supply of spare parts and other related items. Higher echelon servicing, major repair and the assembly of crated AGF aircraft also remained with the AAF, but everyday maintenance and minor repairs were to be handled in-unit by FA mechanics.

There was also AAF involvement in the primary training of FA pilots who, like the AAF's own light aircraft pilots, were officially termed liaison pilots. Upon successfully completing their training course (becoming 'rated' in AAF terminology), pilots of both groups were awarded the same 'L-wings', these taking the form of the standard AAF pilot badge with the letter 'L' superimposed on the shield in the centre. Training up to this point was usually carried out at one of the AAF's civilian contract flight schools, but the operational training that followed was undertaken by the FA itself at Fort Sill, Oklahoma, the home of the Field Artillery School. Here, in addition to training in the adjustment of artillery fire from the air, much practice was given in short field operations and low-level tactical flying. Between August 1942 and August 1945 the school produced 2,769 liaison pilots (2,754 officers and 15 enlisted men) on courses of seven to fourteen weeks' duration, together with 2,269 Airplane Mechanics on courses of five to ten weeks' duration. However, in 1943 a flight school was also established in North Africa to ease the load on FA pilot training in the USA, but graduates of this school were not officially rated as liaison pilots. Accordingly, some were later returned to Fort Sill for this purpose, often after completing many hours of operational flying in North Africa and in due course in Europe.

At FA Battalion level an Air Section normally comprised two liaison pilots, an airplane mechanic, a mechanic's helper (sometimes later upgraded in the field to full mechanic status) and a driver. Observers were not part of an Air Section establishment but were trained FA forward observers assigned to flying duties, usually on a voluntary basis. In practice, however, two observers were often permanently attached to Air Sections, although pilots who were also qualified artillery officers occasionally flew and observed alone. In addition to two aircraft, the equipment of a section comprised a two-and-a-half-ton truck (usually replaced by an M3 half-track in armoured units) and trailer, often augmented by a quarter-ton Jeep. Air Sections were also formed within the Artillery Headquarters at Division, Corps, Army and higher levels, with Artillery Air Officers appointed to supervise Air OP operations in each organisation.

Parallel with the development of FA aviation, the USAAF formed light aircraft squadrons to serve other sections of Army Ground Forces. One Liaison Squadron (LS), as they were called, was assigned to each Army Headquarters, with Flights detached to subsidiary Corps HQs. Squadrons or Flights also served other higher level organisations including, in Europe, HQ 12th Army Group and HQ Communications Zone (Services of Supply). Normally equipped with thirty-two aircraft shared between four Flights and a Headquarters Flight, liaison squadrons were primarily employed on communications duties including the delivery of priority mail and the transportation of key personnel between command posts. They also carried out low-level reconnaissance missions, motor convoy patrols, checks on pipeline installations, telephone wire-laying and the direction of fighter-bomber attacks (known as 'Horsefly' operations) on enemy armour and other close-in targets. If necessary, they could also assist with the direction of artillery fire, but in practice this rarely occurred. Unlike Air OP pilots, who were normally FA officers, the pilots in AAF Liaison Squadrons were, with the exception of squadron and flight commanders, enlisted men, usually with the rank of Staff Sergeant.

Initially five types of liaison aircraft were ordered for service with the US Army, but the two employed operationally in Europe were the Piper L-4 Grasshopper, used mainly by the FA, and the Stinson L-5 Sentinel, favoured by the AAF for its Liaison Squadrons. The two-seat L-4 was of mixed wood, aluminium and steel tube construction with fabric covering. It was powered by a 65 hp Continental O-170-3 (A65-8) engine and, like all liaison aircraft, was unarmed and unarmoured. Its cruising speed was only 75 mph, but an excellent short field performance allowed it to fly from almost any small field or open stretch of road, an essential requirement for operating close to frontline artillery command posts. The first variant to arrive in Europe was the L-4B, followed in greater numbers by the L-4H and later by the L-4J and a number of early L-4As and Bs that had first undergone major overhaul at the Piper Aircraft Corporation factory at Lock Haven, Pennsylvania.

The first L-4s to enter service, the L-4A and B, differed only slightly, the Stevens brake system and Air Associates tailwheel of the L-4A being replaced in the L-4B by Scott brakes and a Scott CST-12 tailwheel. The L-4H, the next military variant, featured a Scott 3-21 tailwheel, a revised shock-mounted instrument panel, and a repositioned ignition switch. (The apparent gap in sub-variants between L-4B and L-4H is because L-4C, D, E, F and G were designations given to former civilian Piper J-3 Cubs, J-4 Cub Coupés and J-5 Cub Cruisers that were impressed into military service and used for training and other non-operational duties.) The L-4J was little more than the L-4H fitted with a Beech-Roby R002 variable-pitch propeller, but this proved unsatisfactory in service and was quickly replaced by the standard fixed-pitch Sensenich 72C42. Late production L-4Js were also fitted with a one-piece windshield in place of the three-piece type of earlier models. One-piece windshields, intended to improve the pilot's view from the cockpit, were also fitted retroactively to earlier variants of the L-4 in service in Europe, these being manufactured locally by a Service Command unit of the 9th Air Force. The L-4A and early production L-4Bs were the only variants that featured a factory-installed radio and electrical system, but this was later removed with the arrival of a portable battery-powered transmitter/receiver. Known as the SCR 610, this was a vehicular version of the standard SCR 609 radio set used by the Field Artillery for short-range communications.

From September 1942, L-4s bound for Britain were dispatched to the US 8th Air Force for onward assignment to Army Ground Forces. Packed in large wooden crates, they were shipped to ports in the north-west of England, destination codename WILDFLOWER, from where the majority went to No. 2 Base Air Depot (BAD 2) at Warton, Lancashire, to be assembled and test flown before going to AGF units. However, in October 1943 this work passed to the newly established IX Air Force Service Command of the 9th Air Force. Depots and other units of this Command were situated in the south of England, and to ease overland transportation problems aircraft were now shipped to southern ports, destination codename SOXO, with Avonmouth Docks, Bristol, the chief recipient. From their arrival port the L-4s, most of which came as deck cargo on tankers, continued by truck or freight train to No. 3 Tactical Air Depot at Grove, near Wantage in Berkshire. Their subsequent onward assignment, mainly to FA units, was in accordance with authorisations issued by the Artillery Air Officers at either HQ First (later renumbered 12th) Army Group or HQ ETOUSA. After D-Day, with the Allies established on the Continent, responsibility for receiving L-4s continued with the 9th Air Force, but others came into Europe via North Africa, Italy and Southern France, the total finally reaching 2,788 and consisting of 213 L-4As, 370 L-4Bs, 1,327 L-4Hs and 878 L-4Js.

As previously mentioned, although officially named the Grasshopper, the L-4 was better known as the Cub, the highly successful civilian light aircraft from which it evolved, but among GIs it also became known by a number of nicknames, among them 'Puddle Jumper', 'Washing Machine', 'Cloth Bomber', 'Flying Jeep', 'Piperschmitt' and 'Charlie Uncle Baker' (C-U-B expressed in the military phonetic alphabet in use at that time). 'Maytag Messerschmitt' was another familiar nickname, and there are two schools of thought on how this originated.

One tongue-in-cheek suggestion was that the low cost Cubs were supplied by Maytag, the 10-cents mail order store, the other being that Cubs were powered by the tiny two-cylinder, air-cooled motor manufactured by Maytag and used by the US Army as a power source for generators, compressors and other devices. Less well known nicknames were 'Giant', used by the HQ staff at Ninth Army Headquarters, and 'Spearhead Stuka', used by men of the 3rd Armored Division, otherwise known as the Spearhead Division. Collectively the FA's Cubs were sometimes referred to as 'the putt-putt air force', but by no means were any of these nicknames used in a derogatory sense. On the contrary, the Cubs and the men who flew them were very highly regarded by frontline infantrymen and tank crews alike.

They first saw action in November 1942, during the North African landings, but their use on a much bigger scale was expected in the forthcoming battles in Europe. In addition to their primary role of locating targets and adjusting fire on them, the duties performed by Air OPs later included the selection of motor convoy routes and monitoring traffic along them. They were also used to find suitable locations for forward command posts and, much like AAF liaison squadrons, carried out courier and communications duties. Later, they regularly flew dawn to dusk patrols along allocated sections of the front line, and also carried infantry officers over future battle areas to observe the terrain.

Although initially equipped with L-4s, the AAF's Liaison Squadrons were quick to adopt the heavier and more powerful L-5 Sentinel, some of which also went to Ground Forces for use by Air Sections at Division, Corps and Army HQs. Like the L-4, the L-5 was a two-seat aircraft of basically similar construction but better equipped for cross-country flying. Its 185 hp Lycoming O-435-1 engine produced a cruising speed of 115 mph, but its field performance, while good by any standard, was slightly inferior to that of the L-4, and its less robust landing gear affected its ability to operate from very rough ground. The initial production model of the L-5 was joined in Europe by the later L-5B, the so-called 'ambulance' version with a 'built-up' rear fuselage that could accommodate a litter ('stretcher' in British army terminology). This shape greatly reduced the rearward view from the cockpit, making it less suitable for artillery 'spotting', but the same fuselage was retained for later versions including the L-5C, -5E and -5G, a few of which also came to Europe. The exact number of L-5s dispatched to Europe is not known but was certainly more than 300. Altogether, approximately 3,200 liaison aircraft (including a few Stinson L-1s, used mainly on air evacuation duties) were shipped to Europe. Handling this large number of crated aircraft presented logistical problems of some magnitude, but careful planning and great expertise in execution overcame them.

CHAPTER 2

The Ninth US Army in Britain, May–August 1944

By the end of May 1944, there were nearly 1.5 million US servicemen in the United Kingdom, trained and ready for the forthcoming battle to free Europe from German occupation. In addition to its two main combat forces – Army Air Forces and Army Ground Forces – this vast US military presence included a huge supply organisation known as Army Service Forces. In the UK this was initially termed Services of Supply (SOS), but in 1944 it was redesignated Communications Zone (Com Z). Its logistics system covered the entire UK which, for administrative purposes including the allocation of camp sites and training grounds, was divided into five regions known as Base Sections. Most AAF units, mainly those of the strategic 8th Air Force but also some belonging to the tactical 9th Air Force, were stationed on airfields in East Anglia and the East Midlands, the area covered by Eastern Base Section. Other 9th Air Force units, mainly troop carrier and fighter groups, were based in the south and south-west of England, where the majority of combat ground troops were also stationed. These areas, together with South Wales, were administered by Southern and Western Base Sections. Elsewhere, troops intended to back up the initial invasion force were spread more thinly in Central and Eastern Base Sections, with others in the Northern Ireland Base Section.

Although the AAF had not then achieved autonomy as an air force, it was already an independent organisation, whereas AGF combat units in the UK came under the control of First Army Group. This Headquarters, retitled 12th Army Group on 14 July 1944, was itself subordinate to Headquarters European Theater of Operations, US Army (HQ ETOUSA), which together with British, Canadian and other Allied armies came under Supreme Headquarters, Allied Expeditionary Forces (SHAEF), with General Dwight D. Eisenhower as Supreme Commander. In total, the US military presence in the UK was enormous, and good communications between the many organisations within it were essential. This was achieved largely through telephone, radio and teleprinter networks, but much also depended on direct contact, mainly by road but also by air, with light liaison aircraft playing an important part.

American participation in Operation *Overlord*, as the invasion was codenamed, was to be led by the First US Army, followed in due course by the Third and Ninth Armies. Before D-Day, the day on which the landings were to begin, most units in Britain had been assigned to the First and Third Armies, the Headquarters of which arrived in Britain in October 1943 and January 1944 respectively. The Ninth Army did not come into existence until 22 May 1944, when the recently formed Eighth US Army was renumbered to prevent confusion with the British Eighth Army. Shortly before this renumbering, three 4-engine Douglas C-54 Skymasters had taken off from Washington, DC, bound for Britain with Lt Gen. William H. Simpson, the new army's Commanding General, and an advance party of key HQ personnel. Most of these officers had previously served with General Simpson, so they came to Britain as an experienced and closely knit team. On arrival they were to familiarise themselves with operating procedures and methods of supply in the European Theater of Operations (ETO), at the same time making arrangements for the arrival of the main body of the Army's Headquarters.

From temporary accommodation at First Army Group Headquarters in Bryanston Square, near Marble Arch in the West End of London, the Ninth's advance party made liaison visits to HQ First Army at Clifton College, Bristol, and HQ Third Army at Peover Hall, Knutsford, Cheshire. Visits were also made to HQ Com Z at Cheltenham, Gloucestershire, to several depots of this vast supply organisation, and to various corps and division HQs in south and south-west England where final preparations were being made for D-Day. It was during this time, too, that arrangements were made for HQ Ninth Army to take over the premises of Clifton College when the First Army departed for the 'far shore', as France was known to the Americans.

Shortly before D-Day – planned for 5 June but postponed until the 6th because of bad weather – participating American units moved into marshalling areas close to their embarkation points on the south and south-west coasts of England. Similarly, British and other Allied forces moved into marshalling areas farther east along the south coast. The initial landing force comprised elements of the First US and Second British Armies, supported by the First Canadian Army and Belgian, Czech, Dutch and Polish units. To prevent German reinforcements reaching the invasion beaches, the seaborne assault was preceded by airborne landings a short distance inland on both flanks. The invasion went largely to plan, despite heavy losses on Omaha, one of the two beaches in the American sector. A beachhead was quickly established and plans then went ahead for the Third Army to arrive in France in July, followed by the Ninth at the end of August.

For Operation *Neptune*, as the D-Day sea- and air-borne landings were codenamed, the L-4s of some participating First Army artillery units were partly dismantled, loaded onto two-and-a-half-ton 6 x 6 GMC trucks and shipped across the English Channel in landing craft. They were to be reassembled on the beaches, but other units were to fly their L-4s to Normandy, a distance of about 170 miles from departure points in southern England, as soon as suitable airstrips became available. However, as L-4s lacked the range to reach the beachhead and, if necessary, divert back to the UK, it was decided to equip them with a temporary auxiliary fuel tank. L-5s serving with Liaison Squadrons and the HQ Air Sections of several participating Corps and Divisions were also to be flown over, but these aircraft had no problem with regard to range.

Despite strong enemy opposition, a 'Cub strip' was quickly established at St-Martin-de-Varreville, adjacent to Utah Beach, and an L-5 and five L-4s of the 4th Infantry Division landed there just one day after D-Day (D+1). That same day, 7 June, a compacted earth emergency landing strip capable of accepting fighter aircraft was opened at Pouppeville, a short distance inland from the southern end of Utah Beach, followed shortly afterwards by more Cub strips. Despite the availability of these landing grounds, some FA units continued to move their L-4s to Normandy by truck and landing craft, some doing so nearly three weeks after D-Day. One such unit was the 3rd Armored Division, which departed the Bruton area of Somerset for Omaha Beach on 24 June. Of this movement Allen H. Knisley, then a lieutenant and the Air Officer of the Division's 67th FA Battalion, recalls:

On June 25, 1944, when we arrived at Omaha, the scene was mass confusion, with a lot of broken equipment, smashed tanks, twisted landing craft, and much half-submerged wreckage. Corpses floated by, one of which became entangled in the propeller of the LST that I was on. Many large ships, part of the invasion armada, sat offshore, still firing big guns over our heads and inland. The first day we spent de-waterproofing our vehicles, but we didn't take our planes off the 6 x 6 trucks until later, when we were inland and could find a pasture big enough from which to take off. There had been some debate prior to the crossing as to why we couldn't just fly the planes across the Channel. The division artillery commander thought that there would be so much air activity and so many barrage balloons around the beach that it wouldn't be practical, and he was right. Thus we removed the wings and placed our two Cubs on 6 x 6 trucks and loaded them aboard the LST.

However, movements by air were more usual by mid-June, and to facilitate this, an Air Marshalling Base had been established at Grove, Berkshire, to brief pilots on their destination airstrip, the route to be flown and other relevant matters. At the same time their L-4s were prepared for the crossing by the Mobile Reclamation and Repair Squadrons that formed No. 3 Tactical Air Depot (TAD), this preparation including the installation of the auxiliary fuel tank. Fabricated from a standard aircraft oxygen bottle, this was installed in the cabin roof, with a supply pipe leading to the main tank in the nose. On arrival in Normandy the auxiliary tank and associated fittings were to be removed and returned to Grove immediately for use on following aircraft.

Other pre-departure work carried out at No. 3 TAD included the application of unit code markings and black and white 'invasion stripes', but these were applied by units themselves on L-4s being moved to Normandy by truck and landing craft. Invasion stripes, officially 'tactical markings' but also known as 'AEF stripes' and 'combat markings', were painted around the wings and rear fuselage of all aircraft belonging to Allied tactical air forces to clearly identify them as friendly to invading army and navy anti-aircraft gunners. The unit codes (more often known as 'squadron code markings') that were applied at the same time consisted of a two-digit number on the side of the fuselage ahead of the star-and-bar national insignia, followed by an individual aircraft identification letter (e.g. 43-E). With ten aircraft in a division, the letters were normally in the range 'A' to 'K', the letter 'I' not being used to avoid confusion with the numeral '1'. However, when the number of aircraft in a unit exceeded ten, the letters were sometimes repeated but either underlined or 'doubled' (e.g. 43-E or 43-EE). Eventually almost every letter of the alphabet was used, including 'I', often when pilots personalised their aircraft by using the first letter of their name. Stencils were normally used for the application of both squadron codes and the much smaller aircraft serial numbers, the latter (minus the first digit and hyphen) being applied across the fin and rudder of the many L-4s that were manufactured without them. Also known as tail numbers, these were used as radio callsigns on non-operational flights and were factory-applied on all L-5s, but only on L-4As and early production L-4Bs, the versions with built-in radios and electrical systems. Non-radio L-4s (late production L-4Bs, L-4Hs and L-4Js) left the factory devoid of tail numbers, their later application being made at USAAF Air Depots following the introduction of portable radio equipment for L-4s operated by the Field Artillery.*

Three weeks after D-Day the main body of Headquarters Ninth US Army arrived at Gourock, near Glasgow, having departed New York on 22 June in the former Cunard liner RMS *Queen Elizabeth*, now serving as a troopship. Then came an overnight train journey to Bristol, where the advance and main parties of the Army Headquarters were reunited in the beautiful Gothic Revival buildings of Clifton College. The historic city of Bristol had long been connected with North America, for it was from there in the year 1497 that explorer John Cabot set sail on a voyage that led to the discovery of Newfoundland, and in so doing initiated a transatlantic link that reached its peak in 1944.

The Ninth's Headquarters, formally activated on 29 June, comprised a number of Sections including an Artillery Section with a subsidiary Air Section commanded by Lt Col. Robert M. 'Bob' Leich, a pre-war private pilot and light aircraft owner. Bob Leich's family owned a long-established wholesale drug business in Evansville, Indiana, but after graduating from Yale University, Bob took a job in New York. This was followed by a period with the US Army's Field Artillery, but in 1929 he returned to Evansville to join the family business. In addition to his aviation interests, Bob Leich was a keen photographer and in the 1930s recorded much that took place at Evansville Municipal Airport. With America's entry into the war he immediately volunteered for active duty, and in 1942 was one of a small group of artillery officers selected to take part in trials using light aircraft to direct artillery fire. All the members of this group, later known as the 'Class Before One', had previous flying experience and after further training with the AAF and Field Artillery they participated in a number of exercises. These proved quite conclusively that light aircraft could be used to direct artillery fire, so following War Office acceptance of this (as reported in Chapter 1) approval was given for a Department of Air Training to be formed within the Field Artillery School at Fort Sill, near Lawton, Oklahoma, to train both pilots and mechanics. Leich, now a Major, subsequently remained at Fort Sill as an instructor, and in June 1942 he became the Department's Engineering and Maintenance Officer. Of Bob Leich's time at Fort Sill, Lt Col. Charles W. Lefever, the Artillery Air Officer at Headquarters 12th Army Group, later said, 'He set standards of pilot and mechanic training that played an essential part in ensuring the success of Field Artillery aviation.'

While at Fort Sill, Bob Leich had flown Piper L-4Bs, Taylorcraft L-2Bs and Aeronca L-3Bs, the three types initially intended for use as Air OPs. Of these, the L-4 became the standard Air OP; the others, with the exception of a few L-3s, were relegated to training and other

---

* Entries in the Ninth's Air Section daily journal and elsewhere in this book do not always indicate the sub-variant of any particular L-4, but if required this can be found by checking its serial number against the list given in Appendix 5.

non-operational duties. As previously stated, for its own Liaison Squadrons the AAF opted for the L-5 Sentinel, but in 1943 a few of these were also made available to Ground Forces and, on 9 August, Leich flew one for the first time. This was with Capt. W. H. Greenleaf, an AAF flight instructor, and two days later, after a second short training session, Bob Leich flew the L-5 solo. From then on his flying was mainly in this type, but on 3 November he broke new ground by flying a Piper J-5D (registration NX41552), a modified military version of the three-seat J-5C Cub Cruiser then being evaluated as an eventual replacement for the L-4. Also known as a J-5CO, the J-5D was the prototype of what eventually became the L-14, but an order for 850 of these aircraft was cancelled when the war ended. Leich continued to fly L-5s, but reverted to L-4s in March 1944, and it was in one of these, on 16 April, that he made his last flight from Fort Sill's Post Field before proceeding to the UK to join HQ NUSA. As Army Artillery Air Officer, Lt Col. (as he now was) Leich was to assume responsibility for all aspects of Air OP operations in the Ninth Army.

From late June 1944 it was expected that reinforcements for the ETO would sail directly from the United States to France, but when the Allies failed to capture the ports of Cherbourg, Brest and Le Havre as quickly as anticipated, units were diverted to Britain. Accordingly, until HQ NUSA itself departed for the Continent it was to receive, accommodate and train new arrivals during their temporary stay in Britain. In preparation for this task, parties from HQ NUSA travelled widely over south-west England and south Wales familiarising themselves with available facilities. Visits were also made to France in order to maintain contact with operations there.

In connection with his duties as Artillery Air Officer (often abbreviated to Arty Air Officer) Bob Leich was also to liaise with other senior Arty Air Officers in Britain, and this brought him into contact with three former 'Class Before One' colleagues. These were Major Charles W. 'Chuck' Lefever, the Arty Air Officer at HQ 12th Army Group; Major Delbert L. Bristol, now Arty Air Officer at HQ First Army (FUSA); and Major Bryce Wilson, in a similar capacity at HQ Third Army (TUSA). Another senior FA pilot in the UK was Major Eugene P. Gillespie, recently arrived from action in North Africa to become Arty Air Officer at HQ ETOUSA. A graduate of FA Pilot Course No. 3, Gillespie was one of the few trainees to leave Fort Sill with 'EX' (Excellent) ratings in both pilot and mechanic categories.

After taking up his new appointment and gaining familiarity with the Bristol area, Leich decided to base his Air Section's aircraft, when received, at Whitchurch, the city's pre-war civil airport. Located on the southern outskirts of Bristol, Whitchurch was the main wartime base of British Overseas Airways Corporation (one of the predecessors of what is now British Airways), and it was from here that Bob Leich made his first flight in the ETO. This was on 3 July, when he flew an L-4H from Whitchurch to Heston, accompanied by Major Chuck Lever of 12th Army Group.

It appears that this L-4H (serial number 43-30299) was on loan to the Ninth's Air Section until it received its own aircraft. The personal flying log books of Leich and Lefever show that neither officer had flown 43-30299 to Whitchurch, so presumably it was delivered, and later collected, by a ferry pilot from No. 3 TAD at Grove, where it had been assembled following its arrival in the UK on 26 April 1944. Records further show that 43-30299 was transferred from No. 3 TAD to Army Ground Forces on 9 July, six days after it was first flown by Leich and Lefever. Heston was the airfield closest to the Army Group's London HQ, and from there the two officers continued to Grove on 5 July, returning to Whitchurch that same day.

On 10 July, Whitchurch experienced its first and only accident involving a US liaison aircraft. This occurred when a Miles Master of the RAF collided with an L-5 while both aircraft were landing. The Master, which was from No. 3 Flying Instructors' School at nearby Lulsgate Bottom airfield (now Bristol International Airport), was about to touch down when it struck the L-5, which was ahead of it. Both aircraft crashed and caught fire on impact, injuring the two crew members in each. These details are given in an RAF accident report, together with the serial number of the Master and the names of its two pilots, but no similar information is given in respect of the L-5, which remains unidentified. It is fairly certain, however, that it belonged to Army Ground Forces as the event is not recorded either in USAAF accident reports or in the unit histories of the two USAAF Liaison Squadrons then in the UK. Nor, somewhat surprisingly, is the incident mentioned in the journal of the Ninth Army HQ Air Section, which was then resident at Whitchurch. Accordingly, with the First Army now on the Continent, it seems most likely that this L-5 belonged to the Third Army, which at that time was still in the UK with its HQ Air Sections at Army, Corps and Division levels each receiving two aircraft of this type.

Lt Col. Leich and Major Lefever flew together again on 15 July, this time to No. 1 Base Air Depot at Burtonwood, Lancashire, for discussions on the future supply of aviation items to FA units. On this occasion they used Chuck Lefever's personally assigned L-5 (42-98565), which the 12th Army Group Air Officer had flown from Heston to Whitchurch the previous day. Following the meeting at Burtonwood, Leich and Lefever returned to Bristol, but because of bad weather at Whitchurch they landed at Filton, on the northern outskirts of the city. Major Lefever's L-5 was used again on 17 July, when the two officers flew to Grove for Lt Col. Leich to collect an L-4H assigned to his Air Section and which he flew back to Whitchurch the same day. Unlikely as it seemed at the time, this aircraft (43-30373) was to remain with HQ NUSA until the end of the war.

In addition to BOAC, Whitchurch was also occupied by No. 2 Ferry Pool of the Air Transport Auxiliary and by the Bristol Aeroplane Company, which assembled Beaufighter Mk II night fighters in premises on the airport's south side. From early 1944 until just before D-Day, the south side also housed a detached Flight of L-5 Sentinels of the 153rd Liaison Squadron, the Ninth Air Force unit attached to HQ First Army. During their stay these L-5s shared a 'T'-Type hangar with newly assembled Beaufighters, and it was here, in what was known as the Flight Shed, that Bob Leich was now able to hangar his L-4.

Among other tasks the Ninth's Arty Air Officer was now busily engaged arranging accommodation and airstrips for FA Air Sections as they arrived in Britain. He was also required to liaise with HQ ETOUSA and certain AAF Depots over the supply of aircraft, spare parts, tool kits and other equipment, and this involved much personal contact. To facilitate this, Bob Leich made extensive use of his recently acquired L-4, his flights in July including several more to Grove and one to Smith's Lawn, the airstrip within Windsor

Great Park that served HQ IX Air Force Service Command and HQ ETOUSA, both of which were located on nearby Ascot racecourse.

Meanwhile, on 28 May, the 125th Liaison Squadron, the USAAF unit destined to provide a courier and general communications service for HQ Ninth Army, had departed the USA, initially assigned to United States Strategic Air Forces in Europe (USSTAFE). Originally known as the 125th Observation Squadron, this unit was formed in July 1940 as part of the Oklahoma National Guard and was activated in February 1941. In July 1942 it became the 125th Observation Squadron (Light), followed by a further change in designation to 125th Liaison Squadron in April 1943. Its overseas deployment began on 15 May 1944, when the ground component of the squadron departed Thermal, California, on a four-day journey to the New York port of embarkation at Fort Hamilton. The squadrons' pilots, who had been attending a briefing at Savannah, Georgia, joined the ground personnel at Fort Hamilton and on 28 May the entire unit boarded the SS *Louis Pasteur*. On arrival at Liverpool on 6 June the squadron, under the command of Capt. Frederick H. Lenczyk, was reassigned to the Ninth Air Force and proceeded to Camp 'G' near Cheltenham, Gloucestershire, to re-equip and gather supplies from depots scattered over the south and west of England. On 19 June, the 125th moved to nearby Chedworth, where it received the first of thirty-two L-5s and began local familiarisation flying and training in UK procedures. However, Chedworth, a busy RAF airfield, was considered unsuitable by the 125th and, on 9 July, the squadron moved to New Zealand Farm, a small grass RAF airfield on the edge of Salisbury Plain, with personnel accommodated in a large manor house in the nearby village of Erlestoke.

The 125th LS was to be attached to the Ninth Army with effect from 17 July, to carry out mail and passenger services between the Army HQ and other HQs and command posts, but some elements of the squadron were to remain on temporary attachment to other organisations. These included 'D' Flight, which was with HQ Southern Base Section at Wilton, near Salisbury, and it was here that the squadron experienced its first accident in the UK. This occurred on 12 July, when one of its L-5s (42-99316) was damaged while on a courier mission from the Relief Landing Ground (RLG) at Oatlands Hill, near Stonehenge, to a short strip located on sloping ground two miles east of Wilton. While landing into wind but downhill, the L-5's brakes failed to hold on wet grass and it overran the strip and crashed into a tree, damaging its left wing, rear left strut and propeller. The pilot, S/Sgt Quentin L. Anderson, was unhurt, but in another 125th LS accident on 17 July both crew members were badly injured. This occurred during a practice message-dropping exercise at New Zealand Farm where, after a low run to drop a message, a second low-speed approach was made to indicate to personnel on the ground exactly where the message had fallen in long grass. However, upon applying power to climb away, the L-5's engine failed, probably due to carburettor icing, and before speed could be regained the aircraft stalled and crashed onto the airfield. The L-5 (42-99356) was destroyed on impact, but fortunately it did not catch fire and 2/Lt Donald K. Neill, pilot, and 1/Lt Frank J. Heineman, observer, were removed from the wreckage and taken to hospital.

Although most of the units coming under the jurisdiction of HQ NUSA were newly arrived from the United States, exceptions were the 82nd and 101st Airborne Divisions, now back in the UK to re-form and re-equip after participating in the initial D-Day landings. On 13 July, the 82nd returned to Leicestershire, where its HQ was re-established at Braunstone Park, Leicester, with the Div Arty HQ and 319th Glider FA Battalion at Market Harborough, the 320th Glider FA Battalion at Husbands Bosworth, and the 456th Parachute FA Battalion at Hinckley. Two days later, the 101st also returned from Normandy and took up residence as before in Berkshire with its HQ at Greenham Lodge, Newbury, and its three FA battalions (327th Parachute, 321st Glider, and 907th Glider) in the Reading/Newbury area. As part of the re-equipment process, arrangements were made for both divisions to collect any AAF-supplied items they might require from No. 1 Base Air Depot, Burtonwood. Approval for this was given by Major Lefever of 12th Army Group, who also arranged for eight replacement L-4Hs for the 82nd Airborne Division and five for the 101st to be collected from Grove. (The serial numbers of the eight L-4Hs assigned to the 82nd were 44-79550, 44-79552, 44-79553, 44-79556, 44-79634, 44-79657, 44-79660 and 44-79667. Those assigned to the 101st were 43-30506, 43-30515, 43-30517, 44-79637 and 44-79664.)

The L-4Hs for the 82nd were subsequently flown to Husbands Bosworth, from where their pilots, who were billeted in a camp on the outskirts of nearby Market Harborough, were to undertake training and communications flights until next required for combat duty. The five allocated to the 101st Airborne, which already had three aircraft on strength, went to RAF Welford, from where they similarly carried out training and communications flights.

Authorisation for the release of these aircraft, together with instructions for their pre-delivery preparation, including the application of tail numbers and squadron code markings, was given to No. 3 TAD by Lt Col. Leich. However, on 24 July, the very day they were collected from Grove, Capt. Shannon C. Powers of the 101st Airborne Division telephoned the Army HQ Air Section to report that one of their new L-4Hs (44-79664) had been badly damaged when struck by a taxiing Douglas C-47A Skytrain of the 435th Troop Carrier Group. This occurred while the L-4 was parked and tied down at Welford, the airfield the 101st shared with the 435th TCG. No one was injured in the accident, but a replacement was required for the wrecked aircraft, which was later collected and returned to Grove by a crash pick-up crew. In addition to approving this replacement, Major Gillespie at ETOUSA released two more L-4Hs (43-30497 and 43-30511) to the 82nd Airborne Division and one (43-30381) to the 101st Airborne. However, the 101st lost another of its newly acquired Cubs on 28 July when, as reported by Capt. Powers, it 'struck vegetation when a slow and low approach was made in gusty weather'. No one was injured, but the aircraft (44-79637) was badly damaged and duly replaced by another L-4H (43-30405). Further L-4H allocations authorised by HQ ETOUSA at this time were two (43-30396 and 43-30541) to XIII Corps, followed a few days later by a third (43-30514), as requested by Major Sheldon M. Smith, the Corps Arty Air Officer.

On 25 July, a second Ninth Air Force unit, the 50th Mobile Reclamation and Repair Squadron (MR&RS), joined the 125th LS on attachment to HQ NUSA. Formerly one of the IX Air Force Service Command units that comprised No. 3 TAD at Grove, the 50th MR&RS was to carry out the higher echelon maintenance and repair of all aircraft assigned or attached to Ninth Army. It was also to prepare and supply aircraft, together with spares and associated equipment, as agreed during a conference at Grove attended by Major Lefever and Lt Col. Leich. A similar arrangement, which proved highly successful, had previously been adopted with the attachment of the 23rd and 43rd MR&RSs to the First and Third Armies respectively.

For some weeks the First US Army had been making only slow progress in Normandy, where the *bocage* countryside – small fields bordered by deep ditches and high-banked hedges – greatly favoured the defenders. In seventeen days FUSA suffered 40,000 casualties in a hard-fought offensive that advanced only seven miles. Although the Allies had overwhelming air superiority, the close air support initially received by ground forces left something to be desired, but lessons were quickly learned and better support was being given before long to FUSA by its attached IX Tactical Air Command (TAC). This Command was part of the Ninth Air Force, and in a similar manner XIX TAC was duly attached to the Third US Army. Later, when the Ninth Army became operational, it was to be supported by XXIX TAC. Consequently, before leaving for France, Air Sub-Sections were formed within HQ NUSA's G2 (Intelligence) and G3 (Training and Operations) Sections for the purpose of maintaining close contact with its supporting Tactical Air Command. In addition to bomber and fighter-bomber missions, this Command was to use fighter-type aircraft to direct the fire of long-range artillery, but within HQ NUSA, now codenamed *Conquer*, there was disagreement on precisely how such Arty/R operations, as they were termed, should be conducted. In view of this uncertainty it was decided to put the Arty/R issue to one side until further information became available. On the other hand, there was no disagreement whatsoever regarding the control and direction of short- to medium-range artillery by FA-operated Air OP aircraft.

While the L-4 was considered highly satisfactory as an Air OP, it was capable of improvement, and on 28 July, Lt Col. Leich was asked to examine and comment on an L-4H that had been modified by No. 3 TAD. The modifications, which consisted of Plexiglas 'eyebrows' (wing-root fairings) and a new, rounded rear upper cockpit canopy (called a 'turtledeck'), were proposed and designed by a corporal at the depot. (Another report states that Plexiglas eyebrows were devised by a Corporal Streeper of the 29th Infantry Division, in recognition of which he was awarded the Legion of Merit by the Commanding General, ETOUSA.) These modifications were intended to improve the all-round view for the crew, with the modified cabin roof additionally improving performance by smoothing the airflow over the existing angular shape. These changes, together with a standard mount for the installation of an SCR 610 radio on the observer's table behind the rear seat, met with the approval of Lt Col. Leich, and this was relayed to both Major Gillespie at ETOUSA and Major Nelson, the Engineer Officer at No. 3 TAD. As a result, it was decided to initiate a programme to so modify all L-4s serving in the ETO.

At the end of July, No. 1 BAD, Burtonwood, anticipating that its association with Ground Forces was coming to an end, released to NUSA all the equipment it was holding for eventual issue to FA air units. At the same time, No. 3 TAD released nineteen L-4Hs to the Ninth Army, but they were to remain at Grove until collected by units as they arrived in the UK. (The serial numbers of these L-4s were 43-30456, 43-30486, 43-30495, 43-30502, 43-30394, 43-30457, 43-30527, 43-30534, 43-30499, 43-30540, 44-79630, 44-79678, 44-79746,

44-79547, 44-79636, 44-79673, 44-79545, 44-79546 and 44-79548.) An advance party from one of these, the 17th Airborne Division, arrived at Camp Chiseldon, near Marlborough, Wiltshire, on 1 August, followed in due course by the main body of the Division and the remainder of the HQ staff including Capt. H. Smith, the Division Arty Air Officer. HQ NUSA now had three Airborne Divisions temporarily under its command, but on 12 August, the 82nd and 101st were to become part of the newly formed First Allied Airborne Army. The 17th Airborne, on the other hand, was to remain with NUSA until 1 January 1945, when it passed to the Third Army.

Advance parties from units now coming to Britain first reported to the Ninth Army HQ at Bristol for details of accommodation, training, equipment and supply procedures. These units included numerous non-divisional battalions in addition to three complete divisions, namely the 9th Armored and 94th and 95th Infantry. Of these, the Advance HQ of the 9th Armored Division arrived at Tidworth, Wiltshire, on 31 July 1944, followed by the Main HQ on 28 August. Training was carried out in the Salisbury Plain area until 23 September, when the Division moved to Dorchester prior to embarking at Weymouth on the 25th. Three days later, the Division arrived at Sainte-Marie-du-Mont and shortly afterwards entered the fray in Brittany. Of the two infantry divisions, the 94th arrived in Wiltshire on 13 August and set up its HQ at Chippenham, but its stay was to be short-lived for it departed for France on 8 September. The 95th Infantry Division's stay was similarly of short duration, its HQ arriving at Winchester on 17 August and departing for France on 15 September.

Other Divisions arriving in the ETO at this time were the 26th Infantry, 104th Infantry, 10th Armored, 44th Infantry and 102nd Infantry. Four of these units were to sail direct to France from the USA, but the fifth, the 102nd, arrived at Gourock, on the Firth of Clyde, on 3 September and then continued to the south coast of England *en route* to France, where it arrived six days later. Between them the divisions now under NUSA's jurisdiction required something like 110 Air OP aircraft, plus others to equip a number of non-divisional FA battalions to be similarly assigned. Of these units, those temporarily remaining in the UK required airstrips in the immediate vicinity of their HQs, but the locations of strips used previously by the First and Third Armies were not known at Ninth Army Headquarters. Accordingly, on 8 August, Lt Col. Leich telephoned Major Lewis, the G3 officer in charge of training areas in Southern Base Section, to determine how land could be acquired for use as airstrips. The acquisition of such land, Leich learned, was carried out under Defence Regulation No. 52, which required the unit commander to first select a suitable field and then give details of its precise location to either the US District HQ (Training Area Liaison Officer) or a British official known as the District Claims Officer, whichever was more convenient. A British Government representative then served notice on the landowner, indicating that the field was to be used by a military unit for a period of ninety days, to be automatically extended if so required. If not in use after ninety days, the field reverted to its owner. In general, Major Lewis reported, British farmers and others readily accepted the requisitioning of land as an important contribution to the war effort, and except in Wales, where there had been terrain problems, no difficulties had been encountered in establishing conveniently located strips of the required size.

For Lt Col. Leich the early part of August continued much like July, including trips in his Cub from Whitchurch to Grove, Smith's Lawn, Heston and Lyneham. On several occasions he was accompanied by either T/Sgt Raymond G. Million or T/4 William B. Hamblen, respectively the mechanic and clerk assigned to the Ninth's HQ Arty Air Section, but when Leich flew to Grove on 4 August, he was accompanied by Col. Hanley, the NUSA Artillery Officer. The purpose of this trip, made in Cub 43-30373, was to attend a meeting with Capt. Haynes of XII Corps and representatives of No. 3 TAD to discuss the continued use of Grove for assembling crated L-4s, the preparation of FA aircraft bound for Normandy, and the use of that airfield as a pre-departure Air Marshalling Base. Major Smith of XIII Corps later suggested that the Arty Air Officer of the 94th Infantry Division, then with its HQ at Chippenham, be appointed Marshalling Area Officer, but ETOUSA's Major Gillespie decided that HQ NUSA should assume this responsibility. In addition to handling FA aircraft bound for Normandy, it was agreed that newly arrived replacement and other pilots would also be briefed at Grove before joining their units in France.

The use of Whitchurch by the NUSA Arty Air Section was a satisfactory arrangement, but on 8 August the civilian Airport Manager, Leonard R. Williams, telephoned the Army HQ to request the removal of poles and overhead wires from the airport's southern boundary. The Airport Manager was under the impression that US Army personnel had erected the wires, which were interfering with the movement of aircraft, but an investigation by Major Goodrich of the Army HQ Signal Section revealed that the General Post Office, the British telephone communications organisation, had actually been responsible and Mr Williams was informed accordingly.

The number of Air OP aircraft required by NUSA continued to increase, and on 9 August, HQ ETOUSA was requested to release another forty aircraft to No. 3 TAD for issue to incoming units. These were the 94th and 95th Infantry Divisions and ten non-divisional FA battalions (the 70th, 193rd, 199th, 211th, 252nd, 259th, 688th, 691st, 692nd and 754th), but another twenty-nine aircraft were soon added to this number to meet the needs of other units expected in the UK by 24 August. Another L-4 was released to NUSA for onward assignment on 14 August, leaving twenty-five still to come to fulfil the initial requirement for that month, but two days later, ETOUSA advised that three L-4s previously released for issue to units were no longer available due to 'emergency far shore replacement requirements'. (On 12 August, these three aircraft had been assigned to FA battalions as follows: 43-30457 to the 199th, 43-30495 to the 193rd, and 43-30536 to the 691st.)

Clearly, developments of some importance were taking place in Normandy. This was further accentuated on 23 August when three Flights of the 125th LS were placed on detached service in France: 'A' Flight (commanded by 1/Lt James C. Young) went to HQ Com Z; 'B' Flight (under 1/Lt Thomas Y. Gardner) to General Patton's Third US Army; and 'D' Flight (2/Lt Preston B. Dumas) to General Bradley's 12th Army Group HQ. The Headquarters Flight (Flight Officer Zaven A. Pachanian) and 'C' Flight (1/Lt William H. Pickles) remained in the UK with HQ NUSA, but an early move to France was expected.

CHAPTER 3

To the Far Shore, September 1944

From hereon each chapter takes the form of a monthly summary of Ninth Army activity, followed by extracts for the same period from the daily journal compiled by Lt Col. Leich, the Artillery Air Officer at Army HQ. This format is adopted from 9 September 1944, on which date HQ NUSA was at Mi-Forêt in Brittany, with its Artillery Air Section at nearby Rennes/ St Jacques airfield. Names, individual letters or numbers that are not clearly discernible in original documents are so indicated by the use of bracketed question marks, while any comments by the author are in square brackets.

A renewed Allied offensive was now developing on the Continent. Progress by the First and Third US Armies, together with the British 21st Army Group and other Allied units, was slow at first but then rapidly gained momentum. Paris fell on 25 August and by the end of the month US troops had crossed the Marne and Aisne rivers. Mons, in Belgium, fell on 2 September and then Brussels, with Amiens, Laon, Rheims and Verdun being taken along the way. Luxembourg was reached on 10 September, and the drive continued eastwards towards Maastricht, Liège and the German border south of Aachen.

Earlier, in anticipation of the Ninth Army's imminent move to France, Lt Col. Bob Leich, accompanied by his mechanic T/Sgt Raymond G. Million, had flown the HQ Air Section's L-4H (43-30373) to No. 3 Tactical Air Depot at Grove to have it prepared for the Channel crossing. The Arty Air Officer and his mechanic then returned to Whitchurch in another L-4H (44-79759), and the next day, 13 August, Bob Leich took two Ninth Army staff officers – Maj. Henry S. Parker and Maj. Morris L. Zimmerman – on local air experience flights in the same aircraft.

On Wednesday 16 August, Bob Leich took off from Whitchurch for the last time. Accompanied by Lt Julian Crocker of HQ NUSA, he was bound for Normandy, routeing via Grove to obtain a cross-channel briefing at the Air Marshalling Base and to collect his original aircraft from the resident No. 3 TAD. Along the way stops were also made at Smith's Lawn and Heston respectively for meetings at SHAEF and 12th Army Group, but after leaving Heston for Grove on 18 August, bad weather forced him to return and complete the journey by road. The poor conditions persisted until the 27th, when an improvement enabled the Arty Air Officer to continue his journey to Normandy. Flying his original L-4H, now displaying invasion stripes and the squadron code markings 63-A, he took off from Grove at 1450 hours, crossed the English coast at 1550 and arrived over Barfleur at 1645. Flying down the east coast of the Cotentin Peninsula he overflew Utah Beach and at 1725 landed at A-21, an Advanced Landing Ground* near Saint-Laurent-sur-Mer, a village situated on the bluffs overlooking Omaha Beach.

His flight time of 2 hours 35 minutes well illustrated the need for the auxiliary fuel tank, as noted by Bob Leich with an entry in his log book that reads 'Aux. gas tank used'. Without this tank he would have run out of fuel at least five minutes before reaching A-21. From this ALG the Arty Air Officer flew three miles along the coast to A-22 at Colleville, followed by a 35-minute flight to a strip near Saint-Sauveur-Lendelin, a small town situated between Périers and Coutances, to await the arrival of his Headquarters. That same day, 27 August, a motor convoy carrying the Staff of HQ NUSA left Bristol, travelling in two sections bound for Southampton on the first stage of a move to the 'far shore', as France was known within the US Army. An uneventful crossing of the English Channel ensued and on 28 and 29 August, *Conquer* and *Conquer Rear*, the forward and rear echelons of the Headquarters, disembarked from landing craft on Utah Beach. Continuing inland, *Conquer* set up a temporary command post (CP) in tents at Saint-Sauveur-Lendelin, with *Conquer Rear* a few miles to the north in a school building at Périers. The Ninth Army was to take over from the Third Army the offensive in Brittany, and in anticipation of this the entire HQ moved almost immediately to Mi-Forêt, a village near Rennes, where both *Conquer* and *Conquer Rear* reopened on 3 September in tents located in the surrounding forest. At the same time Bob Leich, who had earlier met up with his Headquarters at Saint-Sauveur-Lendelin, took up residence with his Air Section on nearby Rennes/St Jacques airfield, otherwise known as A-27.

The events of this time are well recalled by Andrew T. Kennedy Jr, then a Private, First Class (Pfc) on the staff of HQ NUSA. Although not a member of the HQ Air Section, Kennedy was to become closely associated with it, largely because of his previous flying experience. Of that earlier period in his life he recalled:

> I was a pre-war civilian pilot who had learned to fly in Denver in 1940-41, when I was a 15 year old line boy at Old Combs Field. I worked in exchange for flying time, and learned to fly in Aeroncas as we were then the Aeronca distributor for Colorado and Wyoming. We were also Stinson and Beechcraft dealers in the Denver area. Later, in 1942, we dropped Aeronca and took on the Piper distributorship, together with running another airport in

---

* *Advanced Landing Grounds (ALGs), airstrips and airfields opened by American engineer units were prefixed by the letter 'A'. Initially some received 'T' or 'E' prefixes, while others also carried 'C', 'N' or 'D' suffixes to indicate Courier, Night Landing or Air Depot facilities. Other prefixes were 'B' for airstrips etc. prepared by the British, and 'Y' for those opened by American units advancing from the landings in the south of France. At a later date some airfields in Germany used by both British and American units were prefixed 'R'. Light aircraft belonging to Liaison Squadrons and Field Artillery units sometimes made use of ALGs and airfields, but more usually they operated from short strips located close to the unit or HQ they served. Generally known as 'Cub strips', these normally existed only for very short periods and were not numbered.*

Denver, which we renamed Hayden Field, and the airport at Boulder, Colorado. We had the seventh largest Civilian Pilot Training Program (CPTP) in the nation, training army and navy pilots at Hayden Field and navy pilots at Boulder. During the summer of 1942, between graduation from high school and starting college, I was line chief at Hayden Field. I was 18 years old in August and started at the University of Denver in September. In October I took steps to get into the CPTP, and in December I enlisted as a private in the Army Air Corps Reserve through the CPTP. I was supposed to start a Service Pilot course in January 1943, but starting dates were continually pushed back until June, when the type of pilot training I had signed up for was canceled. We were given the choice of volunteering for immediate service as privates in the 'walking air corps' or resigning from the Reserve. I volunteered, completed basic training at Jefferson Barracks, Missouri, and was then sent to the University of Kentucky to take engineering courses in the Army Specialized Training Program. I then went to Fort Leonard Wood to take combat engineer training, after which I was sent overseas as a combat engineer replacement.

Andrew Kennedy was one of several thousand GIs who sailed from New York on 23 July 1944, in the former Cunard liner *Queen Mary*. He arrived at Greenock on the Clyde five days later, and continued to the 11th Replacement Depot at Winsford, Cheshire, to await assignment. He continued:

At Winsford five of us with the highest Army General Classification scores were assigned to Headquarters Ninth Army, then trying to come up to strength before leaving Bristol and becoming operational in France. However, I was at this Headquarters for only about two days before we moved out for France, so I didn't have time to get acquainted with Clifton College. After sailing from Portsmouth on August 30, we lay at anchor all night off the Isle of Wight, and then crossed in a large convoy and landed over Utah Beach late on the night of August 31. Upon arriving in France I was assigned to the Armored Section, but an Artillery Captain in my Section who knew of my interest in aviation, introduced me to our Ninth Army Artillery Air Officer, Lt Col. Robert M. Leich, a pre-war civilian pilot and Aeronca owner. When Col. Leich learned of my background he invited me to fly in his Cubs to observe and get in a little unofficial 'stick time', but I didn't get to fly until later on, when we were in Holland and Germany. At Mi-Forêt the Ninth Army Headquarters was set up in tents in the forest, but our L-4s were kept on a large airport at nearby Rennes, along with air force airplanes. I made one trip to the airport with Colonel Leich and recall that our Cubs were parked close to some P-38s. Bob Leich, one of the Army's first liaison pilots, had been a member of the Class Before One at Fort Sill, where his instructor was Tony Piper, son of the founder of the Piper Aircraft Corporation. Major [as he then was] Leich, then became Engineering/Maintenance Officer in the Department of Air Training at Fort Sill. After the war, when he was a Brigadier-General in the reserve, he was inducted into the Army Aviation Hall of Fame at Fort Rucker.

Ninth Army became operational under 12th Army Group at 12 noon on 6 September, with all US combat forces in Brittany then coming under its command. These units, drawn mainly from the First and Third Armies, included VIII Corps with four Infantry Divisions (2nd, 8th, 29th and 83rd), the 6th Armored Division, and supporting troops. With these units NUSA was to resume the assault on Brest, at the same time protecting the south flank of 12th Army Group along the River Loire as far east as Orléans.

The attack on Brest, a port essential for the reception of units and equipment coming from the United States, was renewed on 8 September, at which time NUSA Air Sections were operating some seventy L-4s, but ten more were expected the next day when the 94th Infantry Division was due to arrive from Britain. The 94th's Arty Air Officer, Capt. Arthur M. Middleton, was already in Brittany and after reporting to the Army Air Section on 5 September he accompanied Lt Col. Leich on a local flight to find a suitable bivouac area for his Air Sections. That same day Bob Leich sent a signal to HQ ETOUSA, asking Major Gillespie to instruct the 94th's pilots, then waiting at Grove Air Marshalling Base, to proceed to A-22 at Colleville, where their Air Officer would meet them.

This was a particularly busy time for Bob Leich, and with his workload likely to increase still further he sought the services of an Assistant Air Officer. More specifically he asked for Lt William R. 'Randy' Mathews, another Class Before One colleague then with the Third Army's 90th Infantry Division. Major Bryce Wilson, the Third's Arty Air Officer, readily agreed to this transfer, adding that he would send Lt Mathews to HQ NUSA by air as soon as he received his August quota of replacement pilots.

The 50th Mobile Reclamation and Repair Squadron, the Ninth Air Force unit attached to HQ NUSA for the major servicing and repair of its aircraft, commenced its move to France on 1 September. From Grove the ground echelon's convoy departed for Southampton, from where it continued to Utah Beach and then on to Saint-Sauveur-Lendelin to join HQ NUSA. As with similar squadrons attached to the other two armies in France, the 50th MR&RS was part of the 2nd Air Depot Area (2nd ADA), an organisation responsible for supplying and supporting Ninth Air Force units on the Continent.

Although its primary task was the higher echelon servicing of Ninth Army Air OPs, a detachment from the 50th MR&RS remained on Utah Beach to assemble partly dismantled truck-mounted L-4s arriving from the UK in landing craft. However, on 14 September, the entire squadron moved to Rennes/St Jacques, but shortly afterwards a detachment returned to the coast near Cherbourg to continue assembling L-4s while another party was detached to an airstrip near Brest to service Air OPs being used in the reduction of that port.

Several supply problems were now being experienced by NUSA Arty Air Sections, chief among them being the acquisition of 73 octane aviation fuel. The use of alternative fuels – including more readily obtainable 100 octane aviation fuel and lower grade motor transport petrol – resulted in engine problems, so every effort was being made by the HQ Air Section to obtain supplies of the correct fuel. Another problem was receiving and assembling crated L-4s that were now being shipped direct from the US to France instead of the UK. With the co-operation of 2nd ADA this matter was resolved quite quickly, but obtaining supplies of 73 octane 'gas' continued to be a problem for some time to come.

By mid-September, HQ NUSA controlled three Corps HQs and twelve Divisions (see Appendix 2 for details), with approximately 140 L-4s on strength, but within a few days the

'Conquer Air Force', as its air component was sometimes known within the Army HQ, had risen to 230, including nearly 100 crated aircraft received direct from the US. In addition, NUSA was served by thirty-two L-5s of the attached 125th LS, which by now was also in Brittany, its ground echelon and Headquarters Flight having been reunited at Saint-Sauveur-Lendelin on 3 September. Two days later, the squadron HQ moved to Rennes/St Jacques airfield, from where HQ and 'C' Flights resumed courier and other missions for HQ NUSA, but shortly afterwards, on 14 September, one of its L-5s (42-99096), flown by Sgt Henry W. Lishaness, was damaged in an accident at Les Nevens. Three Flights had previously been on detached service, but on 15 September, 'B' Flight returned from duty with General Patton's Third Army HQ at Delasse and 'A' Flight returned from HQ Com Z, only to be placed on detached service again with VIII Corps at Brest. 'D' Flight remained with General Bradley's 12th Army Group, now at Buc.

Another Ninth Army connection with the Ninth Air Force occurred at this time with the activation at Vermand of XXIX Tactical Air Command, under Brig. Gen. Richard E. Nugent, on 14 September. Its mission was to provide close air support for NUSA, for which purpose it was assigned four Groups of Republic P-47 Thunderbolt fighter-bombers from the 84th and 303rd Fighter Wings, but XXIX TAC did not become fully operational until early October.

The offensive in Brittany met with strong resistance, but 20,000 German soldiers surrendered at Beaugency (12 miles south-west of Orléans) on 16 September and two days later Brest fell. Isolated pockets of enemy resistance remained in Lorient and Saint-Nazaire, but as they posed no real threat they were bypassed or 'contained', as ordered by 12th Army Group, and did not finally surrender until the end of the war. The main action in Brittany was completed on 20 September, and shortly afterwards HQ NUSA was ordered to move 400 miles eastwards to the Ardennes Forest region of Belgium. It was to take up a position between the First and Third US Armies, along the pre-war German border fortifications known as the Siegfried Line, but this arrangement was changed almost immediately, with the Ninth now to be located between the British and the First US Army. As Andrew Kennedy recalled:

> After Brest was captured we moved east. Most of our HQ personnel went by rail to Arlon, Belgium, and set up a command post there. I moved up in a road convoy, but during the four days we were en route General Bradley decided to switch positions to place Ninth Army on the north end of the line of 12th Army Group. Our destination was changed while we were rolling and we moved into Maastricht, Holland, near the end of October. Although we didn't know it at the time, Maastricht was to be the home of HQ NUSA longer than any other location during its operational life.

The move eastwards was accompanied by changes in the composition of the Ninth Army, with some Divisions being reallocated to the First and Third Armies. Nevertheless, the move was a major undertaking, involving around 80,000 men, and for some weeks the Ninth Army was widely scattered with some elements in Brittany, some on the Belgium-Luxembourg border, and others in transit on roads and railways that were still badly damaged in places by recent Allied bombing. Instructions for the move were issued to the Ninth's FA Air Sections on 27 September, but even the comparatively straightforward movement of light aircraft in small groups was not without its problems. Maps covering the route had to be obtained and issued and arrangements made for several refuelling stops along the way, but weather conditions and operational restraints further complicated the move by the 'Conquer Air Force'.

Following the fall of Brest the detachment of the 50th MR&RS in that area returned to Rennes/St Jacques, but it was soon to depart for Bastogne, Belgium, in advance of the entire squadron. The Cherbourg detachment also rejoined the squadron, which remained at St Jacques until 20 October, when it too departed eastwards.

Extracts from the HQ NUSA Air Journal for 9–30 September 1944, compiled by Lt Col. R. M. Leich (Army Arty Air Section at Rennes/ St Jacques airfield, Brittany)

September 9

(1) News was received that the 2nd Air Depot Area (ADA) of the 9th AF was checking on three replacement L-4s requested by NUSA but not yet received at Rennes. 2nd ADA was also requested to arrange for the delivery of five additional L-4s in the near future (eight were required by VIII Corps and a further two by the Army Air Section).

(2) VIII Corps Arty was notified that six L-4s were ready at Rennes for fly-away delivery by VIII Corps pilots. The balance would be available soon.

(3) Major Lefever (Arty Air Officer, 12th Army Group) was requested to increase the allotment of pilots to Ninth Army.

(4) Major Wilson (Third Army Arty Air Officer), reported that two L-4s currently at A-29 St James, about 10 miles south of Avranches, would be made available to NUSA if they could be collected prior to the departure of the 43rd MR&RS's rear echelon (the 43rd being the servicing unit attached to Third Army). Action was taken to ferry these aircraft to our (NUSA) strip. They will then be available as replacements to complete immediate requirements.

September 12

(1) VIII Corps sent six pilots, including Capt. Hauser, the Arty Air Officer, to take delivery of six replacement L-4s, which were assigned as follows:
44-79776 to 402nd FA Gp, 44-79793 to 174th FA Gp, 44-79775 to 83rd Armd FA Bn, 44-79737 to 8th Inf Div, 43-30531 to 2nd FA Bn, and 43-30332 to 202nd FA Gp.

(2) The following shortfalls currently exist in NUSA units:

Unit	Pilots	Airplanes
8th Inf Div	3	1
83rd Armd FA Bn	1	–
561st FA Bn	1	–
83rd Inf Div	1	1
6th Armd Div	–	2
Total	6	4

Eight L-4s are on order and three are on hand (two less propellers). One aircraft will be retained by the Army Arty Air Section and one will be assigned to the 94th Inf Div.

(3) Five replacement pilots are en route to NUSA.

September 14

(1) Two L-4Hs (43-30207 and 43-30523) were passed to NUSA by Third Army, the first being flown in and the second left near St James in need of repair. NUSA Air Section performed the necessary repairs on this aircraft and flew it to A-27 Rennes/St Jacques today.

(2) Six officers and 118 enlisted men of the 50th MR&RS arrived today and are bivouacked on the Arty airstrip part of Rennes airfield (A-27).

September 15

Lt Col. Leich and Lt Col. Egan made an aerial survey of the locations of FA battalions in the vicinity of Les Pieux, without landing. They then proceeded to A-21 Saint-Laurent-sur-Mer and A-22 Colleville to determine the facilities at those strips for receiving FA pilots flying in from the UK. However, A-21 was abandoned and A-22 is being abandoned by the AAF. Returned via Carteret (20 miles SW of Cherbourg) on 16 September, where an attempt to visit III Corps Exec Officer (Colonel Watlington) failed because of bad weather.

September 17

(1) The truck party remainder of the 50th MR&RS arrived from Omaha Beach and is now located at A-27 Rennes/St Jacques. Major Frank E. Davis is the unit commander.

(2) The availability of 73 octane aviation gasoline for liaison aircraft was taken up with Com Z, basing requirements on data furnished by First, Third and Ninth Army Arty Air Officers and the AAF liaison squadrons attached to those armies. There appears to be some hesitancy on the part of Com Z to complicate its gas supply functions by the addition of 73 octane fuel. In order to reduce maintenance and improve the performance of L-aircraft, it is essential that only 73 octane fuel is used. Pending a decision by Com Z, action has been taken to secure a small stock of 73 octane from the fuel depot (POL 2) near Utah Beach (Capt. Elliott), where some of this gas has been stored. Capt. West is visiting this location today to get as much as he can and to secure the stock for NUSA units.

(3) Accompanied by Major Lefever, Lt Col. Leich visited A-23 Cherbourg, HQ Normandy Base Section, and A-7 Azeville, near Utah Beach, for the purpose of:

(a) Locating a suitable strip for the first landing of FA aircraft arriving from UK.

(b) Locating a field at which FA aircraft arriving in crates from the US could be assembled.

(c) Determining the action to be taken to have crated aircraft delivered from the beach to the assembly point.

Results:

(a) Strip A-7 Azeville was selected for (a) and (b) above. Refuelling of aircraft would be undertaken by the 104th Inf Div (Arty Air Officer Major Clyde Turner), which is located there, pending the arrival of a unit of the 50th MR&RS (104th Div Arty Air sections are there for the purpose of assembling their own aircraft). Major Lefever has secured 9th

AF permission to use A-7 and has confirmed its selection to the Chief of Transportation Section, Normandy Base Section (Colonel J. C. B. Hanley).

(b) Normandy Base Section will direct beach control officers to truck crated aircraft to A-7.

(4) The 50th MR&RS was requested to send an aircraft assembly unit to A-7 Azeville on September 20. One 2½-ton truck and trailer will be provided by this HQ to assist the move. Commanding General III Corps has been notified of these arrangements and will be requested to notify the units concerned to have their pilots and mechanics go to A-7 to pick up their aircraft when they are ready.

(5) Capt. Middleton, Arty Air Officer 94th Inf Div, requested that the 'unflyable' L-4 and spare engine left on his strip by the 6th Armd Div be collected. 50th MR&RS was requested to comply.

(6) Capt. Kerns, Arty Air Officer 83rd Inf Div, stated that his unit required two replacement pilots, that one L-4 was grounded with a burnt out exhaust muffler, that two were grounded with broken props, and that he required valves, spark plugs and aviation oil. He also turned in certain spare parts not required. All items were supplied as requested, and further pilots will be assigned when available.

(7) 104th Inf Div Arty Air Officer (Major Turner) requested that his pilots be sent on temporary duty (TD) to VIII Corps for orientation and 'to get experience' during the periods that 104th Div Arty was being used as a 'trucking organization'. This was not approved, as it appears little could be gained by visiting VIII Corps units at this particular time.

(8) L-4Hs 43-30207 and 43-30513, turned over to NUSA by Third Army, were passed to 50th MR&RS for repair. When completed, these aircraft will be made available to NUSA for assignment as replacements.

(9) The CO of the 50th MR&RS (Engineer Officer, Lt Newbury) was requested to obtain 100 Plexiglas windshields and 160 sets of Plexiglas 'eyebrows' for NUSA units.

(10) Major Davis, CO of the 50th MR&RS, was requested to send three units (1 officer, 48 enlisted men) and necessary spare parts and supplies to VIII Corps Arty on September 20 to perform necessary higher echelon repairs to FA aircraft.

(11) Major Lefever was requested:

(a) To release from ETOUSA (Major Gillespie) all Ninth Army FA pilots now at Grove awaiting instructions to join their units in France.

(b) To have pilots briefed to make their first landing on the Continent at A-7 Azeville, then to proceed to A-27 Rennes to await further instructions from HQ NUSA. This action was taken to relieve the situation at Grove and to get pilots to a location from where they could be dispatched to their units. III Corps have been advised of this and asked to furnish HQ NUSA with the locations to which pilots could be dispatched from A-27.

(12) The following breakdown on the number of L-4Hs in Ninth Army was supplied by 50th MR&RS:

HQ Ninth Army: 3.

83rd and 94th Divs: 20.

VIII Corps: 80.

Arriving from UK: 29.

Arriving from US: 98 (Note. Approximately 60 of these will be assembled by the 50th MR&RS. It is understood that the 104th, 44th and 26th Divs will assemble their own aircraft.)

Total: 230 aircraft.

September 19

(1) Major Lefever was asked to confirm our use of strip A-7 Azeville in the beach area (the MR&RS detachment is to leave for A-7 on Sept 20). Told to consider this confirmed unless further advised.

(2) The OC 50th MR&RS has been requested to have his assembly unit at A-7 prepared to carry out the following on newly assembled aircraft:

(a) Install Plexiglas windshields.

(b) Install Plexiglas eyebrows.

(c) Apply combat markings (invasion stripes).

(d) Apply squadron code markings.

(e) Apply aircraft serial numbers.

(f) Compensate compasses.

(g) He is further requested to refuel Arty L-4s arriving at A-7, remove auxiliary fuel tanks, and re-compensate compasses when necessary.

(3) Major Lefever stated that 2nd AADA (Lt Cunliffe) was tracing the whereabouts of eight replacement L-4s being flown from the UK to A-27 Rennes for this Army. Major Lefever also advised us that:

(a) Another request had been made to the War Dept to authorise the issue of L-5s on the basis of one per Corps Arty, Div Arty and FA Gp HQ. Favourable action not anticipated due to a shortage of L-5s.

(b) That a form of Air OP loss report be forwarded to this HQ. This does not replace the AAF Form 14, Report of Investigation of Aircraft Accidents, which is required by AAF (non combat accidents only in this theater).

(c) That combat stripes should be removed from the wings of all FA aircraft (but not the fuselage).

(d) That no distinctive colors or insignia be applied to FA aircraft other than the required combat stripes and squadron code markings.

(e) That all Ninth Army FA pilots at Grove had been released to proceed across the Channel to A-27 Rennes.

September 20

(1) An unflyable L-4 (43-30310, code markings 55-H) and a stripped engine left at Arzano by 6th Armd Div, were collected by 50th MR&RS for repair.

(2) Three replacement FA pilots (Lts M. J. Kerr, Miller and Frederick A. Zicard) arrived from UK. Kerr and Miller were sent to VIII Corps Arty by truck (to be assigned to 8th Div Arty), but Zicard was retained (attached, unassigned) in the HQ NUSA Arty Section to assist in the Air Sub-Section.

September 21

(1) An L-4 fuselage (43-29768, squadron code markings 37) received from 43rd MR&RS, is being repaired and prepared by 50th MR&RS for reassignment to a Ninth Army unit.

(2) Two pilots and aircraft of the 688th FA Bn arrived at A-27 Rennes and were dispatched to Cöetquidan at 1300 hrs.

(3) Message received from III Corps that 20 L-4s and pilots of separate FA Bns had arrived at Cherbourg/Querqueville (A-23C) and had been instructed to remain there pending receipt of further instructions from NUSA. Lt Zicard was sent to A-23C to lead them to A-27 Rennes, but the pilots of the 207th FA Bn had already reported to their unit and pilots of the 70th, 199th and 259th FA Bns had departed for parts unknown. Pilots of the following units followed Lt Zicard to A-27, spent the night there and were dispatched to the following locations on September 22: 211th, 264th, 275th, 573rd, 754th and 755th FA Bns to Cöetquidan, the 692nd and 777th to the vicinity of Les Pieux, and the 268th to the EAGLE CP (12th Army Gp) airstrip, as requested by Major Lefever. The aircraft of the 691st FA Bn remained for necessary repairs and will depart for the vicinity of Coureville on September 23.

(4) Major Elmer C. Blaha, Arty Air Officer of the 95th Inf Div, reported that aircraft and pilots of the following units would leave Grove for A-27 Rennes on September 27, unless ETOUSA (Major Gillespie) indicated to the contrary: 9th Armd Div, 211th FA Gp, 472nd FA Gp, 81st FA Bn, 252nd FA Bn, 254th FA Bn, XIII Corps Arty.

September 22

Major Middleton, Arty Air Officer 94th Inf Div, requested that pilots of 199th FA Bn proceed to Arzano, if and when they arrived at A-27 Rennes.

September 24

(1) Pilots of the 70th, 259th and 199th FA Bns reported in from Cherbourg and were dispatched, the first two to Cöetquidan and the third to Arzano.

(2) Lt Zicard, accompanied by the Engineer Officer of the 50th MR&RS (Lt Newbury) departed for A-7 Azeville to check with the assembling unit there and to determine their supply requirements. On his return Lt Zicard reported that two L-4s of the 680th FA Bn are being assembled, but 30 aircraft on the beach have not yet been delivered to the strip. Action is being taken to provide additional spare parts and supplies at A-7 for units stationed in Normandy.

(3) Ten L-4s of the 29th Inf Div under Major Swenson, Div Arty Air Officer, landed at our strip to bivouac overnight. The aircraft, pilots and observers were fueled and fed by the 50th MR&RS.

(4) Lt R. Mathews, formerly 90th Inf Div Arty Air Section, arrived on assignment to Arty Air Section as Assistant Army Arty Air Officer.

(5) The Arty Air Officer 26th Inf Div (Capt. D. C. Osborn) arrived at the strip to check supply procedures. His Division had already assembled their own aircraft, received direct from the US. Capt. Osborn was given the necessary information on squadron code and combat markings.

(6) 50th MR&RS (Lt Newbury) was requested to take action to obtain 100 Plexiglas or Lucite top decks for L-4Hs. [Lucite was a form of clear plastic, similar to Plexiglas and Perspex.]

(7) VIII Corps Arty Air Officer (Capt. Houser) reported that 30 FA L-4s would land at our strip on or about September 27.

September 25

(1) Lt Mathews, accompanied by Lt Bovan, Technical Supply Officer at 50th MR&RS, flew to A-42C Villacoublay near Paris to visit 2nd AADA to determine:

(a) Supply channels for L-4 parts as the 10th ADG and 43rd ADG (formerly at Grove) were moving to A-42C and one of these groups would take all L-4H parts.

(b) How long would the aircraft assembling unit of the 50th have to remain at A-7 Azeville, pending the establishment of an assembly base by 2nd AADA. The AADA was also requested to hold up the delivery to A-27C Rennes of eight replacement L-4Hs for NUSA, and to study the situation concerning repacking of Arty parachutes.

(2) Four L-4s, four pilots and two mechanics of units of the 34th Inf Div were requested for temporary duty at Ninth Army HQ to take over message runs Nos 1, 2 and 5 (to Les Nevens, Carteret and Cherbourg) for the HQ Signals Center.

(3) G-3 Air reported that a UC-78 of the 14th LS (attached to Third Army) had been wrecked near St Malo, having run out of gas. Requested 50th MR&RS to collect it, bring to A-27 Rennes and repair it, if possible. Arrangements were completed with the pilot, Lt Thompson.

(4) 81 'K' rations were requested for 21 pilots arriving at A-27 Rennes (17 separately from UK) and 30 pilots and 30 observers from VIII Corps units at Brest.

September 26

(1) 34th FA Bgde (Capt. Keating, Arty Air Officer) was asked to provide this HQ with a complete Air Section (pilots, aircraft, transportation and mechanics), or its equivalent, for temporary duty for an extended period of time.

(2) Lt Mathews and Lt Bovan (50th MR&RS) returned from A-42C Villacoublay with the following information:

(a) L-4H spare parts stocks on the Continent will be carried by 10th ADG at A-42C. Stocks are presently en route from UK.

(b) 2nd AADA will try to hold up delivery of eight replacement L-4Hs to A-27 Rennes and keep the aircraft at A-42C Villacoublay pending receipt of further instructions from this office.

(c) Parachute packing will be available at A-42C.

Action taken: 50th MR&RS (Lt Bovan) was requested to prepare the necessary requisitions for 100 Lucite top decks, 160 pairs of Lucite eyebrows, flying clothing, oil, etc., and all items presently on requisitions from FA units transferred from Third Army.

(3) Pilots 1st Lt Albert Wulf of the 264th FA Bn, 2nd Lt Mathew J. Gilbert of the 207th FA Bn, and Pfc Woodron L. Hamnon (207th FA Bn mechanic) reported from 34th FA Bgde for temporary duty as pilot messengers for NUSA HQ. T/5 Stanley J. Spingler, an Airplane Mechanic with the 275th Armd FA Bn, will report on September 27. This completes action by 34th FA Bgde on our request for four pilots, four aircraft and two mechanics.

(4) Approximately 12 L-4s of 196th FA Gp bivouacked on our strip at A-27 Rennes.

(5) L-4H 43-30513 was assigned as a spare aircraft to HQ 34th FA Bgde. The Bgde Arty Air Officer (Capt. Keating) took delivery of this aircraft at A-27.

(6) Three repair units of 50th MR&RS under Lt Lihme returned to A-27 Rennes from Brest. These units will remain until VIII Corps (Capt. Houser) sends a request for them to move forward to a location to be indicated by Capt. Houser. Organic transport of these units consists of six 2½-ton trucks with one-ton trailers and two ¼-ton trucks with ¼-ton trailers. Additional transportation will be provided by 50th MR&RS.

(7) Scheduled messenger runs to Les Nevens were placed on a 'pilot and plane standby' basis. The Cherbourg run remains as scheduled. Signal Message Center (Lt Miller) reported that these runs would probably be turned over to III Corps after October 1, at which time the four pilots being used would be returned to the 34th FA Bgde.

September 27

(1) The 28th FA Bn and the 44th Inf Div Arty are now using A-7 Azeville as their strip.

(2) An overall estimate of the number of L-4s arriving from the US and requiring assembling at A-7 is as follows:

Inf Divs (10 L-4s each): 104th*, 26th*, 44th, 84th, 102nd.

Armd Divs (8 each): 10th, 12th.

Corps Arty (2 each): III, XVI.

FA Gp HQ (2 each): 401st, 407th.

FA Bn HQ (2 each): 215th, 257th, 280th, 809th, 758th, 776th, 516th, 271st, 514th.

Total: 92.

(The 20 aircraft of units marked * have already been assembled by the units concerned.)

(3) Approximately 30 L-4s of VIII Corps Arty units visited A-27 Rennes en route to the east. Pilots were given maps and their aircraft refueled.

(4) 21 FA pilots of the following units were due to arrive from Grove: 9th Armd Div, 252nd FA Bn, 211th FA Gp, 254th FA Gp, 472nd FA Gp, XIII Corps Arty and 81st FA Bn. Informal message received that the move from the UK was delayed until 28 September.

September 28

(1) 26th Inf Div, which had been with NUSA since August 28 (III Corps from 5 Sept), passed to Third Army.

(2) Lt George K. Hanner, 755th FA Bn, and Lt Shoemaker, 259th FA Bn, reported from 34th FA Bgde for temporary duty with this HQ. These pilots will fly to the tactical command post on September 29. No vehicles or mechanics will accompany them. These pilots will be required for courier missions for an indefinite period.

(3) Engineer Officer 50th MR&RS (Lt Newbury) agreed to the plan that FA units generally recover their own crashed aircraft from the scene of accidents and deliver them to the MR&RS for repair or salvage, rather than leave the wrecked aircraft to the mercy of souvenir hunters and saboteurs pending the arrival of MR&RS trucks which might have to come from long distances. He further stated that the crates in which aircraft arrived should be disposed of by the MR&RS rather than leaving them with the units to which the aircraft are consigned.

(4) XIII Corps reported that Major Sheldon M. Smith, Arty Air Officer, was recovering from pneumonia, with complete recovery expected in six weeks. In the meantime, the transfer of Major Roger N. Ketcham from the 211th FA Gp was requested as a replacement, but the CO of the 211th did not want to release him.

(5) The pilots (total of 20) expected from Grove arrived today and remained overnight.

September 29

(1) Pilots and aircraft that arrived from the UK on the 28th were dispatched as follows:

Unit	Arty Air Officer	Dispatched to
211th FA Gp	Major Roger Ketcham	Cöetquidan
472nd FA Gp	Capt. T. B. Halter	Cöetquidan
HQ XIII Corps Arty	Lt Roark (acting)	III Corps, Carteret
81st FA Bn	–	III Corps, Carteret
252nd FA Bn	–	III Corps, Carteret
254th FA Bn	–	III Corps, Carteret

(2) The Arty Air Officer 9th Armd Div (Capt. Leon Lolo) was dispatched to HQ III Corps at Carteret to obtain further instructions (his seven pilots remaining at A-27 Rennes), although he asserted that previous arrangements had been made with 9th Armd Div for the pilots to proceed to Paris, to remain there pending receipt of instructions. Lts Mathews, Shoemaker and Hanner left for the Tactical CP by air (via Paris).

(3) Lt Mathews carried 30 day supply requisition of 50th MR&RS to 10th ADG at A-42C Villacoublay and was to:

(a) check status of eight replacement L-4s on requisition for NUSA.

(b) check parachute repacking facilities available to NUSA units.

(4) Pvt. Carmen P. Chiampa, HQ Bty, 2nd FA Bn, reported for detached service as Airplane Mechanic for the L-4s of messenger pilots (34th FA Bgde), in place of T/5 Spingler.

(5) 9th Armd Div Arty Air Officer (Capt. Lolo) reported the need for one replacement aircraft and pilot (pilot killed in an accident just prior to movement of the unit from the UK to the Continent).

(6) Present known status of replacement pilots and aircraft in Ninth Army:

	Pilots	Airplanes
8th Inf Div	2	–
9th Armd Div	1	1

Eight aircraft are on order. One spare (each) will be issued when available to III Corps Arty and XVI Corps Arty.

September 30

(1) The only NUSA FA pilot remaining in England is Major Sheldon M. Smith, Arty Air Officer, XIII Corps. His L-4 is at Heston and he is in hospital, awaiting release to fly over.

(2) 9th Armd Div Arty Air Officer, Capt. Lolo, returned from his Division CP at St Marie du Mont (north of Carentan) and led seven other 9th Armd Div pilots, awaiting him at A-27 Rennes, to their strip, departing at 1330 hrs.

CHAPTER 4

Eastwards to The Low Countries, October 1944

Following orders to proceed eastwards, Headquarters NUSA opened its command post at Arlon, Belgium, on 2 October and two days later took over the frontline sector between the First and Third US Armies. Almost immediately, however, the Ninth was ordered to take up a position between the British 21st Army Group and the American First Army. Consequently, shortly after arriving at Arlon the Army HQ moved to Maastricht, Holland, where *Conquer Rear* opened a command post on 14 October, followed by *Conquer Forward* on the 22nd. This changed disposition and the long journey from Brittany resulted in units of the Ninth Army being widely scattered for a while in five countries – France, Belgium, Luxembourg, Holland and just over the border into Germany. The move also resulted in a further exchange of units within Armies, with VIII Corps (now comprising 9th Armored Division with the 2nd, 8th, and 83rd Infantry Divisions) leaving NUSA in exchange for XIX Corps (2nd Armored, and 29th and 30th Infantry Divisions) from the First Army. This new arrangement, with the First Army on its right or south side and British forces to the north, was to be maintained by NUSA until the end of the war.

After organising the eastward movement of the Air OPs under his control, Lt Col. Leich departed Rennes on 11 October in L-4H 43-30373, bound for Laval on the first stage of a flight to Arlon. He was accompanied by Lt Col. John B. Egan of the Army HQ Staff, but bad weather resulted in a return to Rennes ten minutes after take-off. With an improvement in the weather the two officers set off again the next day, reaching Chartres in 2 hours 30 minutes with en-route stops at Laval and Le Mans. Following an overnight stay at Chartres, they continued with a 30-minute flight to A-42C Paris/Villacoublay, followed on the 16th by a flight of 2 hours 20 minutes to Arlon, with an intermediate stop at Rheims. The next day a one hour flight took the Cub to Maastricht, giving an overall flight time of 5 hours 20 minutes to cover 420 miles at an average groundspeed of 79 mph.

The two Ninth Air Force units attached to NUSA were also involved in the move eastwards, the 50th Mobile Reclamation and Repair Squadron duly taking up residence in a large building on the outskirts of Maastricht, and the 125th Liaison Squadron initially moving to Arlon, where its L-5s (minus two Flights on detached service) temporarily operated from a large field just outside the town. Despite atrocious weather, the 125th resumed courier and messenger missions, but the two-mile distance from the strip to the Belgian army barracks where squadron personnel were quartered, frequently walked in heavy rain, left much to be desired. Consequently, a move to Maastricht on 21 October was welcomed, not least because most of the squadron's personnel were then billeted in private homes close to the airstrip. Ten days after their arrival an L-5 (42-99301) of the squadron, flown by Lt Eugene O'Brien, was damaged in an accident four miles north of Heerlen, but it was quickly collected by a crash pick-up crew of the 50th MR&RS and taken to Maastricht for repair.

In addition to Lt Col. Leich, Capt. Mathews and the recently arrived Lt Zicard, NUSA's Arty Air Section at this time included three enlisted men. As Andrew Kennedy recalled:

These were mechanics Cecil E. Tye and Otto F. Roehrich, and clerk William B. Hamblen. The third officer in the Section, Lt Frederick A. Zicard, was the first pilot with whom I flew in an L-4. We had two strips at Maastricht, the artillery Cubs being based at a small strip east of the Maas River (known as the Meuse in Belgium and France). Tye and Roehrich lived on this strip and did the routine maintenance on the airplanes. The 50th MR&RS was also on this strip, which was close to *Conquer Rear*. This was set up in a school building in Wijk, an adjoining town on the east side of the river, with *Conquer Forward* in an old Dutch army barracks, known as the Tappan Kazerne, on the Maastricht or west side of the Maas. The Armored and Artillery Sections were located there, but General Simpson and the General Staff sections were in a school building about two blocks from the Kazerne. General Nugent, the Commanding General of XXIX Tactical Air Command, had his office near General Simpson's, which explains why we had such good air support throughout the war. Our other airstrip was located on top of a high hill west of the river. This was the site of Fort St Pieter, an ancient 12th century Dutch fort situated on one of the highest points in Holland. Our other air force unit, the 125th Liaison Squadron, based their L-5s at this strip. A Cessna UC-78 assigned to General Simpson and its air force pilot, a lieutenant colonel, were also based here, but the UC-78 was wrecked when it ran off the end of the short strip and tumbled down the hill. Fortunately the pilot wasn't injured and the general wasn't in the airplane. British Austers also used this strip occasionally and on one occasion I saw 'Monty' (General Sir Bernard Montgomery, the British commander) take off from here in a Miles Messenger. The only time I saw a Stinson L-1 in the ETO was also at this strip; it was flown by an air force pilot who couldn't find the strip at first, so he landed in a nearby field to locate its position. He later flew out of the field and came into the strip.

It was from the artillery strip east of the Maas that Andrew Kennedy was able to do some flying in the Air Section's Cubs, including some unofficial 'stick time' at the controls. In this connection, Kennedy said:

As I recall, I had to sign a form, agreeing that I was flying voluntarily and that I could not expect to collect flight pay or hazardous duty pay! Lt Col. Leich was a Charter Member of the Aircraft Owners and Pilots Association (AOPA No. 394) and he tried to sign up all his liaison pilots as AOPA members. He also signed me up, although I was a pre-war civilian pilot and not an L-pilot, and my first AOPA membership card caught up with me later on in Germany. I also flew with a couple of pilots who were going back to their divisions after spending some time in hospital, and one of them wanted to first practice his low flying. We flew low down the Maas to Liège and must have gotten there about the time the shifts were changing in the factories as some Belgian civilians were walking along a railroad embankment to our left. We flew by below the level of the people, with them looking down at us and waving. If this pilot had misjudged his distance he could have wiped out a lot of civilians with his wingtip! Lt Col. Leich wanted to use me as a pilot but couldn't do so unless I first got a commission in the Artillery. At one time I was going to transfer from the Armored Section to the Artillery Section, where Leich was considering having Tye and Roehrich teach me more about engines, and then send me as a mechanic to a Division which was having high officer casualties. He thought I might be able to get a battlefield commission with the Division and then bring me back to Headquarters and train me as a Liaison Pilot. However, I was kept in the Armored Section and nothing ever came of that scheme.

At peak strength in Brittany, HQ NUSA had around 230 Air OPs under its control, but the number at any one time varied appreciably. In October the transfer of several units to other Armies reduced the number to about fifty, but by the end of the month the situation had stabilised with some 200 L-4s on strength. However, the move to Belgium and then on to Holland was not without problems, as shown in journal entries for October.

The journal also reveals that the whereabouts of Major Sheldon Smith, the XIII Group Arty Air Officer reportedly en route from the UK, remained a mystery. Following his discharge from hospital, where he had been seriously ill with pneumonia, Major Smith was to collect his L-4 from Heston and resume duty with XIII Group on the Continent. Lt Col. Leich eventually heard that Major Smith was on his way, but several weeks passed with no sign of him. Nor did Major Lefever at HQ 12 Group or Major Gillespie of HQ ETOUSA have news of Smith's progress, but messages between them took on a humorous tone with Bob Leich referring to the missing officer by several nicknames including 'Phantom Smith', 'Disappearing Smith' and 'Vanishing Smith'.

Extracts from the HQ NUSA Air Journal for 1-31 October 1944, compiled by Lt Col. R. M. Leich (Army Arty Air Section at Rennes/ St Jacques airfield, Brittany, until 17 October and then at Maastricht, Holland)

October 1

(1) Lt Zicard, accompanied by the CO of 50th MR&RS (Major Davis), departed Rennes by air for A-7 Azeville to ascertain the situation regarding the assembly of aircraft. Upon his return he reported the following:

(a) Lt Col. Barnum, 9th AF Liaison Officer at Normandy Base Section, has directed delivery from the port of one crated L-4 of the 102nd Inf Div to A-15 Cherbourg/Maupertus to be assembled. The balance of nine aircraft would likewise be sent to A-15, despite previously made arrangements to use A-7 Azeville for assembling purposes. He has further requested that men be sent from A-7 to A-15 to do the work.

(b) Eight L-4s in crates were located in Air Force dumps at Cherbourg. At least two are for XVI Corps, and these will be assembled at Azeville.

(c) Ten L-4s of 102nd Inf Div will arrive at Utah beach in a few days.

Action: Lt Zicard will visit Lt Col. Barnum on 3 October to discuss the situation. It is thoroughly undesirable for assembling operations to be carried out at more than one location in Normandy. Lt Zicard was also instructed to find out the units to which the 10 aircraft are to be consigned.

(2) The Air Marshalling Base at Grove has closed. 2nd Lt Harold O. Svendby and Pvts Albert Yager and Evry Harkin arrived at the CP from HQ XIII Corps on September 30, having accompanied that unit from England. These personnel are Third Army Air OP replacements who remained at Grove to operate the Air Marshalling Base. They will remain at A-27 Rennes until sent for by Major Wilson, Arty Air Officer Third Army. Lt Svendby and the two mechanics are to be forwarded by any Ninth Army transport moving eastward (in fact they left on 3 October in a PX truck).

(3) The air above the city of Paris is hereby declared a restricted area. No aircraft will be operated below 3,000ft within the area, except when operationally required (ETOUSA Instruction dated September 11).

October 2

(Ninth Army Command Post opened at Arlon, Belgium)

(1) Major Tyndall, Signal Section, reported that no further need existed for the services of FA pilots in the NUSA Messenger Service. Accordingly, Lts Troyan, Gilbert, Scott and Wulf (pilots) were instructed to return to their units. Capt. Keating, 34th FA Bgde Arty Air Officer, was so notified.

October 3

(1) Lt Olijar (FA Pilot, 252nd FA Bn, temporarily attached to HQ III Corps Arty pending the arrival of his unit) visited A-27 Rennes, requesting that an auxiliary fuel tank be installed in his L-4H. He wishes to return to the UK to pick up a III Corps Staff Officer (name unknown) who was becoming impatient waiting for a seat on a Channel-crossing C-47. Inasmuch as the installation of an auxiliary gravity-fed fuel tank in an L-4H leaves no room for a passenger, and since weight/capacity limitations would be far exceeded, permission to make this flight was denied. (Also, 12th Army Group frowns upon such things). This was explained in detail to a III Corps Arty pilot (Lt Richardson).

(2) CG XIII Corps Arty (Gen. Shugg) stated that within a week definite word would be received from the UK indicating when his Arty Air Officer, Major Smith, would be released from hospital, and that we should give some thought to a replacement for Major Smith should medical advice be unfavourable. 12th Army Gp (Major Lefever) will be notified, in order that we may act quickly.

(3) Lt Zicard returned from A-7 Azeville and reported that Major Bailey (Executive Officer, Continental Intransit Depots) has instructions to release crated aircraft to units. Before this he was going to send the crates to A-42 Villacoublay. Lt Zicard suggested that a letter be sent to IX Air Force Service Command asking Major Bailey to release the aircraft to Lt Carruba at A-7, to which suggestion Major Bailey agreed.

(4) Air Corps Dump No. 750 (Cherbourg) is to receive crated aircraft from the beach. The crates, which were delivered to A-15 Cherbourg/Maupertus, were released to Major King

(102nd Inf Div) on his demand. The assistant to the CO of Dump 750 (Capt. McCrann) said he would notify Lt Carruba when the crates arrived and Lt Carruba would then arrange for their release.

(5) Major King (102nd Inf Div) said his advance party notified him of the existence of A-15 Cherbourg. He located his 10 aircraft and arranged for their shipment to A-15 through the Air Force Dump and Major Bailey. At that time he had never heard of either A-7 or the 50th MR&RS located there. Lt Carruba finally contacted him at A-15 and after showing Major King his orders from Ninth Army, permitted the crew to assemble the 10 aircraft. The result is that Major King is very pleased and is asking that a letter of commendation from Gen. Busby (CO 102nd Inf Div) be sent in.

(6) Lt Carruba's unit has assembled 18 aircraft in three days at A-15 (10 for 102nd and eight for 10th Armd Div). The eight crates were not for XVI Corps as previously informed, but for the 10th Armd Div.

(7) 9th Armd Div is sending eight aircraft to A-7 for the installation of Lucite eyebrows, windshields and top decks.

(8) Lt Carruba asked about the future of his unit at A-7 when all the aircraft are assembled. Does he remain there to make repairs and operate a fuel dump for aircraft in that area? He has found a supply of 73 octane at Barfleur.

October 4

(1) Lt Mathews called from *Conquer New* and requested that those units of 50th MR&RS formerly with VIII Corps be dispatched as soon as possible to the new CP. 50th was informed and stated they would leave A-27 Rennes on October 6, Assistant Engineer Officer in charge.

October 5

(1) Lt Col. Leich, accompanied by Lt Bovan, Tech Supply Officer, 50th MR&RS, departed 'in a mighty L-4H' for A-42C Villacoublay to discuss supply matters with 2nd AADA and to meet Major Lefever (Arty Air Officer, 12th Army Gp), Major Wilson (Third Army Arty Air Officer), Major Bristol (First Army Arty Air Officer) and Lt Mathews. Time en route was 4 hours.

(2) At the conference at 2nd AADA with Capt. Linn (Exec Officer of Maintenance Division), it was decided that the parachutes of Ninth Army units needing repacking would be turned in to the 50th MR&RS. The 50th would then arrange for repacking to be carried out by 10th ADG at A-42C for units West of Paris, and by 16th ADG, Rheims, for those East of Paris.

(3) The following additional squadron code markings were furnished verbally by Major Lefever: 84 to XXI Corps; 95 to 11th Armd Div; 87 to 84th Inf Div; 96 to 12th Armd Div; 89 to 99th Inf Div.

October 6

Lt Zicard returned from A-7 Azeville and reported on the delivery of aircraft from the beaches to the 50th MR&RS assembling unit (at A-7):

(a) Ten aircraft of 102nd Inf Div and eight of the 10th Armd Div were assembled at A-15 Cherbourg in three days.

(b) Aircraft of XVI Corps and 401st FA Gp have not yet been received from the beach.

(c) 9th Armd Div is arranging to send its eight aircraft to A-7 for certain modifications (it is believed that the necessary parts are not immediately available).

October 7

(1) ETOUSA (Major Gillespie) requested the return to Grove of all auxiliary fuel tanks removed from NUSA aircraft flown to the Continent. They are urgently required at Grove. Lt Bowen of the 50th MR&RS reported that all fuel tanks received to date had been taken to 10th ADG at A-42C Villacoublay for air shipment to Grove. This was reported to Major Gillespie, who will check with A-42C.

(2) Lt Tippen, 2nd AADA Aircraft Allocations Section at A-42C, requested that he be notified as soon as this HQ knows the desired allocation of eight replacement aircraft due at that station for NUSA units.

October 8

(1) Lt Col. Leich flew to meet Capt. Houser, VIII Corps Arty Air Officer, who indicated where he wanted to locate a unit of the 50th MR&RS. Discussed parachutes and the possibility of having all our Air OPs on one field at night and using forward fields in daytime for security when units reach German soil. This practice is being followed by First Army. Returned to Bastogne and led Lt Leimy, CO of a unit of the 50th MR&RS, to a field just ½-mile south of Bastogne. Lt Leimy has a small stock of spare parts on hand, but stocks of clear dope and 30-weight oil are critical.

(2) Arrangements were made to establish a fuel dump on the 50th MR&RS field just south of Bastogne to refuel aircraft along their route.

(3) G-3 Air, Third Army, requested the number of aircraft in this zone and the number operating in Third Army zone. This was given as 51 aircraft in units in this zone, with none in Third Army Zone.

(4) Message from LUCKY (Major Lefever, 12th Army Gp). With regard to the Air OP sections of COUNSEL (26th Inf Div), LUCKY wants complete sections (pilots, aircraft, mechanics and equipment) sent forward as follows: aircraft to A-82C Verdun (Etain/Rouvres), personnel and vehicles to LUCKY CP.

(5) By phone from Lt Col. Leich in 'Paree': 'St James Hotel very respectable – too respectable. Will return tomorrow.' The weather held him up. Reported that we will not get out of the A-7 Azeville Utah Beach assembly business (by the 50th MR&RS) until mid-November.

(6) Major units (divisions, etc.) from the US whose destination was changed from the Continent to the UK; all details regarding their aircraft have been worked out with Major Lefever and Major Gillespie.

(7) ETOUSA Arty Air Officer (Major Gillespie) reported the following with regard to L-4Hs arriving from the USA:

(a) 10th ADG will assemble all L-4Hs received in crates, effective on or about November 15, and put them in a Pool at A-42C Villacoublay.

(b) Pending completion of this, sufficient L-4Hs will be assembled at Grove and flown to A-42C for allocation as follows: 68 for initial issue, 90 for replacements, 24 for establishing emergency Pool. These cover 12th Army Gp requirements to 15 November.

(c) Our assembling unit of the 50th MR&RS at A-7 Azeville will continue to function until further notice.

(8) Five Brodie Devices, complete with operating crews, will be sent to this theater and one may be available to a Ninth Army unit in November for operational test.

(9) The four divisions and four battalions coming from the USA and diverted to the UK will be taken care of (on aircraft supply matters) through arrangements made by ETOUSA. The pilots of these units will be briefed to fly to A-7 Azeville the day after their units move to the Continent (end of October) and that representatives of the units will be notified to meet them there.

(10) Lt Col. Leich returned by air from A-42C Villacoublay. From October 5 to 8 the weather between Paris and Rennes was bad for flying.

(11) Lt Mathews, at *Conquer New*, reported the arrival at Arlon of forward echelons (three units) of the 50th MR&RS, and their subsequent dispatch to VIII Corps at Houffalize.

(12) Major Gillespie requested that Major Ketonamn, Arty Air Officer 211th FA Group, bring his (Gillespie's) aircraft to the FA strip at A-27 Rennes, where he could pick it up on October 10.

(13) Information given to 34th Bgde concerning the routeing of FA pilots to *Conquer New*, for dispatch from there by Lt Mathews to their ultimate destinations. 'Gas' and 'no gas' stops were indicated, instead of assembling at A-7 Azeville.

October 14
(Rear echelon of Army Headquarters opened at Maastricht, Holland)

October 17
(1) Lt Cols Egan and Leich, Major George Cilley, and Lts Zicard and Mathews arrived by air at Arty New (Maastricht).

(2) Pfc Hamblen contacted the 125th LS for the purpose of identifying their strip from the air in case Lt Col. Leich asks where it is located. Told him: 'Fly south of the city along the canal and turn left. The strip is about ½-mile from the canal and on top of a hill (the only hill near the city).'

(3) Call from Capt. Linton at Arlon saying that 84th Inf Div (in the UK) had received ten L-5s, and that action should be taken to ensure assignment of aircraft to the unit when it embarked for the Continent. This was passed to Major Lefever who said he would follow it up with Major Gillespie when he (Gillespie) returned from London. On October 21 this was again referred to Major Lefever who stated he had been unable to confirm the facts and that he would inform this office of the results of his visit to Com Z. He added, 'The assignment of L-5 aircraft to FA units is contrary to War Department policy and it appears that an error might have been made.'

October 20
(1) Major Bristol, Arty Air Officer First Army, forwarded message from 12th Army Gp that five 'Giants' [L-4Hs] for Ninth Army were at A-92 St Trond/Brusthem. Lt Mathews and four borrowed pilots went by truck to A-92, but the aircraft had not yet been delivered from Paris.

(2) Capt. Reed, Arty Air Officer XIX Corps, furnished information concerning the supply of air force equipment. With the exception of propellers, all T/E kits were 'in pretty good shape'. Capt. Reed was Asst Air Officer until October 16, on which date Major Steven E. Hatch, Arty Air Officer, was killed in action near Geilenkirchen when his L-4H was shot down by three low flying Me 109s. Three L-5s (one in Corps, one in 29th Inf Div and one in 30th Inf Div) were returned to First Army on their transfer to Ninth Army.

October 21

(1) Advance party of main body of 50th MR&RS (Capt. Johnson) reported to CP. Main body expected to arrive on October 22. It will include assembly party previously situated in Normandy at A-7 Azeville.

(2) The following units arriving on the Continent will be supplied with aircraft from the Pool at A-42C: XXI Corps; 75th, 78th, 87th and 106th Inf Divs; 351st, 349th and 411th FA Groups; 261st, 281st, 349th, 350th, 351st, 515th, 238th, 666th, 667th and 686th FA Bns. The following units will fly their aircraft from the UK to A-23C: 84th and 99th Inf Divs, 11th and 12th Armd Divs.

(3) Call from XIX Corps Arty (Lt Col. Adams) requesting three L-5s pronto! (This is the number of L-5s in the whole Corps, withdrawn by First Army). Lt Col. Adams was informed of the L-5 situation; none available for FA. Action will be taken for a Flight from the 125th LS to be attached to XIX Corps, the Flight to include photo personnel to accomplish the photo missions required by XIX Corps Arty (for which it had previously been supplied L-5s).

October 22

(Ninth Army Command Post opened at Maastricht)

(1) Discussions took place with Lt Col. Lynn, Asst Arty Officer, XIX Corps, regarding the problem of obtaining an L-5 for taking oblique photos. Lt Lyons of the 125th LS accompanied us and stated that his squadron would provide the Corps with a photographic section of six men, and may be willing to utilise one of their L-5s for taking the pictures.

(2) The Main body of the 50th MR&RS (CO Major Frank H. Davis) arrived at Maastricht today from A-27 Rennes/St Jacques.

October 23

(1) 211th FA Gp requested information on the whereabouts of FA pilots Ketcham, Franke and Huard. On arrival these pilots will be held at the Army CP until contact is made with the unit CO. Later, Major Ketcham was directed from A-92 St Trond to the strip at Tongres.

(2) EAGLE (Sgt Hogan, Air Section) called to say that five 'Giants' [L-4Hs] will arrive at A-92 St Trond before 1500 hrs today. He added that the 84th Div aircraft shipped from the US were not L-5s, as alleged, but were L-4Hs. Lt Mathews flew to A-92 (second time) to take delivery of some replacement aircraft. He will return there on October 24 to actually receive them.

(3) Conference with CO 50th MR&RS (Major Davis), Capt. Knoche (Engineer Section), and Major Moore (XXIX TAC) re improvement of the strip across the river. XXIX TAC

wants to operate four L-5s and two or three UC-78s from this strip, and a runway of 1,400ft would be required. Plans for necessary improvements were finally decided upon. Approval was requested to use matting for the runway, but matting was likewise needed for the 125th LS strip at St Pietersburg and sufficient was not available for both fields. XXIX TAC is being informed that its aircraft cannot operate from the 50th MR&RS strip if matting is not available. The strip is OK for L-4s.

October 24

(1) Lt Col. Leich visited XIX Corps Arty to discuss the matter of L-5s with the Commanding General and others. The CG insists that photo missions be flown by Arty pilots, but the L-4 is not suitable for such missions. The CO 125th LS is sending a Flight of three L-5s (under Lt Peterson and his photo officer, Lt Lyons, with three photo technicians) to XIX Corps. One L-5 will be earmarked for XIX Corps Arty. FA pilots of this Corps will be authorised to fly the L-5.

(2) Report received that Major Sheldon Smith, Arty Air Officer XIII Corps, had been released from the 126th General Hospital in the UK to the 10th Replacement Depot (UK) on October 5. Message sent to replacement system requesting information on the delay of the arrival of Major Smith, stating lack of transportation was no excuse as Major Smith had his own aircraft in England and could provide his own transport.

Lt Mathews took delivery of the following L-4Hs at A-92: 44-79672, 44-30523, 44-79625 and 44-79671. The L-4 (44-79744) assigned to Ninth Army by 2nd AADA had not yet arrived.

(3) Visit by Arty Air Officer 256th FA Gp to 50th MR&RS to pick up parts (tie-down rings, Pyralin, etc.).

October 25

(1) Flying Control at A-92 St Trond reported that an L-4 of Ninth Army was on the field. This, our replacement aircraft (44-79744) due on the 24th, will be picked up on October 26 by Lt Col. Leich.

(2) Flying Control at A-92 also reported that an L-4 had cracked up east of Brussels and that it was being taken care of by A-89 Le Culot. No reports have been received of any missing Ninth Army aircraft. Later investigated (on Oct 27) by two officers, but they could find nothing.

(3) Requested by Capt. Reed, Arty Air Officer XIX Corps, that something be done to get his two unrated pilots rated (legacy from the North African campaign). Similarly, Capt. Haran, Arty Air Officer 2nd Armd Div, is not rated.

October 26

(1) Pilots of the following units arrived at Arty airstrip from points west: HQ 196th FA Gp (Morrison and Lynch), 753rd FA Bn (Sladek and Hayes), 754th FA Bn (Dark and Scott), 70th FA Bn (Black and Valder), 207th FA Bn (Dianich and Gilbert).

(2) NUSA Signal Officer has assigned code name CUBA to 50th MR&RS.

(3) A Liaison Pilot with 258th FA Gp visited CP to discuss squadron code markings (39) assigned by 32nd FA Bgde. Is a change required? In reply, Arty Air Officer XIX Corps (Capt. Reed) will be requested to issue a new squadron code to the unit.

October 27

(1) Progress is being made at the Army Arty airstrip in laying Sommerfeld wire matting by 250th Eng Bn and improving the shop facilities for the 50th MR&RS.
(2) An L-4 of the 357th FA Bn (43-30237: 24-X) flown by 1st Lt Lloyd Abercrombie was damaged in a forced landing, on account of weather and darkness, in vicinity of Varville. The aircraft was picked up by 50th MR&RS and is repairable, but a new aircraft (44-79672) will be sent as replacement. Lt Brown, senior Bn pilot, will submit Air OP loss report direct to this office.

October 28

(1) NUSA Arty Air Section moved from 125th LS strip to the 50th MR&RS strip.
(2) The following confirms an informal conversation with Lt Col. R. M. Leich on October 28 regarding 73 octane aviation fuel requirements for FA Air OPs of NUSA:
(a) 2nd Lt Paul Carruba, 50th MR&RS, informed this section that 40,000 tons of 73 octane (in 85 gallon drums) was on hand at the POL Dump at St Vaast (east of Monteburg on the Normandy peninsula). It is in the charge of Major Bailey, Cherbourg Port Air Corps Supply Officer.
(b) As the 50th MR&RS is the 9th Air Force unit responsible for furnishing Air Corps equipment and supplies to Ninth Army units, the CO of the 50th (Major Frank E. Davis) has been requested to take action to obtain sufficient transportation to haul at the earliest practicable date a minimum of 5,000 gallons of the 73 octane fuel referred to above from Normandy to Maastricht.
(c) The average monthly requirement for 73 octane for FA units in Ninth Army is 60,000 gallons, based on a strength of 200 Air OPs, each aircraft flying approximately 60 hours per month and consuming five gallons per hour. Bad flying weather in the winter could reduce this by as much as 50%.
(d) The O-170-3 engines with which L-4Hs are equipped are designed for operation with 73 octane aviation fuel. The performance of these engines with 80 octane MT fuel is reduced by 5 to 10% (engine rpm on the ground), and top overhauls are required at an average of 30 hours instead of 100-125 hours.
(3) A flak damaged L-4 (43-29831: 59-E), of 258th FA Gp, was picked up by 50th MR&RS between Maastricht and Sittard. It is repairable.

October 29

(1) Major Scott, 7th Armd Div Arty Exec, reported 'Enemy aircraft dropped flares over 7th Armd Div Arty airstrip last night (October 28), then proceeded to bomb and strafe the strip.' One Staff Sgt pilot was killed, one officer pilot was wounded, one aircraft was completely destroyed (burned) and one aircraft damaged (extent unknown).
(2) Replacement aircraft assigned from our Pool for above losses are 44-79626 (56-E) and 43-30523 (56-F). Lts Davis W. Crockatt and Marvin L. Graff, who arrived today, will be sent

to 7th Armd Div, whose Arty Air Officer (Capt. Neal) will furnish a pilot to lead them to his strip. Capt. Neal reported that the mechanic was not needed and the requisition for him had been canceled.

(3) Report on assembly and assignment of L-4s:

(a) The following L-4s were assembled by the unit of 50th MR&RS at A-7 Azeville (Lt Carrub, officer i/c) and assigned as follows:

280th FA Bn: 44-79953 and 44-79889.

44th Inf Div Arty: 44-79935, 44-79945, 44-79936 and 44-79939.

102nd Inf Div Arty: 44-80128, 44-80095, 44-80161, 44-80145, 44-80049, 44-80149, 44-80124, 44-80133, 44-80083 and 44-80061.

10th Armd Div Arty: 44-79939, 44-79926, 44-79929, 44-79921, 44-79919, 44-79916, 44-79904 and 44-79911.

HQ and HQ III Corps Arty: 44-79905 and 44-79691.

HQ and HQ XIV Corps Arty: 44-79949 and 44-79954.

(b) The following units have aircraft to be assembled, but the 50th MR&RS assembling unit moved before the crates arrived: 84th Inf Div Arty*, 11th Armd Div Arty*, 12th Armd Div Arty*, 401st FA Gp HQ, 407th FA Gp HQ, 514th FA Bn, 25th FA Bn.

* Information received from Arty Air Officer ETOUSA (Major Gillespie) indicated that aircraft of these units would be flown from the UK by unit pilots.

(c) Eight Lucite eyebrows, windshields and top decks were installed for the 9th Armd Div.

(d) Combat markings, AAF serial numbers and squadron code markings were applied to all aircraft assembled. Also the markings were applied to aircraft belonging to 9th Armd Div, 44th Inf Div and 26th Inf Div (these units had previously assembled their own aircraft).

(4) Major Lefever advises squadron code markings of aircraft transferred from one Army to another should not be changed. Will also try to check the whereabouts of Major S. M. Smith, the 'phantom' XIII Corps Arty Air Officer.

(5) Informal concurrence given by this HQ for the return to Fort Sill of three unrated FA pilots (Welch and Pechar of the 2nd Armd Div and King of the 65th FA Bn).

(6) Report submitted to 12th Army Group on shortages found in aircraft received from Air Forces as replacements (cushions, covers, first aid kits, records, etc.).

(7) Message received indicating that Lt Zicard would depart by air from Rennes on October 30. He was held up by weather on October 28 and 29.

October 30

(1) Call from MASTER (First Army) Arty Air Officer, Major Bristol, reiterating request that the First Army L-5 retained by 29th Inf Div be returned PRONTO! However, 29th refused to relinquish the ship without a written order. XIV Corps Arty Exec said that this matter should be handled through command channels, but 29th still refuse to give up without a fight.

(2) Capt. Neal, 7th Armd Arty Air Officer, arrived at strip to pick up two replacement pilots and two aircraft. Remained overnight to have flak damage to his L-4 repaired by 50th MR&RS.

(3) Telecall from Major Wilson re parachute packing, adding news on the birth of his daughter (Carolyn, born October 23, brown curly hair, chubby, dimples!).

October 31

(1) Visit from 258th FA Gp Arty Air Officer to discuss Air OP matters. He requested Lt Heath, if sent to Ninth Army as a replacement pilot, be sent to his unit. (Lt Heath had been his assistant, was shot down over enemy territory, made his way back to friendly civilians and turned up in a military hospital in Paris.) He was requested to furnish an Air OP Loss Report on his L-4 (43-29831, turned in to MR&RS for repair of flak damage).

(2) 7th Armd Div Arty Air Officer (Capt. Neal) and Lts Crockatt and Graff departed for 7th Div strip. At 1615 hrs Lt Crockatt returned in a British Jeep, having made a crash landing. This occurred after knocking off a wheel on taking off from a pasture after becoming separated from the other two pilots in 'stinko' weather. Called 7th Armd at 1620hrs. Lt Hoffman reported it was hailing there and that Capt. Neal and Lt Graff had not yet arrived. Notified him that Lt Crockatt would be furnished a new aircraft and would remain here until sent for. 50th MR&RS notified to pick up 43-30523 (56-F) on November 1 and prepare another aircraft for Lt Crockatt.

(3) Pilot from 29th Inf Div reported that the Div Commanding General had ordered the Div Arty Air Officer to return their L-5 to First Army at once, rain or shine. As the weather was not good, the L-5's wings were removed and it was loaded on a truck and hauled to First Army.

(4) Major Lefever reported that ETOUSA Air Officer (Major Gillespie) was hot on the trail of Major Smith, but results were uncertain.

CHAPTER 5

Maastricht, November 1944

The move by HQ Ninth Army to Maastricht was accompanied by a lull in activity along the entire front line. Nevertheless, despite poor weather conditions, 230 combat missions were flown by the Army's Air OPs in the first eleven days of November, but about one quarter of these took place in just one day, the 4th. There were no casualties among Air OP personnel during this period, but five L-4s sustained major damage in operational accidents. Four of these were replaced immediately, while the fifth was repaired and returned to its unit. This left the 50th Mobile Reclamation and Repair Squadron with one serviceable and five repairable L-4s as reserves, although another twelve replacements were on order. During this same eleven days the 50th carried out five engine changes, together with minor overhauls on thirty aircraft and major overhauls on another eight. In addition, eight major and nine 'top' engine overhauls were completed.

Maastricht, a quaint old-world town with narrow cobbled streets, had many rest and recreation facilities, but was now under the path of German FZG-1 'flying bombs' intended for Antwerp. These weapons had first been used against London in June, and were now being used in attacks on the vitally important Belgian port. As Andrew Kennedy recalled:

Maastricht was right on the 'buzz bomb alley' to Antwerp and one day, when I was flying east of Aachen in an L-4, I noticed a gunner in one of our half-tracks following us with his quad fifties. I well remember hoping that he recognised us as a friend, but as I looked out of the left window I saw a 'buzz bomb' off our wingtip, heading in the opposite direction and so close it could have been a midair collision. It was probably my imagination, but I still think I could hear the sound of its motor over the roar of our mighty Continental!

Bad weather with poor visibility persisted during the period 12-18 November, although Air OPs were again able to operate most of the time. No L-4s were lost in combat, but three that received major damage in accidents were collected for repair by the 50th MR&RS and replaced by aircraft from the Army Pool. A crash pick-up crew of the 50th also collected an L-5 (42-99285) of the 125th LS. Flown by Lt John S. Wall, this aircraft was badly damaged on 14 November in an accident at Wolk, Belgium, but following repair it was returned to the squadron at Maastricht on 1 December.

Ninth Army reserve pilot strength was now better than of late, with nine in excess of establishment, including four recently received from the Ground Forces Replacement

System. By 18 November the situation had improved still further, with surplus pilots now totalling eleven, of whom six were with units and five in the Army Pool. To maintain or improve their flying proficiency, the latter were given cross-country administrative flights and regular short-field operating practice.

On 16 November, NUSA launched a new offensive, but bad weather continued to affect air operations. The cold, wet conditions that prevailed for much of the month also made life difficult for mechanics servicing aircraft in the open on FA strips. The heavy rain also created problems for the 50th MR&RS, its low-lying strip beside the river becoming a quagmire, and considerable effort was required to keep it usable. The mechanics' living quarters were no better, with their tents in a sea of mud, but despite these difficulties the 50th managed to service or repair about 40 per cent of NUSA's L-4s during the month.

The saga of Major 'Disappearing' Smith continued into November, with reports of him being sighted at Villacoublay and elsewhere in the early part of the month. And then, on 19 November, the long-lost XIII Group Arty Air Officer turned up at Lt Col. Leich's HQ airstrip at Maastricht, and his whereabouts for the last few weeks were revealed. Apparently Major Smith's flight from the UK had been prolonged by bad weather, and poor or no communications facilities at some of his en-route airfields had been responsible for the lack of news on his progress.

An after action report covering 19-25 November reveals that at the end of this period 220 Air OP aircraft were with NUSA. Of these only one L-4 was non-operational, this aircraft having received major damage from enemy shell fire on a forward airstrip. During the same period no Air OPs were lost in combat, but one that was badly damaged in an operational accident was collected, salvaged and replaced by the 50th MR&RS. This left nine L-4s in the Army Pool, three having been received during this period, with seven more on order from 12th Army Group. Work completed by the 50th that week included fifty-two minor and twenty-three major repairs to aircraft, six engine overhauls (four top and two major), and three engine changes. Spares holdings included fourteen engines. Personnel reserves were also good, with seven surplus pilots in units and nine in the Army Pool. Five replacement pilots who arrived on 24 November underwent refresher and orientation training before being assigned to units.

For some time the NUSA Arty Air Officer had been trying to obtain formal flying status for FA air observers, an essential requirement for them to receive flying clothing, and this status was now authorised by IX AFSC. Progress was also made with the acquisition of 73 octane aviation fuel; by 25 November 21,000 gallons had been obtained and reallocated to units, with approximately another 35,000 gallons expected shortly. Other Air OP matters receiving urgent attention by the Army Air Section were the condition of landing strips, the camouflage of Air OPs on the ground at forward airstrips, the procurement and installation of Lucite windshields and 'turtledecks' on L-4 aircraft, the inspection, repacking and repair of parachutes, and the procurement and distribution of non-detergent aviation oil.

Several changes were now being made in the disposition of the 125th Liaison Squadron, with 'D' Flight arriving at Maastricht on 19 November from detached service with 12th Army Group, 'A' Flight moving from VIII Corps to XIII Corps, and 'B' Flight being detached from

HQ NUSA to XIX Corps at Heerlen. Another event around this time was the mysterious disappearance of an L-5 of 'A' Flight while on a courier mission from Heerlen to Merkelbeek, a distance of only ten miles. According to the squadron's official history, this aircraft was never found, and its pilot S/Sgt Fred G. Stoeker and passenger Sgt William H. Hunt are still shown as 'missing in action'. However, further details of this incident are to be found in other records, including a USAAF missing air crew report dated 30 November. This states that the L-5 (42-99123), which carried the name *Hot Box*, took off from Heerlen at approximately 1230 hours on 26 November, but failed to reach its destination. (The unit history incorrectly gives the date of this incident as 11 November. It also gives the destination as Merkelsbeck, but this is an incorrect spelling of Merkelbeek, a small community situated about eight miles north of Heerlen.)

Weather conditions at the time were reported as 'CAVU' (ceiling and visibility unlimited), effectively ruling out bad weather as a possible case of an accident. A search for the missing aircraft was organised by 1/Lt Eugene O'Brien, the 125th's Operations Officer, who notified all Army and Air Force HQs and G-2 Sections in the area that the L-5 was missing. In addition, a search of the area between Heerlen (where the airstrip was located two miles south of the town) and Merkelbeek was carried out by aircraft of 'A' Flight, but no trace of the missing L-5 was found. Consequently, on 29 November, Lt O'Brien called upon the NUSA HQ Arty Air Section for assistance, and this resulted in S/Sgt Vandemeer, a pilot with the 84th Infantry Division, reporting that he had seen an aircraft shot down by enemy anti-aircraft fire at the time the L-5 was in the air (between 1300 and 1400 hours). No location was given, but a pilot with the 30th Infantry Division also reported seeing a 'Cub' shot down that day, about 500 yards east of Laon. This 'Cub' might actually have been an L-5 – they were often misidentified – but as Laon is about 140 miles from the Heerlen/Merkelbeek area it is most unlikely that this was the missing L-5. As for its occupants, the records of the US Army Graves Registry Service confirm that they were killed, thereby becoming the first fatalities suffered by the squadron. Sgt Hunt, a recipient of the Purple Heart, was buried on 27 November at Margraten Cemetery, six miles south-east of Maastricht, while S/Sgt Stoeker was buried some twenty miles distant at Neuville-en-Condroz Cemetery, Liège, but was later moved to Iowa, USA. The fact that they were initially buried some distance apart, and well away from the Heerlen/Merkelbeek area, heightens still further the mystery of where and why their L-5 crashed.

In recent weeks L-4 engine maintenance difficulties in NUSA had increased threefold, and this was explained by the use of 80 octane motor transport fuel instead of still difficult to obtain 73 octane aviation fuel. Aircraft performance had also deteriorated substantially and incorrect fuel was also seen as the reason for this, as well as contributing to accidents. Consequently, a major effort was made by the Ninth's Arty HQ Air Section to obtain a steady flow of the correct fuel from Petroleum, Oil and Lubricant (POL) Dumps. Small stocks had been located and approximately 30,000 gallons (one month's supply) were obtained and issued to units. This followed several meetings with major subordinate units and Air Force agencies, but there was no assurance that the supply of 73 octane fuel could be maintained. Other items continuing to be discussed at these meetings were modifications to aircraft and their winterisation, shortages of 30-weight non-detergent aviation oil, shortages of winter flying clothing for pilots and observers, and the physical condition of pilots.

Towards the end of November the renewed Allied ground offensive continued to make progress, with NUSA units reaching the Roer River on the 28th, but in the period 26–30 November heavy enemy flak and the shelling of forward airstrips resulted in major damage to six L-4s, five of which were repaired and returned to units with the sixth salvaged and replaced. Another L-4 was hit in flight by a 'friendly' 155-mm shell, without injury to pilot or observer, but the major damage sustained by the aircraft made a replacement necessary. A replacement was also required for the only aircraft badly damaged in an operational accident in this period. No pilot casualties occurred in the last week of the month, but three pilots from the Pool were used as temporary replacements for pilots who were sick in hospital. Overall, within NUSA there were now eight surplus pilots in units, with five in the Army Pool. With regard to surplus aircraft, on 30 November there were still nine L-4s in the Pool, with seven on order.

Extracts from the HQ NUSA Air Journal for 1-30 November 1944, compiled by Lt Col. R. M. Leich (Army Headquarters Air Section at Maastricht)

November 1
(1) 1st Lt Roach (196th FA Gp pilot) took off from A-42 Villacoublay heading eastwards for Belgium, but he soon returned because visibility varied from zero to half a mile.
(2) LUCKY (TUSA) Arty Air Officer, Maj. Wilson, requested we pick up three replacement aircraft at A-83 Denain/Valenciennes that had been ferried there for TUSA by mistake. However, it was pointed out that TUSA was closer to A-83 than we were. He had apparently confused A-83 with A-93 Liège/Bierset.
(3) Lt Crockatt (7th Armd Div pilot) went with a pick-up truck of 50th MR&RS to collect an L-4 that had crashed the day before. A replacement L-4 (44-79671: 56-F) for Lt Crockatt is ready.
(4) The 50th MR&RS picked up L-4 43-30352 and the engine from another L-4 (serial number unknown until 7th Armd Div submits a Loss Report). These two aircraft were lost by bombing, and 7th Armd Arty Air Officer will be requested to turn them in. The instruments had been stripped from one of these aircraft.

November 2
(1) Maj. King of 102nd Inf Div arrived today with seven L-4s. Another two had been forced down just outside Paris due to engine failures, and a third was thought to be with them as it was missed just after take-off. The reason for the failures, according to Maj. King, was the use of 80 octane motor fuel. Maj. King has dispatched a vehicle with two mechanics and an officer to locate these L-4s, repair them and bring them up.
(2) With the return of the Arty Air Section's Lt Zicard from Rennes, the 'Conquer Arty Air Force' is once again complete. Lt Zicard had taken off from Maastricht on October 21,

bound for Rennes to check on the whereabouts of some missing aircraft. His trip proved to be quite an epic, as the following report, which he made on November 3, reveals:

'October 21. Left Maastricht at 0915. Landed at 1140 in a field 60 miles north of Rheims, because of weather. After several attempts to leave, decided to remain overnight. The field was in the Ardennes Forest.

'October 22. Took off at 1315. Landed at Rheims at 1400 hrs. Arrived at A-47 Paris/Orly at 1800. A-42 Villacoublay was closed on account of weather.

'October 23. Ground fog – no flying. Another night in Paris. Met the 211th FA Gp pilots who were headed east.

'October 24. Left A-47 Paris/Orly at 1330. Arrived at 1730. Visibility was 1-2 miles.

'October 25. Pulled 25 hour inspection on aircraft.

'October 26. Flew 15 mins. Weather bad.

'October 27. Flew Lt Col. Kenney. Carburettor heater broke. Landed on a strip south of Jouleville. Lt Col. Kenney walked through a mine field to get gas. At Barneville – had carburettor heater welded and oil changed by XVI Corps. Capt. Hallstein asked me to see Maj. Gillespie about units that are in Normandy without aircraft. No arrangements had been made for the pilots to pick up aircraft. Remained in Barneville overnight.

'October 28. Arrived at Rennes from Barneville.

'October 29. Took off for Maastricht – turned back at Laval. Cloud was on the deck.

'October 30. Left Rennes; arrived at A-42 Paris-Villacoublay. Rain all the way from Le Mans.

'October 31. Refused clearance to take off by A-42. Tried to see Maj. Gillespie but he was not in. Met the pilots who were there to pick up aircraft (the ones I was to see Maj. Gillespie about). Capt. Wallister had sent Lt Kelter and Lt Williamson (XVI Corps pilots) with the other pilots to see that they received aircraft (evidently Capt. Wallister had contacted Maj. Gillespie before I did). The units, pilots, aircraft serial numbers and squadron codes were as follows:

407th Gp. Capt. Burman, 1st Lt Cline: 44-79789 (82-I), 44-79731 (82-J).

401st Gp. Capt. Davison, Capt. Mcorley, 1st Lt Fox: 44-79743 (82-G), 44-79671 (82-H).

349th Gp. Capt. Rickham, Capt. Pfeifer, 1st Lt Fields: 44-79665 (82-E), 44-79741 (82-F).

776th Bn. 1st Lt Bryan, 1st Lt Hancock: 44-79733 (82-O), 44-79762 (82-P).

758th Bn. 1st Lt Shepherd, 2nd Lt (?): 44-79561 (82-M), 44-79999 (82-N).

514th Bn. 1st Lt Seymour, 2nd Lt Pillsbury: 44-79560 (82-S), 44-79664 (82-T).

25th Bn. 1st Lt Capes, 1st Lt (?): 44-79661 (82-K), 44-79991 (82-L).

808th Bn. 2nd Lt Politella, 2nd Lt Ford: 44-79713 (82-Q), 44-80044 (82-R).

Aircraft Allocations Section, 2nd AADA at A-42, said six aircraft will be forwarded to A-92. The propeller on my aircraft was changed.'

November 4

(1) Capt. Mathews and Lt Duffy, preceded by 3 Me 109s (!), visited 29th Inf Div Arty Air Officer (Maj. Swenson) and informed him that two of his aircraft were ready at the MR&RS. The Me 109s took no action.

(2) Eng Officer, 50th MR&RS (Lt Newbury) made the following report on the condition of aircraft:

Serial No.	Obtained from	Condition
43-30310	6th Armd Div (Arzano)	Salvaged
43-2976	5th Inf Div (43rd MR&RS)	Repairable, awaiting parts
43-30523	7th Armd Div (not previously assigned)	Repaired
43-30237	557th FA Bn	Repaired

(3) Visit from 102nd Div Arty Air Officer (Maj. King). His air sections are bivouacked at Arty airstrip but he has already reconnoitered a strip near the front and plans to move today. His missing aircraft have arrived.

(4) Lt Zicard with Col. Nisely and the Arty Air Officer at 12th Army Group departed for Verdun but were grounded by weather near Luxembourg. Motor transport was obtained for Col. Nisely to complete his trip. Lt Zicard returned to the Arty strip.

(5) Maj. Lefever (EAGLE Arty Air Officer) called with regard to Maj. Sheldon Smith (XIII Group Arty Air Officer), reporting 'He has been located. The Replacement Depot in which he had been hibernating has been notified to release him so that he could fly to Maastricht, via A-42C Villacoublay, as soon as weather permits. This is positive – well, fairly positive!'

November 5

(1) Capt. Mathews accompanied by Col. Hamley on a visit to FUSA CP obtained the following information from the Army Arty Air Officer (Maj. Bristol):

(a) A-40 Chartres will be the new L-4H assembly point instead of A-42C Villacoublay. Lt Cramer, formerly in charge of work at Grove, will be there. He will again be prepared to produce 1/8" Lucite windshields and eyebrows.

(b) He is sending one of the officers in his section to camp on the doorstep of 2nd AADA at A-42C to ensure his requisitions are actioned.

(2) Message from XVI Corps: 84th Inf Div Arty notified Corps that 11 Div Arty aircraft were being flown from the UK to France on November 4.

(3) Authorisation was secured for the issue of one SCR 593 radio receiver to each Corps Arty HQ, Div Arty HQ, FA Brig HQ, and FA Group HQ for use at airstrips to receive anti-aircraft warnings.

November 6

(1) Visit by Capt. Good (RAF), British 30th Corps Air OP pilot. He wanted to base his squadron (16 Taylorcraft Austers) at our strip. Told him that the strip would not accommodate this number of aircraft in addition to those already there, but we could handle them for one night while he prepared his own strip closer to his CP. He stated that his Corps controls the squadron, allocating Flights of 4 aircraft to each Division when requested to do so, that many 'ridiculous missions' (such as hunting for one sniper) had caused casualties in the squadron since D-Day, that they never performed courier missions, that their aircraft were not too satisfactory (not enough power [130 hp], not enough maneuverability and not enough climb). He indicated that he might help to obtain 30-weight aviation oil from the RAF when he gets in position, and that the RAF didn't like the fact that their pilots flying for the Arty wore Army khaki uniform.

(2) An Air OP pilot of 472nd FA Group visited the Arty strip and brought his L-4 (44-79701: 68-O) to the 50th MR&RS for major repairs to flak damage. Flying over enemy lines this

morning this aircraft was hit, but is repairable. The pilot was not injured but the observer (1st Lt Domwel) suffered minor wounds. An Air OP loss report will be filed.

(3) Visit from 30th Inf Div Arty Air Officer (Maj. Blohm) to discuss supply matters. He believes it imperative than an L-5 be assigned to Div Arty HQ (the Commanding General weighs over 200 lbs and likes to fly).

November 7

(1) Visit by Arty Air Officer XIX Corps (Capt. Reed), who reported that Air OP traffic at the front has been too heavy, with the result that Corps has ordered that all flights be cleared at Corps Fire Direction Center (FDC) to reduce air saturation. Flights to the rear (25 miles) are authorised for training purposes. This is a temporary measure and does not indicate Corps desire to 'take over'.

(2) 94th Inf Div aircraft reported grounded due to having used detergent oils. 200 gallons non-detergent oil critically needed.

(3) ETOUSA (Maj. Gillespie) reported that no further word had been received from Maj. Smith, but he was expected at A-42C Villacoublay at any time.

November 9

Capt. Mathews departed by air for A-20C Lessay and Chartres to follow up AF supply matters (unfilled requisitions of 50th MR&RS for Lucite windshields, eyebrows and turtledecks, observers' flying jackets, trousers and helmets).

November 10

(1) Lts Kistler and Lillibridge, 2nd Armd Div Arty pilots, visited Arty strip to pick up replacement aircraft for 14th FA Bn. L-4s 43-29641 and 43-30229 were wrecked in cross-wind landings on the Battalion strip and will be picked up by the 50th MR&RS on November 11. L-4s 44-79744 (49-M) and 44-79768 (49-P) were assigned as replacements. Weather and darkness prevented delivery today.

(2) Message from XIII Corps (Lt Roark, acting Arty Air Officer) reported that an L-4 of 196th FA Group had been 'disabled'. No further details reported. We are having a replacement prepared for delivery. L-4s on hand are 43-30237 (earmarked for 196th FA Group) and 43-30523.

(3) A War Correspondent, Mr Banker, arrived to arrange a visit to the front by L-4H.

(4) Eleven pilots and aircraft of 84th Inf Div arrived at Arty airstrip. Capt. Paschall departed for unit HQ, the other ten pilots remained overnight.

(5) Lt Duffy visited A-92 St Trond to check the arrival of six replacement L-4Hs. None had arrived.

November 11

(1) XIII Corps Acting Arty Air Officer (Lt Roark) reported a disabled L-4 of 196th FA Group at Group airstrip. Aircraft iced up, went over on its back in forced landing. 50th MR&RS crash crew departed to pick it up; 43-30237 will be ready on November 12 as replacement. Capt. Morrison, Group Arty Air Officer, will file a loss report.

(2) EAGLE Arty Air Officer (Maj. Lefever) called with regard to replacement aircraft: 'Six are at A-42C awaiting availability of AF ferry pilots. Will be flown to A-92 St Trond sometime. Additional NUSA requirement for six is being put in today for earliest possible delivery. With regard to Maj. "Phantom" Smith, ETOUSA (Maj. Gillespie) reported that he was to leave (or had left) Paris for Maastricht yesterday (November 10). Re conditions at EAGLE airstrip, my L-5 was sitting in 18 inches of water at the strip this morning.'

November 12

(1) Maj. Smith ('Vanishing Smith'), XIII Corps Arty Air Officer, has still not checked in from A-42C Villacoublay.

(2) Capt. Mathews arrived back and reported on his trip to A-42C. Among other things the matter of obtaining rear-vision mirrors from P-38s was taken up, but he was told none were available. Also, a new memorandum will be published by ETOUSA regarding combat markings on Cubs. They will either be completely removed or just a 6" stripe left to aid new units identify friendly aircraft. Visited Lt Cregar at A-40 Chartres with regard to Lucite windshields, eyebrows and turtledecks for L-4H aircraft. His equipment for this work is in the process of being shipped to the Continent. Lt Cregar has only a small quantity of material on hand at the present time. He expects to set up his unit at A-42C Villacoublay or A-40 Chartres, and be ready for production in the next two weeks.

Lt Tippin of Aircraft Allocations Section, 2nd ADAA, has six Cubs for NUSA, but is snowed under with fighter planes and has no ferry pilots. The Aircraft Allocations Section is being transferred to A-93 Liège. Aircraft will be sent to A-92 St Trond until the field can accommodate C-47s (for returning ferry pilots to their base). From Maj. Lefever: 'Nine aircraft only were left at A-42C before transfer of activities to another location. These are on their way up. FUSA needs six, so you (NUSA) can have three for the Pool. If the situation on ferry pilots gets tight again, I will arrange for NUSA pilots to go get 'em.'

November 13

(1) No current reports concerning the whereabouts of Maj. ('Disappearing') Smith, XIII Corps Arty Air Officer. He is believed to be weathered in somewhere west of here.

(2) Lt Sladek, 753rd FA Btn took delivery of L-4 43-30237 as a replacement for 44-79545, damaged in November. The latter is repairable.

November 15

(1) Lt Col. Leich and Lts Mathews, Duffy, Coolan, Bergman and Norton flew to A-95 Nancy/Azelot to pick up three replacement L-4s, serial numbers 44-80022, 44-80037 and 44-80042. Report of missing seat cushions (100%) was made to Flying Control and will be relayed to EAGLE.

(2) The number of Air OPs in NUSA is as follows:

Army HQ: 3

XIX Corps: 92 (includes one in excess in 2nd Armd Div)

XIII Corps: 51 (includes 12 with units attached to the British and one in excess in 84th Inf Div Arty)

34th FA Bgde: 3
Units in Normandy: 22
Units on Forecast: 42
50th MR&RS Pool: 3
50th MR&RS under repair: 4
Total: 220

(3) Conference with Lt Newbury, Engineer Officer, 50th MR&RS, concerning rear-view mirrors, winterization of aircraft, microphone switch in control stick, jigs for transporting wings and fuselages of crashed aircraft, increasing the effectiveness of the cabin heater, mooring rings, tailwheel springs, and other technical matters.

(4) No report from Maj. Smith ('Evanescent Smith'), but believed headed this way.

(5) Visit to Arty strip by Lt Kistler, Asst Army Air Officer (Engineering) 2nd Armd Div Arty, to report their third wrecked L-4 in a week. This was 43-30495 (49-C), cracked up on November 14 by Lt Miller in a forced landing apparently caused by carburettor icing. Lt Kistler requested that the wrecked aircraft be picked up at Hansbach. Replacement L-4H 44-80042 (squadron code 49-C) was prepared and delivered to Lt Kistler. No assignment to the 2nd Armd Div will be made as it was learned (later) that the unit had one L-4 in excess of number authorised.

November 17

(1) Capt. Reed, Arty Air Officer, XIX Corps Arty, stated that British Air OPs (without squadron code markings) flying in or near XIX Corps units were repeatedly reported to Corps as 'enemy Cubs'.

(2) Lts Coonan and Moran flew to A-95 Liège to check on replacement L-4Hs delivered there. Six were on the field: 44-80013, 44-80036, 44-79559, 44-80030, 44-80031 and 44-80118. Allocation of the first three was not known, but the last three were consigned to LUCKY. This was reported to EAGLE Arty Air Officer, Maj. Lefever, who will arrange releases to MASTER and NUSA on November 19.

(3) Lts Bergman and Norton visited A-92 St Trond to attempt (through Flying Control) to check airfields to determine possible location of Maj. Smith. Communication lines were tied up due to heavy air support operations, so nothing was accomplished.

(4) The squadron code markings and serial number of Maj. Smith's L-4 were reported to MASTER for them to check if it was in their area.

(5) A-62 Rheims reported no record of a visit there by Maj. Smith.

(6) Flying Control 9th Air Force has been notified of the missing aircraft and pilot by Maj. Lefever.

(7) An officer of this section will visit A-69 Laon/Athies on November 19 to make a further check.

(8) Lt Zicard reported that 43-30091 (43-A) was picked up from 29th Inf Div for major repairs. The unit did not want a replacement, but preferred the return of the same L-4. It should be ready on November 21. Five O-170-3 engines for L-4Hs were ready for pick-up by 50th MR&RS at A-42 Villacoublay. Lt Zicard also reported the following activity by the 50th MR&RS during the week November 11-17. Crash pick-ups: five L-4s, one L-5. Repairs:

30 minor, 6 major. Engine overhauls: 9 top, 6 major. Parachutes exchanged for repacking: 120. Replacement aircraft received: 3. Replacement aircraft turned out: 3.

(9) The search for Maj. Smith, XIII Corps Arty Air Officer, continues.

November 19

(1) Maj. Smith ('Nomadic Smith'), XIII Corps Arty Air Officer, arose out of the 'Belgian Fog' and reported to the CP. In 48 hours he would have been declared 'AO'. Reason for his delay in arriving from A-42 was weather. He was grounded at a British field from where he could communicate with practically nobody.

(2) Lt Kistler, 2nd Armd Div Arty Air Officer (Engineer), visited Arty strip and requested the loan of three aircraft pending the making of minor repairs to two flyable aircraft of the unit.

(3) Report from Arty Air Officer XII Group (Maj. Ketcham) on the crash of 43-30304 (33-V), 256th FA Bn, Lt Swan pilot. The aircraft failed to clear trees on a cross-wind take-off and suffered severe damage. 50th MR&RS will pick up the aircraft at XII Group strip on November 20, repair it and return it to unit. No replacement will be made. No injuries to personnel reported.

(4) Maj. Ketcham (see preceding) later requested that 43-30304 be replaced. 43-29642 (33-V) will be furnished as a replacement.

November 21

Maj. Lefever called to report that 10th ADG at A-42C Villacoublay would stock immediately 100 Lucite windshields and 100 sets of Lucite eyebrows, available on requisition to MR&RSs.

November 22

2nd Armd Div Asst Arty Air Officer (Eng), Lt Kistler, brought two L-4s to the Arty strip, one for replacement of a wing (bullet hole through spar), the other for exchange 'because it is not in good condition'. Repair work initiated on one ship and Lt Kistler informed that if the other ship was not flyable it could be turned in without replacement as the Division had one aircraft in excess of authorised allowances. XIX Corps Arty Air Officer, Capt. Reed, concurred with this action.

November 23

(1) Lt Col. Leich and Maj. Lefever visited 2nd ADG at A-93 Liège to discuss parachute repacking, delivery of replacement L-4Hs, and the dispatch of FA pilots to the Arty air strip. Maj. Hanning, Engineer Officer, stated that he could handle 500 parachutes per month for us (or 50%) and that in two days time he would train FA mechanics of all major units in methods of making required 10 day inspections. Lt Lamonte, Operations Officer, stated that he would take care of replacement aircraft received there and notify this section of their receipt, and that he would instruct FA unit pilots arriving there from the UK to proceed to Maastricht. S/Sgt Roehrich was taken along to check over the three aircraft at A-93 Liège, released to NUSA by EAGLE. One requires a new aileron, another a new propeller,

carburettor air filter, brakes, etc. New parts will be flown to A-93 together with a mechanic on November 24 and when repairs are completed the aircraft (serial numbers 44-80013, 44-80036 and 44-79559) will be picked up.

(2) Maj. Lefever stated that 78th Inf Div FA pilots would be briefed by ETOUSA to fly from the UK to A-93 Liège, to obtain further instructions upon arrival there.

November 24

(1) Lts Coonan, Bergmann and Norton with S/Sgts Roehrich and Tye flew to A 93 Liège to complete repairs to and pre-flight check six L-4Hs at that strip. Three were allocated to NUSA, the other three to TUSA.

(2) Call from LUCKY Arty Air Officer, Maj. Wilson, asking if we could fly his three replacement aircraft from A-93 to LUCKY airstrip, if he provided return air transportation for our pilots. Answer: yes.

(3) Authority was received from 12th Army Gp for the issue of flying clothing (helmets, jackets and trousers) to FA air observers. Total requirements for the Army (based on approximately 240 observers) were given to 50th MR&RS in order that a bulk requisition could be sent to 2nd ADG tomorrow.

(4) FA replacement pilots 2nd Lts Coppock, Fergusson, Fulkerson, Gordon and Hunter reported at CP. Their orders mistakenly assigned them to HQ NUSA, but they will be retained here as attached until assigned to units.

November 25

(1) Lt Bergmann flew S/Sgt Tie to A-93 Liège to complete repairs on replacement aircraft 44-79559 and 44-80119. The latter was absent, having been borrowed by a P-51 pilot to go to Brussels. Operations Officer at A-93 signalled Brussels for immediate return of the aircraft.

(2) Lt Anderson, Asst Army Arty Air Officer at TUSA, and two pilots picked up three replacement aircraft at A-93, relieving NUSA pilots of the task of delivering then to Nancy.

(3) Lt Col. Leich, Capt. Mathews, Lts Cooman, Bergman, Coppock, Gordon and Hunter and S/Sgt Tie flew to A-93 to pick up and bring back three replacement aircraft.

November 26

2nd Armd Div Asst Arty Air Officer (Eng), Lt Kistler, visited the strip and reported major damage to 44-80113 (87-J) of 84th Inf Div, caused when enemy aircraft dropped anti-personnel bombs near the 2nd Armd Div Arty airstrip. A crash crew was sent to pick up this aircraft. No replacement will be furnished as the 84th has one aircraft in excess of authorised allowance.

November 27

Capt. Mathews and Lt Bergmann visited 228th Group strip to discuss repairs to aircraft damaged on November 25. Also discussed the matter of air observers being relieved after completing 35 missions and being replaced by new personnel (to spread out the Air Medals) in 755th Bn.

November 29

Lt O'Brien, Operations Officer, 125th LS, requested information concerning L-5 42-99123 missing on a flight from Heerlen to Merkelsberk between 1300 and 1400 hrs on November 26. This aircraft was in the Flight attached to XIII Corps. Capt. Paschall, 84th Inf Div Arty Air Officer, was requested to follow up the rumour that one of his pilots, S/Sgt Vandeveer, had seen an aircraft shot down by enemy ack-ack at about the time indicated.

November 30

(1) Lt Kistler, Asst Arty Air Officer (Eng), 2nd Armd Div, reported that an Air OP of 65th Armd FA Bn had been struck by a 'friendly' Arty shell which did not explode. The L-4 suffered damage requiring major repairs but returned to its strip, its occupants unharmed. The aircraft (43-29629) is repairable, but 43-30495 has been supplied as a replacement.

Lt Moran flew a radio mechanic to AFID at A-89 Le Culot but returned alone. This technician seems to prefer the dangers of traveling in a Jeep to the safety of flying in an aircraft, this being the second time this has happened.

(2) Maj. Hallstein, XVI Corps Arty Air Officer, and Capt. Welter and Lt Williamson, Corps Arty pilots, visited the CP to discuss Air OP matters. Their unit will be closed at Tongres this date. L-4 44-79559 (82-A) was assigned to XVI Corps.

(3) Capt. Mathews and Lts Coppock and Hunter made reconnaissance flights in the vicinity of Aachen.

(4) Maj. King, 102nd Div Arty Air Officer, visited the strip to pick up a new L-4 (44-80013: 76-A) to replace 44-80049 which suffered major damage in an operational accident. The latter will be picked up by the 50th MR&RS on December 1 at the Div Arty airstrip.

(5) Lt O'Brien, Operations Officer, 125th LS, was informed that no further information had been obtained concerning the missing L-5 referred to in yesterday's Journal. He had received an additional report through G-2 channels that a 'Cub' (which could have been an L-5) had been seen shot down 500 yards East of Laon on 26 November. This report was attributed to a 'Lt Reed, 30th Div Arty pilot' (who doesn't exist – possibly this could be Capt. Reed, XIX Corps Arty Air Officer). Lt Williams, 125th LS, asked that our pilots keep a look-out for the wreckage when, as, and if possible.

CHAPTER 6

The Battle of the Bulge, December 1944

During the first two weeks of December a total of 177 L-4 aircraft were operational in Ninth Army units, with another thirteen in the Army Replacement Pool. During this same period the Army experienced no losses through enemy action, but two L-4s that were badly damaged in operational accidents were subsequently salvaged for serviceable parts. According to a NUSA after action report, another three were so badly damaged that replacements were issued while they were being repaired. There were no crew casualties, but three pilots were reassigned from the Army, including one transferred to the rear as 'war weary'. This left five surplus pilots in units and another five in the Army Pool, but extensive use was made of the latter on administrative flights for various Sections of the Army Headquarters.

A seemingly strange event on 9 December was the assignment of the 75th Infantry Division to NUSA, 'strange' because at this time the 75th was located in Wales, where its HQ had arrived at Tenby on 2 November. Casting his mind back to this time, Ed 'Skeeter' Carlson, then a mechanic with the Air Section of the Division's 899th FA Battalion, recalled:

> Early in November we departed New York in the British ocean liner *Aquitania* and a few days later arrived in Scotland. A steam train then took us south to Cardiff, where our Air Section occupied an airstrip adjacent to Camp Heath. Each morning we went to the local airport to uncrate and assemble the eight L-4H Cubs that had been shipped there earlier. All were ready for test hops by the time the pilots arrived, these being the same lieutenants we had trained with in the States, with Lts Mann and Wallin assigned to the 899th.

Following assembly the eight L-4s were flown to the Camp Heath airstrip (located on what is now Heath Park, adjacent to the University Hospital of Wales. The local airport mentioned by Carlson was the pre-war Cardiff civil airport at Pengam Moors.) A week or so later they departed for the 'far shore', routeing via Beachy Head to Rouen. They were led by Capt. (later Col.) Edward L. Wolff, the Division's Arty Air Officer, who recalled, 'we were escorted by a British seaplane, to rescue any of us who went into the drink, but luckily none of us did'. More precisely the escorting aircraft was a Supermarine Walrus amphibian of No. 277 Squadron, an RAF Air/Sea Rescue Service unit based at Hawkinge, Kent. While most of the Division arrived at Le Havre, the Air Section mechanics disembarked at Rouen and then drove their weapons carriers to Liège, where they caught up with their aircraft on 19 December. On Christmas Eve they went into combat at Grand-Halleux, but three days later the 75th

Infantry was transferred to the First US Army in a reshuffle of units brought about by an unexpected development.

In recent months the battle for Europe had gone well for the Allies, but before dawn on 16 December, the Germans launched a surprise counter-attack on a 60-mile front against weakly held First US Army positions in the Ardennes Forest of Belgium. Enemy tanks and infantry pushed quickly between Maastricht and Luxembourg city, aiming to retake the vitally important port of Antwerp while at the same time cutting off large forces of American, British and other troops in Holland and Germany.

Within 48 hours, in what was to become known as the Battle of the Bulge, the Germans had bypassed and isolated 9,000 American troops. At first there was much confusion and it took some time to fully appreciate the seriousness of the threat. Intelligence on the precise whereabouts of the enemy was poor, and heavy snow and poor visibility during the early stages of the offensive robbed the Allies of their usually very effective air support. To contain the situation, the Allies were forced to fall back, regroup and throw in their strategic reserves, with NUSA, now isolated from HQ 12th Army Group, relinquishing some units before organising its sector for a defence in depth.

On 15 December, the day before the German offensive began, 235 L-4s were either in service with the Ninth Army or about to join it, and as the land battle developed it became clear that many aircraft in forward positions would have to be flown back to safer areas. Of this period Andrew Kennedy, the pre-war private pilot at that time a combat engineer with NUSA's HQ Staff, recalled:

> Colonel Leich, who had more airplanes on hand than he had rated L-pilots, knew that First Army had to destroy some of their L-4s to stop them falling into German hands, but if a similar situation arose he did not want to do this. He told me that if the Germans got close to Maastricht he was going to have me fly one of the Cubs back to France, so he wouldn't have to destroy it. As it happened, we didn't have to pull out, so I didn't get my chance to fly solo in an L-4.

However, there were now reports of 'enemy Cubs' flying over the Allied lines, and these were believed to be former First Army aircraft captured by the Germans.

A major change resulting from the German penetration was the transfer on 20 December of both the Ninth and First US Armies to General Sir Bernard Montgomery's British 21st Army Group, despite opposition to this by General Omar Bradley. Nevertheless, this arrangement was to remain in force for NUSA until 4 April 1945. With this reorganisation some Ninth Army units were transferred to the First Army, which was mainly engaged in reducing the German salient from the north while the Ninth Army held the line along the Roer. Accordingly, on 21 December, XIII Corps took over the XIX Corps sector, with the latter taking over the VII Corps sector (which remained under the First US Army). This was followed the next day with the transfer of the 8th Infantry Division from the First Army to NUSA's XIX Corps.

Another movement at this time involved the 407th Field Artillery Group, an advanced detachment of which had arrived in France on 9 September, but the main party of the

Group's HQ and HQ Battery did not leave New York until 24 September. After landing at Gourock, the 407th continued by train to Southampton to board a freighter bound for France, and off the coast of Normandy transferred to an LCT which reached Omaha Beach on 3 October. After one night in nearby Transit Area No. 2 the 407th moved by motor convoy to the Valognes staging area, but the very next day, 5 October, the Group was ordered to move 'without delay' to Tongres, Belgium, where it was to join the Ninth Army's XVI Corps. However, the departure was delayed and the Group's motor convoy did not leave Valognes until 7 December, when it began a three-day journey to Wellen, Belgium. Morale, already high, was further boosted by the advance parties obtaining good billets along the route, the first night being spent in a thirty-five-room mansion and the second in a French army barracks. At Wellen the 407th experienced action for the first time when its HQ was strafed by enemy aircraft. Several V-1 flying bombs also fell in the area. From Wellen the Group continued to Stolberg, Germany, where it arrived on 23 December, the 60-mile journey being made in cold, clear weather, and the next day section chiefs and officers were sent to adjacent frontline units to become 'combat-wise'. The Air Sections of units assigned to the 407th at this time, together with those of the HQ and HQ Battery, were under the control of Capt. (soon to be Maj.) Henry M. Burmann, the Group Arty Air Officer, with a Group airstrip established close to the HQ command post.

In the meantime, the 101st Airborne Division, resting at Rheims after the ill-fated Operation *Market-Garden*, had been ordered to proceed to Bastogne, where it was to earn fresh laurels fighting alongside elements of the 9th and 10th Armored Divisions. Despite being completely surrounded and sustaining heavy casualties, the 101st stood firm in the beleaguered city and for the first time since it was launched on 16 December the enemy offensive faltered. However, it was not fully contained until 17 January, following attacks on the north side of the 'bulge' by the Ninth Army and on the south side by General Patton's Third Army. Had the thrust into Belgium succeeded, the consequences for the Allies would have been extremely serious.

During the period 1-15 December the 50th Mobile Reclamation and Repair Squadron completed eleven major and thirty minor repairs on Ninth Army aircraft. In addition, its crash pick-up crews collected five L-4s, and engine changes were accomplished on five aircraft. This left four serviceable engines on hand, together with eleven repairable spare engines. This was followed, during the second half of the month, by five engine changes, eight crash pick-ups, major repairs to fourteen aircraft and minor repairs to another sixty-two. At the end of the month, twenty-two serviceable spare engines were on hand, together with seven spare engines needing repairs. In addition, the 50th MR&RS was also involved in the repair of three aircraft of the attached 125th Liaison Squadron. On 1 December, two of the 125th's L-5s (42-99307 and 42-99318), flown by T/Sgts Israel H. Rosner and Samuel D. Brose, were accidentally damaged on the Maastricht strip, followed three days later by a non-flying accident to another L-5 (42-99306), also at Maastricht, but this aircraft was quickly repaired and returned to the squadron. Another L-5 was involved in a crash landing in the Amby district of Maastricht, where it came down in a pasture owned by a dairy farmer named Van den Born, but little more is known about this incident. Contrary to what might be expected, this aircraft did not belong to the locally based 125th LS, nor did it belong to any other liaison squadron in the ETO. This is confirmed by unit histories, supported by the fact that no relevant USAAF accident report was raised. This would seem to indicate that the L-5 belonged to an AGF unit, yet there is no mention of the incident in Ninth or other US Army records. Due to its location, this aircraft would normally have been collected by a crash pick-up crew of the nearby 50th MR&RS, but no such recovery took place as within hours of its crash landing the aircraft had disappeared, its many parts being taken by souvenir-hunting local civilians. Some of these parts still exist, including the L-5's partly damaged propeller and its six-cylinder Lycoming engine, which was partly restored in the 1970s by the son of the person who originally acquired it. Many years later, ownership passed to the late Rob Delachaux of Saint-Pancras who, in 2008, completed its restoration and succeeded in starting and running the engine for the first time since 1944. However, details of the L-5 and the unit to which it belonged remain a mystery to this day.

A worthwhile experiment during the month had been the installation of a K-22 camera in one of the 125th's L-5s. This was accomplished by removing the rear door of the aircraft and placing the very large camera on a flexible mount in the doorway. On 17 December, the first photographic sortie for the Ninth Army was carried out over the area between Barmen and Linnich in Germany, the results of the mission subsequently being used by the Infantry, Artillery and G-2 Intelligence Sections of XIII Corps. Subsequent missions covered the Roer River and the entire Ninth Army front, the pilots being T/Sgt Robert P. McGaw, T/Sgt Samuel D. Brose – previously a recipient of the Air Medal, awarded for meritorious service in the air over Europe – and Capt. Eugene O'Brien, with Capt. William M. Lyons and Lt Frank Haneman acting as camera operators. With a move to Kornelimünster on 18 December, the 125th's 'B' Flight became the first section of the squadron to operate in Germany, but almost immediately its stay was threatened by the German offensive.

At the end of December the authorised strength of Air OPs with the Ninth Army, including units about to be assigned to it, was 197. Of these, 150 were in operational units and ten in the Army Pool (of which six were flyable, with four undergoing repair). No aircraft were lost due to enemy action in the period 16-31 December, but one was damaged beyond repair in an operational accident and salvaged for spares. Another seven aircraft that were damaged in accidents were replaced from the Army Pool, and five more were supplied to First US Army as replacements. One pilot, the 102nd Infantry Division's Arty Air Officer, was listed as a combat casualty, another pilot was hospitalised as a result of an operational accident, and a third was lost by transfer to the First Army. Nevertheless, there remained five excess pilots in the Army Pool, with three more in units. An FA mechanic with the 104th Inf Div Arty was also a casualty, but he was immediately replaced through the Ground Forces Replacement System.

The increased number of accidents in recent weeks was cause for concern and as a result every effort was made by the Army HQ Air Section to impress upon personnel the need to improve both flying and aircraft maintenance standards. The reception, routeing, dispatching and escorting Arty pilots who were joining their units or moving to new areas also received close attention, as did the better co-ordination of crash pick-ups and the carrying out of major repairs by the 50th MR&RS. Attention was also being given to more reports of 'enemy Cubs'

– captured L-4s being flown over Allied lines by the enemy – together with a more effective means of supplying spare parts and other Air Force items to Arty units by 50th MR&RS.

Extracts from the HQ NUSA Air Journal for 1-31 December 1944, compiled by Lt Col. R. M. Leich (Army HQ Arty Air Section at Maastricht)

December 1

(1) After many weeks trying to obtain 73 octane aviation fuel, it has at last been agreed that the AAF will supply it in 55-gallon drums, starting in about three weeks, in sufficient quantity to allow approximately 50,000 gallons per Army per month. The AAF will also bring in approximately 1,000 gallons of 30-weight aviation oil per month.

(2) 45th Air Depot Group will start production of an unknown number of Lucite turtledecks in the near future and supply them to 10th ADG, from where MR&RS requisitions will be filled. The AAF has been requested to revise manufacturing specifications of L-4s to provide for factory installation in future production.

(3) Ten L-4s of the 78th Div Arty Air Section are at Y-29 Asch, having been flown over from England.

(4) Maj. Smith, Arty Air Officer at XIII Corps, reported major damage to 44-80061 (76-D) of the 102nd Inf Div at the Corps strip (used by the 102nd Div as a forward strip). A pilot and observer were in the L-4 which was still on the ground with its engine running ready to take off when enemy aircraft started to strafe the strip. In evacuating the aircraft one of the occupants knocked the throttle forward. The unoccupied aircraft took off down the field, crashing at the end of it. No casualties.

December 2

(1) 102nd Inf Div Asst Arty Air Officer (Eng) reported the location of L-4 44-80061, which suffered major damage yesterday, and requested that it be picked up and a replacement supplied. The 50th MR&RS sent out a crash pick-up crew. 43-30229 (76-D) was assigned in its place from the Army Replacement Pool.

(2) L-4 43-29629 (59-I), which was being flown by Lt White when a 'friendly' 155mm shell passed through it, was brought in for major repairs. 43-30495 was assigned as a replacement from the Army Pool.

December 3

(1) Visit from Capt. Reed (XIX Corps Arty Air Officer) to discuss, among other things, rest periods for pilots. He believes some really need it, such as the pilot who was installing a 30-caliber machine gun in his L-4, but believes that all units in the Corps have a scheme. He will check and advise further on this.

(2) Maj. Lefever called to say that L-4s for NUSA with the following serial numbers were being delivered to A-93 Liège by 45th ADG: 44-80187, 44-80188, 44-80239, 44-80245, 44-80368 and 44-80226. This leaves just one aircraft on order. Also, ETOUSA has arranged

for pilots of units in the UK to fly to France and join their units before proceeding to the Army Arty airstrip.

December 4
(1) Maj. Horn of the 78th Inf Div started bringing in his aircraft to have their serial numbers painted on their tails.

(2) Lt Coppock, NUSA replacement pilot, flew to A-93 Liège to check on aircraft there for NUSA. He returned with information that the following five L-4s were there, assigned to us: 44-80187, 44-80188, 44-80226, 44-80239 and 44-80245. NUSA replacement pilots flew four of these to the *Conquer* Arty Air strip. 44-80239 was not there, but two aircraft were discovered on the field that the operations office knew nothing about. A check will be made to determine the units to which they belong. L-4s for FUSA were also on the field, their serial numbers being 44-80024, 44-80206, 44-80345, 44-80358 and 44-80380. These aircraft were equipped with the old 3-piece windshields and did not have Lucite eyebrows; they were complete in every other respect, except that a tie-down kit was missing from one of them.

December 5
(1) Lts Coonan and Moran, replacement pilots, went to A-93 Liège and located two L-4s (44-80239 and 44-80368) which they brought in, making six new aircraft in the Army Pool in addition to those already on hand.

(2) Lt O'Shaughnessy of the 252nd FA Bn wrecked an aircraft on take-off when he stalled into the ground while trying to make a turn to avoid some trees. His L-4, 44-79630, was replaced by 44-79545.

(3) Lt Kerr of the 83rd Armd FA Bn crashed on a crosswind take-off when a wheel hit a log and threw him into a fence. His L-4, 44-79737, was replaced by 44-80036.

(4) Lt Beadling of the 78th Inf Div brought in four more aircraft to have serial numbers painted on their tails. They will finish this on all their aircraft tomorrow.

December 6
Lt Zicard reported that 2nd AADA had ordered the 50th MR&RS to transfer the personnel of two of its nine repair units, complete with equipment, to another station. It is understood that each of the three MR&RSs in 12th Army Group will be reduced by such transfers of cadre personnel to form a new MR&RS for the newly arrived 15th US Army.

December 7
(1) Visit by Maj. Davis, CO of the 50th MR&RS, who has just returned from a visit to 2nd AADA (Paris) with the following information:

(a) The Chief, Maintenance Div, 2nd AADA, has stated definitely, without a shadow of doubt, that detergent oil should not be used in O-170-3 engines.

(b) Turtledecks etc. Production still not under way.

(c) Loss of two units (36 men) and equipment as cadre for new MR&RS; only the equipment of one unit will be required. One unit will be replaced by untrained or semi-trained personnel (this is a better break than we expected).

(d) Transfer of 45 glider mechanics from MR&RS: 2nd AADA and IX AF Service Command have resisted this but have been overruled by USSTAF. They recommended that since the loss of these men would seriously cripple MR&RS operations, the Army should initiate action through Army Group to settle the situation. It does not seem likely that these glider mechanics could be replaced in the near future with adequately trained personnel. 2nd AADA will hold up action for a few days. This was taken up with 12th Army Gp Arty Air Officer, Maj. Lefever, who, together with Col. Redekin, decided to handle the matter informally with USSTAF (Maintenance Division, Capt. Purman) through ETOUSA Arty Air Officer (Maj. Gillespie). The Army Group could not initiate a formal letter to the Air Forces on an AF personnel admin matter, particularly since the War Dept was beating the drum for the use of Army Air Depot Units, designed primarily for the job which the MR&R Squadrons are doing in the Armies. The Army Air Depot Unit has 4 officers and 54 enlisted men.

(2) Call from Maj. Parker, Surgeon Section, requesting information concerning capabilities of L-1 aircraft in evacuating wounded from forward Arty airstrips. Several L-1s are available to the Army as flying ambulances.

(3) 104th Inf Div had lost two aircraft, two pilots and two observers since being with First Army.

(4) A visiting FA pilot from the 84th Inf Div Arty was asked to which base went the salvaged parts of 44-80119, which was wrecked near Caen, France, on November 4.

(5) Two FA pilots (2nd Lt G. J. Pechar and 1st Lt W. M. Emerick) and a mechanic (Tec 4 Louis E. Yarbrough) had been declared surplus by the 2nd Armd Div and shipped to the 18th Replacement Depot at Tongres. Arrangements were made for the pilots to be attached unassigned to NUSA and for the mechanic to be made available to First Army (he was previously the mechanic of Maj. Bristol, the First Army Arty Air Officer, who requested the man to fill one of two mechanic vacancies in First Army units). Lt Emerick duly went to 2nd Armd Div, but Lt Pechar was to remain here until orders are received for his return to the States.

(6) Maj. Lefever on Lucite products: 'Materials are short on the Continent. Windshields and eyebrows will have first priority. Have ordered 800 turtledecks. '

December 9

(1) Fifteen (of a requisition for 100) one-piece windshields were received today from 10th ADG and were allocated as follows: one to 2nd Armd Div, two to XVI Corps Arty, eight to Replacement Pool, and four to 84th Inf Div.

(2) Engineer Officer 50th MR&RS (Lt Newbury) reported that L-4H 44-79737, wrecked by 83rd Armd FA Bn pilot Lt Kerr, could not be repaired and would have to be salvaged. He also indicated that 44-80119, wrecked by the 84th Inf Div at Caen, was salvaged. (See December 7, Item 4.)

December 10

Received a call from Flying Control at A-93 Liège, asking if we had taken delivery of 44-80198. The answer was 'No'.

December 11

2nd Armd Div (Lt Wistler) reported an operational accident to 43-29512 at the Div Arty strip, with no personnel injuries. 50th MR&RS will pick up the aircraft on December 12 and bring it in for repairs.

December 12

(1) Maj. Lefever called regarding the new light-weight radio case: 'A pilot plastic model is now ready in Paris. Would like you to see it, and will try to get it to you soon so that production can be started if it is satisfactory.'

(2) Re the loss of 45 glider mechanics in 50th MR&RS, Maj. Gillespie (ETOUSA) reported that USSTAFE refused to change its mind, but IX AFSC had agreed to immediate and rapid replacement of the personnel.

December 13

Maj. Lefever reported that ETOUSA is getting out a letter directing the removal of combat markings (not to be confused with squadron code markings) from all aircraft (instructions will be published in Air OP Memo No. 2).

December 14

(1) L-4 43-30540 of 211th FA Bn (Lt Troyan, pilot) was damaged in an operational accident. No personnel injuries. 50th MR&RS was requested to send a crash pick-up crew to 250th FA Gp airstrip to collect it. It has not yet been determined whether a replacement is needed.

(2) XIX Corps Arty Air Officer (Capt. Reed) visited the Army Arty strip to discuss Air OP operations when POZIT (a proximity fuze) is being used. The Corps plan is based on units clearing use of POZIT with Corps Fire Direction Center (FDC), which will clear Air OPs from the particular area involved. (Similar plan subsequently adopted by Maj. Smith of XIII Corps).

(3) Visitors to the Army strip included Arty Air Officers of 196th FA Gp (Capt. Morrison) and 302nd FA Gp (Maj. Murrell).

December 15

(1) Quartermaster Section reported that word had been received from Com Z that 50,000 gals of 73 octane aviation fuel would be made available to this Army each month.

(2) Sufficient 1/250,000 scale maps have been supplied to 94th Inf Div Arty Air Officer (Maj. Middleton) by EAGLE Arty Air Officer to enable units' pilots to proceed to Maastricht, routing through A-70 Laon and A-57 Charleroi.

December 16

(On this day the Germans launched a counter-attack against First Army positions in the Ardennes).

(1) Maj. Lefever called regarding the new model light-weight plastic case for the SCR 609 radio. Stated this was about 5 lbs lighter than the standard case, but a redesign would save an additional 2 lbs. Therefore, he is not sending the sample for NUSA consideration, as previously proposed.

(2) The following Arty Air Officers visited the Army strip: Maj. Smith, XIII Corps; Capt. P. J. Keating, 34th FA Bgde; Maj. Baigan, 258th FA Gp; Capt. Warren J. Walter, 472nd FA Gp.

(3) Lt Pechar flew MP Sgt Shultz to Freebak to recover a wandering Jeep(!).

December 17

(1) Eight pilots and one observer of 7th Armd Div arrived at Army strip en route to First Army. Remained overnight.

(2) First Army Arty Air 0fficer (Maj. Bristol) reported that their Air OP personnel Rest Center at Liège was operating smoothly and effectively in spite of certain 'temporary' discomfiting interruptions. He reported the loss of 14 Air OPs this morning and requested possible assistance by providing him with two from our Pool. Maj. Bristol had just returned from the UK (Burtonwood) where he had picked up a C-47 load (Gen. Hodge's aircraft) of flying clothing and had arranged to pick up four more loads. He stated that flying clothing to fill our requisitions was on hand at Burtonwood awaiting air lift (which cannot be provided through usual channels).

(3) Capt. Mathews visited Town Major to determine availability and suitability of hotels or houses in Maastricht for an Air OP Rest Center. Nothing appeared to be available or suitable.

December 18

(1) Call from First Army Arty Air Officer (Maj. Bristol) concerning replacement aircraft: 'We need two urgently.' (Lt Col. Leich, Capt. Mathews, Lts Coppock and Hunter delivered 44-80049 and 44-80226 to the 23rd MR&RS strip at Spa at 1100 hrs). FUSA Air OP Rest Center at Liège: 'We closed it up temporarily. It's too hot.'

(2) At 1600 hrs Maj. Bristol called again to say: (a) that his air section was operating 'tactically' for the first time; (b) that he had found it necessary to move his strip and MR&RS; (c) that he was in the middle of moving his 'office'; (d) that if he could get two L-4Hs (which we delivered to him this morning) out of the old strip, these might be of some use to him.

(3) Call from Lt Dratwell, Flying Control at A-93 Liège, with the information that aircraft and pilots of 7th Armd Div, 2nd Inf Div and 99th Inf Div were at that field. He wanted to notify Maj. Bristol (FUSA Arty Air Officer), but could not contact him. He was told that this information would be passed on, if we could contact him, but guessed that Maj. Bristol had sent them there.

December 19

(1) Maj. Lefever called: 'Will arrange for five replacement aircraft to be sent to you on second priority. FUSA to get 17 on first priority. Lightweight radio cases: A 3-ply wood job will be made in Paris. 1,000 are expected in first month. Will notify you when yours are ready and 50th MR&RS can pick them up at the factory. Installation instructions will accompany each case. Let me know if NUSA Signals Supply can furnish any Lord shock mounts as none are now available in Com Z. If these are not available, the MR&RS will probably have to design a simple gadget for mounting the antennas.'

(2) Capt. Mathews departed for Burtonwood in the CG's C-47 to pick up winter flying clothing. Lts Zicard, Coppock and Gordon flew Capt. Mathews, Lt Col. Lineman and WO

Coss to Y-29 Asch, from where the C-47 departed. Capt. Burman, Arty Air Officer 407th FA Gp, and one of his pilots flew to Alsdorf, in tow of Lt Gordon, to visit a 'front line airstrip'.
(3) Maj. Bacon, 280th FA Bn, requested that he be notified when his Battalion pilots arrive at Maastricht from Normandy.

December 20

7th Armored Div Arty Air Officer (Capt. Neal) visited CP looking for his air sections. Was told they were at A-93 Liège and had been there since the FUSA strip was abandoned on December 18. He departed for Liège.

December 22

(1) Maj. Bristol (FUSA) requested that the 50th MR&RS pick up a wrecked aircraft of the 78th Inf Div at map reference K-908287. He has already replaced it.
(2) Air OP Loss Report of December 16 from 349th FA Gp states that L-4H 44-79665, wrecked on December 15 in the vicinity of Caen, was left at B-17 (the British field at Caen/Carpiquet). Maj. Lefever said that the 50th MR&RS should pick up the wreckage and that a replacement L-4 was issued to the unit by ETOUSA.

December 23

(1) 78th Inf Div Arty Air Officer, Maj. Horn, called concerning the pick-up of two L-4s, 44-80283 (previously reported by FUSA Air Officer) and 44-80295. The latter was at the 78th Arty airstrip. Two crash pick-up crews were dispatched by the 50th MR&RS.
(2) Call from 12th Army Gp (T/Sgt Hogan, Air Section) concerning destinations for replacement L-4 deliveries. He was told that we and FUSA want ours delivered to A-93 (Liège) until further notice.

December 24

(1) FUSA Arty Air Officer (Maj. Bristol) called. Gave him information regarding elimination of combat stripes on aircraft by December 31,1944.
(2) 78th Div Arty Air Officer reported loss of L-4 44-80298 due to enemy action. Pilot OK. Crash crew will pick up aircraft on Christmas Day.
(3) 83rd Inf Div Arty Air Officer, Maj. Byrd, and Lt Baker, pilot, visited strip to pick up replacement 44-80061 (the wreck had been turned in to 23rd MR&RS).
(4) 472nd Gp Arty Air Officer reported crash of 44-79701 (68-C) by Capt. Steagald at unit strip. No personnel injuries reported. Crash pick-up crew dispatched and 44-79630 assigned as replacement.
(5) Lt Zicard reported the return last night of two crash pick-up crews with 44-80283 and 44-80295 from 78th Inf Div. Both L-4s are repairable and will be put in the Army Pool, replacements already having been made by FUSA.
(6) 50th MR&RS sent a signal to 2nd AADA, Paris, requesting it arrange for a crash crew to collect 44-79665 left at Caen by 349th FA Gp.
(7) Maj. Lemasters and Capt. Dunn, 369th FA Gp, visited the Section. The Information Copy of the Air OP Loss Report on 44-79665 from Gp Arty Air Officer was returned to

Capt. Dunn (informally) for resubmission 'without trying to pull the wool over our eyes'. (See entry for December 22).

December 25

(1) XVI Corps Arty Air Officer, Maj. Hallstein, called and reported the location of his strip. He will notify Capt. Halter (472nd Gp Air Officer, who is on the same strip) that a replacement aircraft is ready for him at Army. He reported the return of the Air OP Loss Report of 349th FA Gp to Capt. Dunn of the Group (entries on December 22 and 24 refer).

(2) FUSA Arty Air Officer, Maj. Bristol, reported that his Asst Arty Air Officers, Capt. Stevenson and Lt Wilson, were shot down in an L-5 by enemy aircraft yesterday but are back on the job today.

(3) 8th Inf Div Arty Air Officer, Maj. Berger, was informed that we would furnish a replacement L-4 43-39629 (38-G) for one of his aircraft turned in to 23rd MR&RS for repairs, and that he could send for it on December 26.

(4) 78th Inf Div Arty Air Officer, Maj. Horn, called, requesting a replacement for 44-80298, which was picked up today at his strip. L-4 44-80158 (86-K) will be prepared for him to collect on December 26. He stated that FUSA had not replaced aircraft 44-80238 and 44-80295 and requested they be returned to him after they have been repaired.

(5) XVI Corps Arty Air Officer (Maj. Hallstein) called concerning 102nd Inf Div Arty Air Officer, Maj. King, who was shot down by enemy action but landed his L-4 safely although wounded. He has been evacuated to hospital.

(6) 472nd FA Gp Arty Air Officer, Capt. Halter, visited the Army strip to pick up a replacement L-4. Similarly, 83rd Inf Div FA pilot Lt Baker visited the Army strip to pick up a repaired aircraft.

December 26

(1) XVI Corps Arty Air Officer (Maj. Hallstein), operating under XIII Corps, called to say that squadron code markings for 516th FA Bn aircraft, 82-KK and 82-FF, had previously been assigned to the unit by him while in Normandy.

(2) Following a visit to 401st FA Gp, the S-3 at NUSA reported that a Cub was wrecked while he was there.

December 27

(1) XVI Corps Arty Air Officer (Maj. Hallstein), in answer to our inquiry, stated that the L-4 of 401st FA Gp reported as 'wrecked' (see Journal for Dec 26) had received only minor damage and was repaired by the unit.

(2) XXIX TAC Flying Control (Lt Duffy) and an MP officer reported the crash of an L-4 (82-(?)) at approx 1100 hrs near the Arty airstrip. The pilot was removed to 41st Evac Hospital by an Engineer unit. Further investigation revealed that 908th FA Bn pilot Lt Politella, on a local flight from the 125th LS strip to the Arty airstrip, made a forced landing on account of 'engine stoppage', wrapping up 44-79713 in a tree, and apparently suffered only minor injuries. Action: 472nd FA Gp Asst Arty Air Officer (Lt Cook), who was at the Arty strip to lead Lts Politella and Ford forward to join their unit, requested a replacement L-4 and

stated that an Air OP Loss Report would be sent in. L-4H 44-79701 will be furnished as a replacement.

(3) XIX Corps Arty Air Officer (Capt. Reed) reported that 43-29610 of 228th FA Bn had been wrecked and that a replacement L-4 would be required. A pilot of the unit will call this afternoon for the new aircraft, 44-80187 (32-(?)).

(4) Called G-3 (Maj. Taylor) and discussed the matter of FA pilots of all Ninth Army units in France being dispatched to Maastricht, as soon as they are ready, without waiting for their units. He will notify XVI Corps today of above.

(5) In answer to our inquiry, informed that empty POL drums and jerricans not required by us could be turned in to W Depot. Action: Requested G-4 to furnish 16 trucks at 0800hrs, 28 Dec, to Arty air strip to haul approx 2,600 jerricans and 225 drums to W Depot.

(6) Three FA pilots of the 78th Inf Div visited the Army strip to pick up two repaired L-4s (44-80283 and 44-80295) and one replacement (44-80186).

(7) Maj. Bristol (FUSA Arty Air Officer) reported an excess L 4 in 2nd Armd Div. Told him 'Will pick it (44-80042) up tomorrow and return it to you.'

December 28
8th Inf Div Arty Air Officer (Maj. Berger) requested that the L-4 (43-29629) assigned to his unit as a replacement, be held at the Arty airstrip until he can send for it.

December 30
(1) Maj. Ketcham, Arty Air Officer, 211th FA Gp (attached to FUSA) visited CP to report an accident to L-4 44-79788 (65-BB). Lt Zicard was requested to arrange for the wreck to be picked up on 31 December and to assign 44-80245 as a replacement.

(2) XIX Corps Arty Air Officer (Capt. Reed) visited CP to discuss a number of matters. Among other things he said, 'In some respects, the ease with which higher echelon repairs or replacement aircraft can be obtained has done some harm. Many pilots are beginning to get careless in their flying, which wouldn't happen were they more on their own.'

December 31
(1) 349th FA Gp Arty Air Officer (Maj. Rickker) visited CP to discuss Air OP supply matters. He submitted a new Loss Report for the accident which occurred to 44-79665 at Caen (see entries for December 22, 24 and 25).

(2) 258th FA Bn Arty pilot (Lt Tate) visited the Arty airstrip for the third time to pick up 43-29502, which was in 50th MR&RS for repair and promised for delivery on three different times. The matter was taken up with the CO of the 50th MR&RS (Maj. Davis) by Lt Zicard. On completion of repairs the aircraft will be delivered to the unit by one of our pilots. 12th Army Gp Arty Air Officer (Maj. Lefever) informally notified this office that a few L-5 aircraft might be made available to FA units on the Continent during the next 90 days.

CHAPTER 7

The Allied Offensive Resumes, January 1945

Although blunted by the gallant defensive action at Bastogne, the German thrust through the Ardennes continued to pose a major threat, but an improvement in the weather on Christmas Day enabled the Allied tactical air forces to resume their close support. In a desperate attempt to nullify this, the Luftwaffe launched maximum effort attacks on British and American airfields and airstrips on New Year's Day, and although this failed to achieve its main purpose, it succeeded in damaging and destroying many aircraft. Among these were eight Ninth Army L-4s, damaged in varying degrees on the Maastricht airstrip, but all were subsequently repaired and returned to service by the resident 50th Mobile Reclamation and Repair Squadron. Of these attacks, Andrew Kennedy of HQ NUSA recalled:

> During the Luftwaffe's last big show in our area, we were bombed at midnight on New Year's Eve and then strafed during the morning of New Year's Day. The Germans were mostly after fighter strips in Belgium, to the west of us, but they also strafed our headquarters and our artillery strip. None of our people were wounded, but the boys at the strip had a problem that made them even more miserable. It seems that some civilians had stolen some L-4 gasoline from us, bottled it and sold it back to our guys as Calvados, to use in celebrating the New Year! We had some pretty sick people for a while.

Another incident on New Year's Day was the loss of an L-5 of the 125th Liaison Squadron, shot down by two Bf 109s while on a flight from Maastricht to Liège. Both crew members were wounded, but while S/Sgt Owen Stafford survived, S/Sgt William D. Fletcher died shortly afterwards in an army hospital. This was followed on 5 January by the loss of another L-5 (42-99303) in an accident at Kornelimünster, a suburb of Aachen. This aircraft, which was being flown by Sgt Harry R. Eilrich, was badly damaged, but it returned to the squadron a month later following repairs by the 50th MR&RS. Another incident involving the 125th LS occurred on 12 January, when T/Sgt Jack S. Pridgen was injured when his L-5 (42-99284) crashed in south-eastern Holland near Heerlen, although a USAAF accident report gives the date as 13 January and the location as Kornelimünster, about 15 miles from Heerlen. T/Sgt Pridgen was later awarded the Air Medal for meritorious service over continental Europe.

At one time during the Bulge offensive it seemed likely that 'B' Flight of the 125th, which was attached to XIX Corps at Kornelimünster, would have to pull back to Belgium in a similar manner to some FA units, but this became unnecessary when the enemy thrust was finally halted at Malmedy. This occurred on 17 January and followed a Ninth Army attack on the north flank of the 'bulge' while General Patton's Third US Army, having moved north, attacked the enemy's south flank. It had been a hard-fought battle, with American losses totalling 19,000 dead and 47,000 wounded, but even heavier casualties were suffered by the enemy. When the First and Third Armies finished reducing the salient, they returned to the command of 12th Army Group, but the Ninth Army remained under the British 21st Army Group for the remainder of the Rhineland Campaign. The 153rd Liaison Squadron had been serving the First US Army since August 1944, but on 18 December it was attached to HQ 12th Army Group, then at Spa in Belgium. However, although Ninth Army was now under 21st Army Group control, the L-5s of the 153rd LS were frequent visitors to Ninth Army command posts, mainly carrying priority and other mail to and from Group HQ.

NUSA Air OP casualties during the Bulge offensive were surprisingly light, but an observer injured by enemy action on 31 December later died in hospital. On a happier note, authorisation was received to send five Air Section officers to Paris on 72 hours' leave. This was the first of several steps intended to overcome the problem of pilot fatigue, a subject being studied with some urgency throughout the ETO.

On 15 January, there were six surplus FA pilots in NUSA, five of whom were in the Army Pool where they performed courier, liaison and ferry missions, at the same time becoming more proficient in navigation and short field work prior to assignment to units. Of these excess pilots one was transferred to the Third Army, another went to the First Army and three who were graduates of the Fifth Army Air OP School in North Africa were returned to the United States to be formally 'rated' as liaison pilots. This took place at the FA Department of Air Training at Fort Sill, Oklahoma, after which they were to be reassigned to combat duty.

High winds on 19 January caused damage to a number of Ninth Army aircraft on the ground including two Stinson L-1Cs (41-19006 and 41-19021) and an L-5 (42-99311) of the 125th LS at Maastricht. This led to a reappraisal of existing tie-down equipment and the issue of instructions and advice to units on how to counter this problem.

After overcoming the German thrust, the Allies regrouped and prepared to resume their advance into Germany. For Ninth Army, which now comprised XIX Corps (8th, 78th and 104th Infantry Divisions) and XIII Corps (29th and 102nd Infantry Divisions), together with units attached to them, the offensive began on 26 January, when the 102nd Infantry Division staged a limited objective attack along the Army's north flank in support of a British 2nd Army attempt to clear the Roer River in their zone. Four days later, the 78th Infantry Division began an attack along the Ninth Army's south flank in conjunction with an attack by the First Army on the Roer River dams.

Despite the events of recent weeks, at the end of January all NUSA Air Sections were fully up to strength in aircraft and pilots, with 180 of the latter in units and eleven surplus. Five additional pilots arrived as reinforcements during the month and one pilot reported missing in action was replaced. As the month came to an end there was another incident at Maastricht, a forced landing on the 30th, resulting in damage to an L-4H (43-29770) of the 119th FA Group flown by Lt Philipp Kuhn.

For some time there had been discussions on the advantages of providing Air OP support to tank destroyer units, and as an experiment it was now decided to make the Air Section of the temporarily non-operational 620th FA Battalion available to the 771st Tank Destroyer Battalion (then attached to the 102nd Infantry Division). Preliminary results were excellent, but one aircraft, together with its pilot and observer, were lost due to enemy action.

Reports had recently reached the NUSA HQ Air Section that an 'enemy Cub' had been operating over the Ninth Army sector, but where and how this L-4, which was still carrying US nationality and squadron code markings, came into German hands was something of a mystery. Also receiving attention at the Army HQ were reports that a number of Stinson L-5s were to be expected in the near future as replacements for L-4s, and arrangements were put in hand to cover their arrival. This included preparations for the transition training of pilots and aircraft mechanics, together with an assessment of spare parts requirements and procurement procedures. In connection with this development, Andrew Kennedy recalled, 'About mid-January Ninth Army Arty HQ received its first L-5, and I was one of the first people to fly in it, riding with both Lt Col. Leich and Capt. Mathews on the same day.' However, a number of Arty Air Officers and other pilots were opposed to the introduction of the L-5 for Air OP work, the lighter L-4 being preferred because of its better short field performance and its ability to operate from very rough, unprepared strips. The less complex L-4 was also preferred from an 'in the field' repair and maintenance viewpoint.

As in the previous month, January had been a busy time for the 50th MR&RS. In the first two weeks the squadron made nine crash pick-ups, carried out 149 repairs on aircraft (fourteen major and 135 minor), and completed five engine changes. Spares holdings were generally good, with twenty-seven serviceable and ten repairable spare engines on hand, but some items, notably tachometer drive shafts, spark plug inserts, air filters, engine oil, and hand tools, were in the critical 'short supply' category. Action was taken to resolve this, but a quick solution seemed unlikely.

At the end of the month there were 177 L-4s in the Ninth Army, of which fourteen were in the Army Pool (four flyable and the other ten undergoing repair). During the month five aircraft had been damaged in operational accidents, six damaged by high winds, and one destroyed by enemy action. Of these, six were replaced and the remainder repaired. Snow and ice persisted throughout the second half of January, during which time a few pairs of aircraft skis were received and issued to units for test purposes, but despite the bad weather, the 50th carried out seven engine changes, made nine crash pick-ups and completed 348 repairs to L-4s (thirty-six major and 312 minor). Spares now held by the squadron included nineteen serviceable engines and seven undergoing repair.

Since first becoming operational in September 1944, 96 per cent of Ninth Army aircraft that received major damage (including all eight damaged by enemy action on the Maastricht airstrip at midnight on 31 December) were repaired and made airworthy again. This compared well with the results obtained by other US Armies on the Continent, and says much for the efforts of the 50th MR&RS. Nevertheless, in an attempt to focus the attention of personnel on the need to avoid operational accidents, with their tremendous cost in personnel, aircraft, repair facilities, and efficiency of units, the Army Arty Air Officer devoted much effort to 'fighting a belief that away from the training fields anything goes'. To this end an Air Memo covering the requirements for investigating and reporting aircraft accidents was distributed to all units. Attention was also paid to the problems of winter weather and its effect on efficient and safe Air OP operations, and this resulted in the manufacture of new engine baffles to raise operating temperatures, mooring rings for permanent installation on aircraft, oil sump lagging materials, and mooring stakes. Experimental tests on these items were carried out by the Army Air Section, as were preliminary test flights to determine the value of a new telephone wire-laying reel for L-4 aircraft.

Extracts from the HQ NUSA Air Journal for 1-31 January 1945, compiled by Lt Col. R. M. Leich (Army Headquarters at Maastricht)

January 1

(1) Enemy aircraft bombed and strafed the Army Arty airstrip (3 bombs), damaging eight L-4Hs including all three of this Section. Operations building windows were shattered and walls 'dislocated'. There were no personnel injuries. Action: The aircraft are being repaired, bomb craters (which were not on the runway) are being filled in and buildings repaired.

(2) 125th LS Operations Officer (Capt. O'Brien) stated that no enemy action had been taken against their strip.

(3) 102nd Inf Div Arty Air Officer, Capt. Dobbs, visited the strip to report a combat loss. L-4 44-80095 (76-C) with Lt Larue, pilot, and Lt Stephens, observer, were shot down this morning by three enemy aircraft. The pilot and observer were seriously injured, but a crash landing was made. 44-80239 was assigned as a replacement and collected by Capt. Dobbs. The wrecked L 4 will be picked up on January 2 by the 50th MR&RS. A replacement pilot will be transferred to the unit by XIII Corps.

(4) 36th FA Bgde Arty Air Officer, Maj. Keating, and 472nd FA Gp Arty Air Officer, Maj. Halter, were promoted this date from the grade of Captain.

(5) Maj. Lefever called with regard to sightings of 'enemy Cubs'. 'Will check with Third Army on a Cub with the unit code markings 42 (28th Inf Div), reported in your area today.'

(6) A series of conversations took place with G-2 and AA Sections about reports of a Cub with invasion markings operating suspiciously in XIII Corps Zone. A Cub with unit code markings 42 was doing likewise about the same time. In at least one case, Air OP pilots did not succeed in pressing home an 'attack' to chase the suspicious Cub to the ground. Everyone wanted to shoot them down. 42 is the number assigned to 28th Inf Div, a Third Army unit. Neither G-2 nor this office could get through to LUCKY. The matter was referred to 12th Army Group, which will furnish by teletype a list of missing Cubs. Upon its receipt, the pertinent information will be disseminated to our units. The situation is being brought to concert pitch.

January 2

(1) Pilots of NUSA Arty Air Sub-Section flew 145:20 hrs during the month of December.

(2) Army Engineers completed filling in bomb craters at Army strip.

(3) 102nd Inf Div Arty Air Officer (Capt. Dobbs) reported that the Air OP shot down yesterday was apparently at 400ft at the time. The pilot reported that he never did see the enemy aircraft. The pilot, in hospital, will probably recover, but the observer is in a critical condition.

(4) FUSA Asst Arty Air Officer (Capt. Stevenson) reported that the following replacement L-4s were awaiting our pick-up at A-93 (Liège): 44-80211, 44-80215, 44-80233, and 44-80240. L-4 44-80235 was at the 23rd MR&RS strip (4 miles west of Liège, north side of road). These will be collected by our pilots. Receipt of these aircraft will complete the filling of all outstanding orders.

(5) With regard to Lt Zicard's development of an attachment for laying wire from an L-4H, two DR-6 reels of w130 wire were released by Signals Officer for this purpose.

(6) Third US Army Arty Air Officer, Maj. Wilson, called and stated that he had not been able to check on an L-4 with the code markings 42. Report from 12th Army Gp indicated that one aircraft (42-A) had been destroyed on the ground by the 28th Inf Div.

January 4

(1) Medical Section (Maj. Parker) reported that Lt Larue, 102nd Inf Div pilot, had been sent from 41st Evacuation Hospital to a General Hospital. Lt Stephens, observer, was in the Evacuation Hospital, still in a critical condition. (See Item 3 of January 2.)

(2) Five new L-4s (44-80211, 44-80215, 44-80233, 44-80235 and 44-80240) were shuttled from Liège to the Army Pool by Lt Col. Leich, Capt. Mathews, Lts Zicard, Merriman, Coppock, Gordon, Pechar and Stockwell (the latter borrowed for the occasion).

(3) At 1730 hrs the 125th LS Operations Officer (Capt. O'Brien) reported receipt of a gale warning (between midnight and morning) from GYPSY. Army Arty airstrip personnel and Arty Air Officers of XIII and XVI Corps were notified.

(4) XIII Corps Arty S-2 called concerning 'enemy Cub' scare. He proposed publishing something on the subject and was referred to FA and Tank Destroyer Summary of this HQ published December 28.

(5) Lt Newbury, Engineer Officer, 50th MR&RS, notified Lt Zicard that the L-4 (44-79665) wrecked and left by 349th FA Gp at B-17 Caen (Carpiquet) would be picked up by 43rd MR&RS. This information was given to 12th Army Gp Arty Air Officer (Maj. Lefever) who will pass it on to ETOUSA Arty Air Officer (Maj. Gillespie).

(6) Information received from 50th MR&RS indicates the arrival of 36 one-piece Lucite windshields and a fairly large quantity of flying clothing. Ten windshields will be allocated to 102nd Inf Div and balance spread around to units needing them.

(7) 78th Inf Div Arty Air Officer (Maj. Horn) states that he needed no Lucite windshields and that he would send in tomorrow for oil and clothing.

January 6

(1) Maj. Lefever (12th Army Gp Arty Air Officer) called concerning the L-4 coded 82-P, reporting:

(a) 'The 43rd MR&RS (Third Army) picked up this L-4; it was sitting in VIII Corps area for a week, complete with covers, tied down, etc., with no guard anywhere around. Can you find out to which unit it belongs?' Answer: It belongs to the 776th FA Bn, which was transferred to First Army on December 7, 1944.

(b) 'Radio cases: Manufacture is coming along and yours should be ready in about a week.'

(2) 'Fifteenth US Army (Maj. Thornton, Army Arty Air Officer), is on the Continent.' Further to Item 1 above (the L-4 with squadron code 82-P), Maj. Lefever reported: 'The mystery deepens. The 776th FA Bn, to which it belongs, is in III Corps (Third Army).'

(3) XIX Corps Arty, Lt Gray, reported that a Cub with the squadron code markings 89 had been reported by one of the 8th Inf Div's forward observers. The Cub was in their sector, flying too far in front of the lines. A check indicated that this aircraft had the markings of the 99th Inf Div, but when asked about it the 99th Div stated that it had no aircraft in the air.

(4) NUSA G-2 periodic report No. 121, dated January 4, 1945, gave the information that L-4 89-W (44-80102) was left in enemy hands and that it could not be positively verified by photo interpretation that it had been destroyed. Noted and reported to G-2 (Intelligence), Lt Col. Kirks. (See Item 2.)

(5) XIII Corps Arty Air Officer, Maj. Smith, requested the following allocation of one-piece Lucite windshields: one to 29th Inf Div, five to 202nd Gp, one to 472nd Gp, two to 196th Gp and seven to 102nd Div. He was told to have two aircraft brought in at a time to have the installations made.

(6) 102nd Div pilot, 1st Lt Mathias, reported an incident that happened to him a couple of days ago. Two Me 109s attacked him from slightly above his altitude of about 1,000ft. One Me 109 peeled off and overshot Lt Mathias when he went into a dive, which he continued down to ground level and then flew contour. The Me 109 returned but only came down to about 500ft and did not try to make further passes. Lt Mathias returned to his field safely. [The correct designation for this Messerschmitt fighter was Bf 109, but it was widely known to the Allies as the Me 109. The other principal fighter in service with the Luftwaffe at this time was the Focke Wulf Fw 190.]

(7) 196th Gp Arty Air Officer, Capt. Morrison, reported that he needed three more one-piece windshields as the three he received were broken or cracked.

January 7

(1) XIX Corps Arty Air Officer, Capt. Reed, asked that we check to see if an Air OP (47-(?)) of the 83rd Inf Div, had been operating in 8th Inf Div Arty area about 0800 hrs today. Called First Army Arty Air Officer, Maj. Bristol, who checked and stated that the 83rd Inf Div Arty Air Officer, Maj. Byrd, had reported that none of his aircraft had been in that area, either yesterday or today.

(2) Maj. Lefever, 12th Army Gp Arty Air Officer, called re squadron code markings as follows: 'Please notify XVI Corps Arty that 82-O and 82-P can be used again. The unit in Third Army which had them has changed markings.'

(3) XIII Corps Arty Air Officer, Maj. Smith, called. He stated that AA spotters, etc., get in a 'twissy' every time a 125th LS L-5 appears in the area, because this unit has no squadron code markings and its aircraft are always being reported as unidentified Cubs.

January 8

(1) XIX Corps Arty Air Officer, Capt. Reed, called concerning 'enemy Cubs'. He asked whether Army Group had had a change of heart about not shooting down liaison aircraft with friendly markings. Answer: No, as of January 7.

(2) 12th Army Gp Arty Air Officer, Maj. Lefever, called and requested number and status of aircraft in the Army Pool. Answer: 13, of which two are undergoing repairs. He stated he would probably ask us to pick up a few wrecks for repair.

(3) FUSA Arty Air Officer, Maj. Bristol, called concerning surplus aircraft in 2nd Armd Div. Requested 'please assign aircraft 44-80042 to FUSA. We will assign it to 2nd AD and pick up a wreck, repair it and return it to your Pool.'

January 9

(1) XIII Corps Arty Air Officer, Maj. Smith, called to request permission to 'white wash' tops of wings, fuselages, etc., of Air OPs while snow is on the ground to aid concealment from enemy aircraft, both while in flight or on the ground. Answer: No objection, if proper materials are available. No white camouflage paint is on hand or immediately available, but white obtained from local sources could be satisfactory.

(2) Maj. Lefever called to say, 'If January quota of L-5s comes in, we'll do our best to get four to NUSA, but we are not sure that ETOUSA will give the whole quota to 12th Army Gp. Also, we are having the following aircraft (now at B-58 Coulommiers/Voisins, a British airfield near Brussels) assigned to NUSA: 44-80480, 44-80232, 44-80209, 44-80162 and 44-80200. They were intended for Third Army, but got off track. Don't know their condition, but they can't be flown. Will you arrange to repair and pick up?' Answer: Yes. We'll check them and see if repairs are too difficult to be made at B-58. If so, we'll truck them in; if not, we'll fly them in.

January 10

The 125th LS Operations Officer, Capt. O'Brien, called and asked for information as to who issued squadron code markings for liaison aircraft. He was told that Lt Snaime, Traffic Control, IX AFSC, had charge of putting this information out and was referred to Lt Duffy, Traffic Control, XXIX TAC.

January 11

(1) XIX Corps Arty Air Officer, Capt. Reed, reported crash of 44-79938 (77-E) of 104th Inf Div on January 10. No personnel injured when this L-4 hit a snow drift while landing and went over on its back. Lt Zicard will have wreck picked up at 104th strip and a replacement L-4 (44-80368) prepared for a unit pilot to pick up.

(2) 78th Div Arty Air Officer reported crash of 44-80188 (86-KK). No personnel injured when the L-4 crashed in a forced landing due to carburettor icing. Lt Zicard will have the wreck picked up and a replacement (44-79788) prepared for a unit pilot to pick up.

January 12

(1) Capt. Reed, 228th FA Gp Arty Air Officer, reported that an aircraft had forced landed due to carb icing in a small field. The wings were removed and the aircraft trucked out, reassembled and put back in service, with no damage.

(2) Lts Zicard and Collins and S/Sgt Roehrich departed by vehicle for B-58, near Brussels, to check on the condition of five aircraft being held there for us to collect.

78th Div Arty Air Officer, Maj. Horn, reported that the 50th MR&RS had collected the L-4 (44-80188) that he had reported wrecked (Item 2 of January 11 refers.)

January 13

(1) 12th Army Gp Arty Air Officer, Maj. Lefever, reported, 'It appears that all L-4 contracts have been canceled and replacement aircraft coming to the Continent will be L-5s. A teletype will request your recommendations for basic issues.'

(2) With regard to the issue of L-5s, Capt. Reed, XIX Corps Arty Air Officer, believes definitely that each major HQ (Corps, Divs, Gps) should have at least one L-4 and that L-4s should be the standard in all battalions, except possibly in Armd Divs, where one L-4 and one L-5 might be useful. The matter was discussed in some detail with particular emphasis on transition pilot training, supply, maintenance, etc. Maj. Smith, XIII Corps Arty Air Officer, has the same views as Capt. Reed.

(3) The CO of 50th MR&RS (Maj. Davis), was notified of possible receipt by Arty of L-5s instead of L-4s and was alerted to the problems which will arise (e.g., seat pack parachutes instead of back packs, higher fuel consumption, need for new Tech Orders, stock lists, longer time for higher echelon maintenance, etc., etc.).

(4) Capt. Mathews visited 125th LS with a view to obtaining additional information on L-5s. The Squadron agreed to allow our mechanics (Roehrich and Tye) to spend some time with them to pick up information on inspection and maintenance procedures on this type.

(5) Lts Zicard and Collins and S/Sgt Roehrich returned from Brussels with the following report: Only L-4s 44-80232, -80206, -80162 and -80200 were at B-58 (44-80480 was missing). Three had major damage (caused by wind and enemy strafing and bombing) and will have to be trucked in for repairs. One is repairable on the spot and can be flown in (but needs new wings). The 50th MR&RS will be notified to send crash pick-up crews for three aircraft, taking along two new wings (and one mechanic) for the repair of the fourth Cub. A pilot will be flown to Brussels to pick up this aircraft later.

(6) 104th Inf Div Arty Air Officer (Maj. Turner) visited the CP to discuss Air OP matters including the possible acquisition of L-5s. He stated that his unit would not want more than one L-5, was not even enthusiastic about that, and hoped the chances of receiving one were slim.

(7) Third US Army Arty Air Officer (Maj. Wilson) stated that his HQ probably would recommend the following authorization for issue of L-5s received as replacements for L-4s: one per Air Section of Army, Corps, Brigade, Division and Group.

(8) First US Army Arty Air Officer (Capt. Stevenson) stated that his HQ would probably recommend the authorization for issue of L-5s as replacements for L-4s as two aircraft per Air Section of each major HQ (as listed above). In a message to 12th Army Gp (in answer to

an inquiry) he recommended the same basis as indicated by Third Army, i.e., one L-5 per Air Section of each major HQ (see two previous items).

January 14

(1) 78th Inf Div Arty Air Officer (Engineer), Capt. Brill, reported crash of L-4 43-30292 (86-J) on Div Arty strip on account of snow. No personnel injuries. Lt Zicard to have aircraft picked up today and replacement aircraft 44-80211 prepared for delivery to unit pilot.

(2) XIII and XVI Corps Arty Air Officers, Majs Smith and Hallstein, visited CP to discuss various Air OP matters including L-5s and the transition training of pilots and mechanics.

(3) 78th Inf Div Arty Air Officer (Maj. Horn) visited Arty strip to pick up replacement L-4 44-80211.

January 15

(1) NUSA Arty pilot losses (as advised to 12th Army Gp) for the period June 1-December 31, 1944, were: 3 killed, 1 wounded, 0 missing, 3 non-battle losses (disease or injury), 2 transferred to other duties, total – 9.

(2) Called G-5, Col. Perry, to request concurrence in placing entire Air Section (two pilots, two mechanics and two vehicles) of 690th FA Bn (which is on Military Government duty in Aachen) on special duty with this HQ. Col. Perry informally agreed, but will get Col. Cragie's approval and notify us on January 16.

(3) Third US Army Arty Air Officer, Maj. Wilson, called concerning aircraft skis. He stated care should be taken in their use to prevent bending of shock struts.

(4) M/Sgt McCrea, Tech Supply Sgt, 50th MR&RS, stated that approximately 38 B-10 jackets (for pilots) had been received and requested priorities for their issue to units.

(5) Maj. Lefever, 12th Army Gp, visited the CP to discuss various matters. He reported:

(a) 'Ten L-5s will arrive in Theater in Feb and 20 in March. Spare parts are supposed to come too. Will arrange for Army to ferry them from assembly point.'

(b) 'Lucite turtledecks. AAF hasn't started production yet.'

(c) 'Skis. Your share will be 30 pairs.'

(d) 'Reinforcement pilots. Situation will be very tight between February and June.'

(e) 'Aircraft replacements. Situation will be critical. Only about 25 more L-4s are in sight. Conserve what you have.'

(6) Two units of the 50th MR&RS (32 men and 4 vehicles) were transferred to Rheims today.

January 16

(1) Concurrences were obtained from G-5, Provost Marshal and CO 690th FA Bn (Lt Col. Willis) to use the Battalion's complete Air OP Section for an indefinite period. L-4s 44-80233 and 44-80240 will be issued to pilots Lts Jameson and Badura, their own aircraft having been turned in to First US Army on December 17.

(2) Lt Helms called from Brussels to report that one of the wings transported there by the 50th MR&RS for the repair of an aircraft (which Lt Sprague planned to fly to Maastricht) was damaged en route. He was told to return here, when weather permitted, and not to await receipt of a new wing.

(3) XIII and XIX Corps Arty Air Officers were notified of the granting of 72 hour leaves in Paris to Air OP personnel on basis of 2 EM and 3 officers respectively per day.

January 17

(1) XIX Corps Assistant Arty Air Officer, Lt Moran, reported the crash of L-4 44-79950 (77-D) at 104th Inf Div Arty strip. No personnel injuries. Lt Zicard to arrange for the pick-up of the wreck and the preparation of 43-29810 as a replacement.

(2) Maj. Moore, A-4 Section, XXIX TAC, stated that they were increasing the length of the Arty air strip to 2,000ft (and were cutting down trees) in order to accommodate two C-78s and one AT-6 there.

(3) 690th FA Bn pilots Lts Jameson and Badura reported to the CP complete with mechanics (T/3 Peimann and Pfc Hamey), driver (Pfc Snyder) and trucks (¾-ton and ¼-ton). L-4s 44-80233 (63-J) and 44-80240 (63-K) have already been assigned. This Air Section will be placed on Temporary Duty with the Tank Destroyers of 102nd Inf Div.

(4) Sgt Tye returned from Brussels by truck with three wrecked aircraft. A 50th MR&RS truck will leave on the 18th to pick up the fourth aircraft. Plans to fly it here have been abandoned.

(5) Called XIII Corps Arty Air Officer, Maj. Smith, to discuss the use of an air section with 771st Tank Destroyer Bn and the 'buzzing' of a XIX Corps Battalion while being inspected by General Shea (allegedly by a XIII Corps aircraft).

(6) Capt. Mathews and Maj. Zimmerman visited XIII Corps CP and talked to CO 6th Tank Destroyer Group, Col. Searcy (and Maj. M. B. Johnson) with regard to placing an air section with one of the TD Battalions in their Group. As the 29th Inf Div gave them reason to believe more aircraft were not necessary for the TD Bns attached to this Div, it was decided to use the 771st TD Bn attached to 102nd Div. A concurrence was obtained from Col. Williams, XIII Corps Artillery. Col. Searcy, accompanied by Maj. Zimmerman and Capt. Mathews, visited 102nd Div Arty and talked to General Busby as well as 771st TD Bn C0, Lt Col. Smith, and Maj. Cilley, TD Officer. All concerned gave a hearty OK and details were discussed as to employing and using the section.

January 18

(1) FUSA Arty Air Officer, Maj. Bristol, called to say they were moving back to their old strip at Spa today. Also, reported that the 23rd MR&RS is going into quantity production on auxiliary baffles to increase cylinder temperature and produce more heat for carburettor and cabin. (Comment: There is no means of determining cylinder head temperatures. The amount of oil temperature increase does not necessarily reflect accurately the increase in head temps. This is a very ticklish affair. Having already inspected the cylinders of an engine, Lt Zicard is installing auxiliary baffles and will operate the ship for ten hours in the air, then tear down the engine to see if there have been any ill effects from too high head temps before going ahead with quantity production of baffles).

(2) XIII Corps Arty Air Officer, Maj. Smith, reported that two Me 109s had made a pass at an Air OP of the 102nd Div, chasing it to the deck but getting no hits. Evasive action by the pilot was successful.

(3) Receipt for 11,632 gallons of petroleum spirit in non-returnable tins obtained from the Officer Commanding 133 Petrol Depot, Royal Army Service Corps, on December 27, signed and turned over to M Sec, POL, for processing under reverse lend-lease.

(4) 29th Inf Div Asst Arty Air Officer (Capt. Merry) visited the Arty strip to exchange an unserviceable K-20 camera for a good one.

(5) Maj. Thames, *Conquer* Signals Section, gave information that light-weight radio cases were on the way here from Paris.

January 19

(1) XIII Corps Arty Air Officer called re:

(a) Wind damage to aircraft of the 691st FA Bn. Repairs will be made locally.

(b) Squadron code markings. He will send corrected list of all 68 markings issued by him.

(2) 34th FA Brigade Arty Air Officer called re wind damage to aircraft of 265th FA Bn. Lt Zicard will have new left wing delivered to unit at the Brigade Arty air strip.

January 20

(1) T/3s Roehrich and Tye are assisting 125th LS mechanics daily in L-5 maintenance to gain some experience with this type of aircraft.

(2) 8th Inf Div Arty Air Officer (Maj. Burger) reported wind damage to two aircraft at Div Arty strip. One, of the 8th Div, is repairable locally; the other, of 25th FA Bn (44-79681: 82-C) requires replacement. Lt Zicard will have wreck picked up and 44-80095 prepared for assignment to unit.

(3) 78th Inf Div Arty Air Officer (Maj. Horn) reported wind damage to 44-80292 (86-K) at Arty strip. Lt Zicard will have wreck picked up and 44-80298 prepared as replacement.

(4) XIII, XVI and XIX Corps Arty Air Officers were notified to take action with lower unit Air Officers to prevent, in the future, damage to parked aircraft during high winds. No unit which had wind damage to aircraft during the past few days had taken all the precautions that could have been taken.

(5) FUSA Asst Army Arty Air Officer (Capt. Stevenson) called to say that their strips are no good on account of snow, but were being bulldozed today.

(6) Maj. Lefever called to say that 99 reinforcement pilots are due to arrive in next 30 days, and asked what is our current status. Answer: 159 assigned, which is six in excess of number authorised.

(7) In view of 12th Army Group's recommendation that two L-4s in the Arty Air Sections of Army, Corps, Brigade, Division and Group HQs be replaced by L-5s as the latter are received as replacements, the comparative information below should be of interest.

	L-4H or L-4J Cub	L-5 Sentinel
Horsepower	65	190
Speeds (IAS) (mph)		
Cruising	75	110
Max diving	130	206
Stalling, with power	35	45 (full flap)
Rate of climb (fpm)	600	900

Gross weight (lbs)	1160	2200
Payload (lbs)	340	500
Service ceiling (ft)	11,000	16,000
Fuel capacity (gals)	12	36
Fuel consumption (gph)	4-5	9-10
Oil capacity (gals)	1	3
Electric starter	None	Yes
Landing lights	None	Yes
Navigation lights	None	Yes
Landing gear	Shock cords	Hydraulic
Flaps	None	Yes
Slats	None	Yes
Parking brake	None	Yes

Other advantages of L-5 over L-4:

(a) Is more spacious and comfortable, therefore less fatiguing for pilot and observer.

(b) Has improved visibility.

(c) Has greater stability in rough air, therefore binoculars may be used.

(d) Has adjustable pilot's seat.

(e) Has improved engine cowling fasteners.

(f) Has four moveable windows, therefore better ventilation.

(g) Has greater horsepower, therefore more payload, better maneuverability and more safety in take-offs.

(h) Is better for photo missions because of greater stability and width of unobstructed view.

(i) Can perform evasive maneuvers better because of higher climbing, top and diving speeds.

(j) Can operate from fields farther back from the front, or can go farther into enemy territory (dubious).

(k) Is less liable to damage on the ground from high winds.

Disadvantages:

(a) Is difficult to manhandle on the ground.

(b) Tyre flotation is impracticable in soft or rough landing field conditions.

(c) Tail cone is too close to the ground, consequently subject to damage when taxying over rough terrain.

(d) Wheel brakes are inadequate (too small for the weight and for the amount of use in short fields).

(e) Longer and more refined air strips are generally required.

(f) Ignition switch-magneto-ground circuit causes excessive electrical interference with 600 series radios.

(g) Landing gear construction causes excessive fuselage damage when gear is damaged or strikes bad ruts.

(h) Use of carburettor heat seems to reduce power unduly.

(i) Oleo shock strut cylinders break after hard usage.

(j) Generator shaft tends to wear (which requires more frequent maintenance inspections of accessory case).

(k) Parking brake cannot be left on when aircraft is taxying or left standing overnight because of causing deterioration of the rubber in the expanded tubes.

(l) Use of battery for radio, navigation and landing lights and electric starter makes special care of electrical equipment necessary.

(m) Extremely careful use of carburettor heat must be made to prevent engine failures when icing or low temperature conditions prevail.

(n) Increased fuel consumption.

(o) Impossibility of making field structural repairs and necessity for relying more on the higher echelon maintenance unit.

(p) Increased necessity for using 73 octane fuel.

(q) No cabin heater (we're working on a correction to this situation).

(r) Requires more flying skill in short field flying.

January 21

(1) Called XIII Corps Arty Air Officer, Maj. Smith, re installation of Bazookas in 102nd Div Air OP. He has stopped it.

(2) L-4H 44-79938 being substituted for 44-80298 as replacement for 78th Inf Div. MR&RS had not been able to complete repairs to the latter ship.

(3) L-4 44-80208, left by 50th MR&RS at Brussels pending delivery of new wing, blew away because of inadequate moorings into a shell crater, suffering serious damage. It may be repairable. (The Air Forces appear not to believe that their D-1 mooring kit is no good for Cubs in high winds).

(4) Test of baffles submitted by 252nd FA Bn has been discontinued inasmuch as they did not raise oil temps to normal. The FUSA baffle is now being tested. It raised oil temp to 160 degrees after ½-hour flight (normal 160-180).

(5) A tie-down ring for installation on L-4s has been submitted for approval by 50th MR&RS.

(6) Called 12th Army Gp Arty Air Officer, Maj. Lefever, concerning quota for Riviera Rest Center. 'None specifically set for pilots. That will have to be earmarked by Army from Army general quota. Re L-5s, the model coming over has the ambulance feature and visibility for the observer is not good. He can, with difficulty, look past (or through) the head of the pilot and out the front windshield. Modification at assembly point will be necessary to correct this.'

January 22

(1) A second wing was sent by 50th MR&RS to 34th Bgde strip for damaged L-4 of the 265th FA Bn (see January 21). It, too, would not fit the aircraft.

(2) 472nd FA Gp Asst Arty Air Officer, Capt. Steagald, reported that 44-79710 (68-CC) had been rolled up on 258th Gp strip. No personnel injuries. Lt Zicard to pick up the wreck and to prepare 44-80215 for assignment to unit.

January 23

(1) 472nd FA Gp Asst Arty Air Officer, Capt. Steagald, requested that 44-79710 wrecked by Lt Cook be repaired and returned to the unit instead of being replaced by 44-80215. Lt Zicard will comply with this request.

(2) 78th Inf Div Arty Air Officer, Maj. Horn, reported major damage to 44-79788 (86-KK) when it went over on its back on the Div Arty airstrip during a crosswind take-off on a slick surface. Lt Zicard to arrange for pick-up of wreck and prepare 44-80292 as a replacement. (Does not require assignment as the aircraft formerly belonged to this unit and had not been relieved from assignment.)

(3) Lt Hunter flew 44-80298 of the Pool to A-93 Liège to have it de-magnetized, but facilities were not available at that field. The MR&RS has given it up as a hopeless case!

(4) 50th MR&RS requested to produce sufficient tie-down rings (to be installed on the front lift struts of L-4s) for 350 aircraft, and 100 sets of winter baffles.

(5) III Corps Arty Air Officer, Capt. Reed, reported crash of 44-79960 (77-H) of 104th Inf Div in a forest near the Div Arty strip. The aircraft forced landed due to engine failure. Aircraft was badly damaged but no personnel injuries. Lt Zicard to have wreckage picked up and 44-80215 prepared for assignment to unit.

(6) 12th Army Gp Arty Air Officer, Maj. Lefever, called concerning:

(a) MR&R Squadrons. They have been placed under operational control of Arty Officer, 12th Army Gp, who will shift repair units of the squadrons from Army to Army as required. At present only Fifteenth Army will suffer, 5 units having been dispatched today from its MR&RS to Third Army.

(b) Aircraft Accidents and Losses. During period December 1 to January 10 the breakdown is as follows: Engine failures – 17; enemy aircraft – 19; enemy AA – 14; enemy arty (aircraft on ground) – 14. The engine failures are probably evenly divided between Armies and the situation needs some 'professional' attention, etc.

January 24

Maj. Lefever called concerning:

(a) Light-weight 610 radio cases. 'Tell your Signals Officer that these have been released and can be picked up.'

(b) Tie-down rings. 'Can you bring along a few samples to show the other Armies?' Answer – Yes.

January 25

(1) XIX Corps Asst Arty Air Officer (Lt Johnson) called to report 43-30051 (32-B) was damaged on a down wind, down hill take-off that ended in a ground loop into a fence. This aircraft will be picked up by 50th MR&RS, but no replacement will be made until the repaired aircraft can be returned as there are only two replacements ready at the present time.

(2) III Corps Arty Air Officer, Maj. Smith, called to request information as to brushes and soluble white camouflage paint for his aircraft. After checking with Engineer Section, he was told this equipment is available at Engr Depot No. 4. The technique used by pilots in cross-wind conditions on snow covered strips was discussed to prevent more of the large

number of accidents that have already occurred. It was decided that a tail low take-off was best as it gives the pilot more control until flying speed is gained and will prevent drifting off the strip. Maj. Smith is also checking on the progress of the pilots attached to the 771st Tank Destroyer Bn.

(3) The cold weather is causing low engine operating temperatures and to counter this some of the baffles designed by the 50th MR&RS have been issued to XIII Corps. Lagging material for oil sumps is still lacking but a further search is being made of both Engineer and Ordnance Depots for anything suitable.

(4) Lt Zicard reported that the wire reel for laying wire works. It is very satisfactory except it is hard on the reels when they are dropped after finishing the laying process.

(5) C-78s of the 125th LS are now using the Arty airstrip, it having been lengthened.

January 26

(1) XIII Corps Arty Air Officer, Maj. Smith, called to report that L-4 44-80233 (63-J) assigned to 771st TD Bn was missing. He later reported locating this aircraft down at coordinates 9560-7050. No positive identification could be made but the L-4 was badly wrecked. Forward elements will try to reach it and determine the condition of the pilot and observer. The aircraft appears to be too far forward to salvage it at this time.

(2) Maj. Smith also reported that after renewing application of white camouflage on the Corps aircraft with materials recently drawn from the QM Depot, three glowing balls of fire were found in the dark as they had applied luminous paint!

(3) Lt Cook, 472nd pilot, visited the strip to pick up the repaired aircraft in which he had recently crashed.

(4) Report to Assistant Chief of Staff by HQ 102nd Inf Div, dated February 1, 1945, reads as follows:

Subject: US Arty Observation aircraft shot down on January 26, 1945.

The following information on the above subject was obtained from the interrogation of a PoW (Obergefreiter Johann Leis), captured January 31, '45. PoW saw the aircraft crash directly across the Roer River from his position, and led three men across the river to capture the officer who survived the crash:

(a) The aircraft crashed on the left bank of the Roer at RR bridge in the vicinity of Map Ref 961703. It approached this point about 1000 hours from the East at an altitude of about 100ft. It was fired on by LMG of the 59th Fusilier Bn in position on the right bank of the river some distance south of the bridge. The aircraft dived gradually, landed on its nose and turned end over several times.

(b) The observer, said to be a 1st Lt (who had been seated in the rear cockpit) was thrown clear of the plane. The Germans saw him pick himself up, limp back to the plane, and remove something from the cockpit which he concealed or buried. The Germans succeeded in crossing the river by laying tree trunks over the destroyed RR bridge, but by the time they reached the officer he had completed his task and they were unable to find the object he had concealed. He was badly shaken up by the crash and had injured his thigh, but was not otherwise wounded by MG fire. He was evacuated to the Aid Station of the 59th Fus Bn/59th Inf Div, in Ball.

(c) The pilot, also said to be a 1st Lt, was found dead in the cockpit. He had been shot through the chest by MG fire and apparently killed instantly.

(d) The aircraft bore the markings 'C7' on the side; to the rear of this marking was an insignia in the form of a crown.

(e) On the evening of the crash a patrol was sent out by the 59th Fus Bn to look for the object concealed by the observer, and to salvage gasoline and equipment from the wrecked plane.

(f) This was said to be the second US Arty Observation aircraft shot down by the one MG of the 59th Fus Bn, the first having been scored about ten days previously. The gun crew was given leave as a reward.

> Samuel Reich
> 1st Lt, Corps of Engineers
> OIC, IPW Team 103

January 27

(1) XIII Corps Arty Air Officer, Maj. Smith, called to report action taken to reach the aircraft of the 771st TD Bn. A daylight patrol was unable to reach the aircraft, but a second night patrol finally reached it and reported the following:

(a) No personnel in or around plane.

(b) Radio was missing.

(c) Aircraft was burned except for left wing and tail.

(d) Tracks leading from aircraft towards Roer River.

(e) Patrol immediately drew heavy MG fire and had to throw away parachute and one wheel they salvaged to make possible their escape.

Action: Another aircraft, 44-79938, was assigned to the 690th FA Bn and another pilot will be dispatched to the unit tomorrow (attached unassigned to the 690th FA Bn and on temporary duty with the 771st TD Bn). Lt Badura was the pilot and Lt Woodard the observer of the aircraft lost.

(2) 102nd Inf Div Arty Air Officer, Capt. Dodds, visited section to turn in an Air OP Loss Report on the 690th FA Bn L-4 and to discuss past performances of this section with the TDs. He gave the information that this Bn's pilots were a little cocky, which may be the cause of the recent occurrence. Capt. Dobbs also expressed desire to obtain a K-20 camera for use in his air section. He was told we hope to make these available to all divisions in the near future.

(3) XIII Corps Arty Air Officer, Maj. Smith, called to ask how soon we can supply baffles designed by the 50th MR&RS as they are very effective and raise oil temp of engines from 140 to 160 degrees under current conditions. These baffles are being made as fast as material is available and aircraft will be brought in from both Corps to have them fitted at a rate of five a day.

January 28

(1) XVI Corps Arty Air Officer called to check on availability of baffles. (Same reply as above.) The engine on which the baffle plates were tested has been torn down and no ill

effects were apparent. The MR&RS can produce 60 sets of baffles at about 6 per day. They will be issued to units immediately.

(2) Five reinforcement Arty pilots arrived today, having landed first at Naples, Italy, and then making the trip here.

January 29

(1) NUSA S-3 visited 102nd Inf Div Anti Tank Officer (Maj. Gilley) and 771st Tank Destroyer Bn (Lt Col. Smith) and obtained reports on loss of Cub 63-J with pilot and observer.

(2) Lt Hunter, reinforcement pilot, was dispatched to the 771st TD Bn but was unable to reach the unit because of poor weather conditions and other difficulties. He will try again tomorrow.

(3) Several L-4s, including 44-80186, 44-80235, 44-79681 and 44-80200, were test hopped today by Capt. Mathews and Lt Zicard. All were returned to 50th MR&RS because of small items of maintenance that have been overlooked but which detract from the appearance and safety of the aircraft.

January 30

(1) Ordnance Section asked to requisition 600 shoulder holsters for FA pilots and observers. These are authorised for 'Flyers, AAF', which term, by Theater decision, is to be interpreted to include FA flying personnel. It is the intention to issue holsters through the MR&RS.

(2) Aircraft 43-30292 was picked up by 78th Inf Div instead of 44-80292, and 44-80298 was picked up instead of 44-79936. In each case the latter aircraft had been assigned as a replacement. Corps Arty Air Officer, Capt. Reed, was requested to notify the 78th Inf Div Arty AO that aircraft were still assigned by the Army and not by the unit sending in for replacement.

(3) XIX Corps Arty Air Officer, Capt. Reed, reported that 119th FA Gp had damaged an aircraft in a forced landing. No personnel injuries reported. Further details will be furnished later.

(4) Called 34th Brgde Arty Air Officer, Maj. Keating, concerning night flying. Maj. Keating thought good work could be done with counter-battery fire on moonlight nights. When confronted with the difficulties involving AAA, night fighters, untrained pilots, modifying aircraft and danger to pilots and aircraft, he agreed that it presented too many difficulties to warrant the effort. Comment: Army Arty Air Officers in this Theater unanimously indicated lack of success in attempts at night operations.

January 31

(1) Lt Collins flew Capt. Spofford, Armored Section, on a reconnaissance flight in the vicinity of Vaals.

(2) FUSA Arty Air Officer (Maj. Bristol) called to say action was being taken by his HQ to have a pilot replace the observer, who presently is Arty Air Officer in 2nd Armd Div, in order to comply with FM 6-150.

(3) XVI Corps Arty Air Officer (Maj. Hallstein) called. He was informed that he could pick up a limited number of baffles for his unit. He will turn in 44-79954, issued in excess of TO&E, as he finds it more of a hindrance than a help.

(4) The following developments in Air Force supply methods and procedures for FA are in the offing (as learned at ETOUSA Meeting):

(a) A test pilot will be assigned to each MR&RS, with additional duty as Asst Engnr Officer. (This may be a help, but will not relieve us of test flying aircraft before accepting them.)

(b) One Air Depot will probably be assigned to back up the MR&RSs working for Armies and will specialise in aircraft parts, etc.

(c) Switching of repair units between MR&RSs to assist in clearing up backlogs, etc., will probably not be done; the Air Depot referred to in (b) being charged with equalizing the burdens.

(d) Emergency requisitions to obtain parts needed to repair grounded aircraft, when marked AOG, will get priority.

(5) Called Maj. Lefever concerning:

(a) L-5B. When will we get it? Answer: 'Our own shipment will probably get in before the sample deal gets through all the HQs.'

(b) Aircraft 44-79665 wrecked by 349th FA Gp and left at Caen. 'Can you get Fifteenth Army Arty Air Officer to try to pick it up? The MR&RS has thrown up its hands.' Maj. Lefever: 'Will notify them to see what can be done.'

Above left: 1 Lt Gen. William H. Simpson, Commander Ninth US Army, leaving the Headquarters of the 30th Infantry Division, accompanied by the Division's Commander, Maj. Gen. Leland S. Hobbs. (*R. M. Leich*)

Top right: 2 Major (as he then was) R. M. 'Bob' Leich (centre), with Lieutenants Lloyd M. Bornstein and M. J. 'Jake' Fortner at Fort Sill, Oklahoma, prior to Leich becoming Artillery Air Officer at Headquarters Ninth US Army. (*C. W. Lefever*)

Above right: 3 Lt Allen Knisley, Artillery Air Officer with the 3rd Armored Division's 67th FA Battalion, with his observer, Lt Ted Marick, in the rear seat of a Piper L-4. (*A. Knisley*)

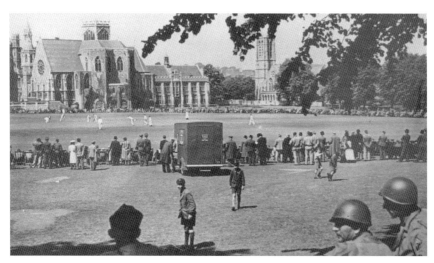

4 Part of Clifton College, Bristol, was occupied in turn by the Headquarters Staff of the First and then Ninth US Armies. No doubt the GIs seen here were totally mystified by the game of cricket being played by resident schoolboys. (*Bristol Evening Post*)

5 Map 1: England and Wales. (*P. V. Wakefield*)

6 The Stinson L-5 Sentinel was widely used by USAAF Liaison Squadrons and in smaller numbers by Artillery HQ Air Sections. The aircraft seen here (serial number 42-98989) belonged to 'B' Flight, 153rd LS. (*L. Shrum*)

7 Major Charles W. 'Chuck' Lefever, Artillery Air Officer at HQ 12th Army Group, at the controls of an L-5. (*C. W. Lefever*)

8 Pilots and observers of the 125th LS. The officer on the right of this line-up is 1/Lt Frank H. Heineman, the observer badly injured in an L-5 crash at New Zealand Farm, Wiltshire, on 17 July 1944. (*R. Haynes*)

9 Bristol (Whitchurch) Airport. The 'Flight Shed' that housed the Ninth Army Air Section's L-4 is the hangar to the left of the buildings in the foreground (the airport's south side). (*KGW Collection*)

10 The 'long range' auxiliary fuel tank installed in Cubs for the Channel crossing can be seen quite clearly in this photograph of 28-V (serial number 44-79549), an L-4H of XII Corps. (*B. Moyes via D. Summers*)

11 Map 2: Normandy. (*P. V. Wakefield*)

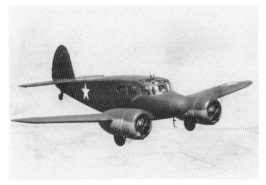

Above left: 12 Cherbourg, with Barfleur faintly visible in the background, photographed from an L-5 of the 125th LS. This was the position on the French coast first reached by many pilots of L-4s and L-5s making the Channel crossing from southern England. (*KGW Collection*)

Above right: 13 The Cessna UC-78 Bobcat, the type of light personnel transport assigned to Gen. William H. Simpson, the Officer Commanding Ninth US Army. (*KGW Collection*)

14 A Ninth Air Force P-38 Lightning fighter on ALG 21, the Advanced Landing Ground at Saint-Laurent-sur-Mer, adjacent to Omaha Beach. (*KGW Collection*)

15 An L-5 on a beach in Brittany in September 1944. This aircraft almost certainly belonged to the 125th LS, the Ninth US Air Force unit attached to the Ninth US Army. (*KGW Collection*)

Above left: 16 Pilots and mechanics of the 125th LS. (*R. Haynes*)

Above right: 17 An L-4 of the 9th Infantry Division, with Pfc Paul Matarazzo talking to some young refugees from Brest, the port in Brittany recently captured by the Ninth US Army, 10 September 1944. (*R. M. Leich*)

Above left: 18 T/5 James Hancock applying paint to the 'invasion stripes' of an L-4 of the Air Section, HQ Ninth US Army, 8 December 1944. (*R. M. Leich*)

Above right: 19 This L-4H (43-30400: 28-M) of XII Corps displays the first change to 'invasion stripes', this being their removal from the top of the fuselage and upper wing surface. (*R. Haynes*)

Left: 20 Although barely visible, the serial number on the tail of this L-4H is a clue to its history. On 24 October, HQ Ninth Army took delivery of this aircraft (44-79672) from the 50th MR&RS at St Trond. Three days later, it went to the 357th FA Battalion as a replacement for a damaged L-4 (43-30237: 24-X) but was itself damaged on 13 April 1945, when it struck some trees on take-off. (*R. Haynes*)

Above left: 21 To hide it from enemy aircraft, camouflage netting has been placed over this L-4 of the 188th FA Group, seen here at Maastricht while undergoing maintenance by the 50th MR&RS. (*R. Haynes*)

Above right: 22 This field, with trees on two sides and houses on the other two sides, was used as an airstrip by L-4s of the 899th FA Battalion while temporarily stationed near The Heath Hospital, Cardiff, in December 1944. (*KGW Collection*)

23 Following a take-off accident on 11 December 1944, this L-4 of the 2nd Armored Division's 78th FA Battalion is being pulled from mud at the end of a strip in Germany. (*R. M. Leich*)

24 Mechanics of the 50th MR&RS installing a replacement one-piece windshield on a ski-equipped L-4 (33-Z) of the 9th Infantry Division. (*R. Haynes*)
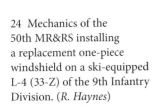

25 L-4H (44-79723: 63-B) of the Artillery Air Section, NUSA, on Geusselt airstrip, Maastricht, where it arrived for servicing by the 50th MR&RS on 1 January 1945. That same night it was damaged in a German air raid, but was quickly repaired and returned to its unit on 2 January. (*H. N. Bronkhorst*)

26 Capt. Wilbur Berry, the pilot of this L-4 of the 29th Infantry, prepares to patrol his Division's sector of Germany with his observer, 1/Lt George D. Maxwell, holding a K-20 aerial camera. (*R. M. Leich*)

27 A badly damaged German motor convoy, photographed from a low-flying L-4. (*KGW Collection*)

Above left: 28 This hilltop French château provided temporary accommodation for some personnel of the 50th MR&RS during the German offensive in December 1944. (*R. Haynes*)

Above right: 29 A Stinson L-5 (42-98681) of the 125th LS on a snowbound French airstrip in January 1945. (*C. W. Lefever*)

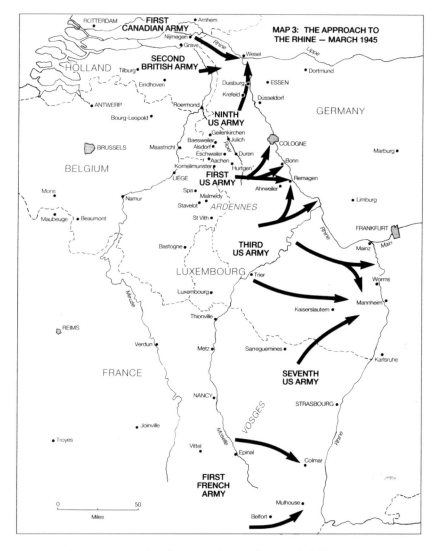

30 Map 3: The Approach to the Rhine, March 1945. (*P. V. Wakefield*)

31 An L-4H (44-79717: 68-B) belonging to a XIII Corps FA Battalion about to depart from a snow-covered airstrip at Alsdorf, Germany, in January 1945. (*US National Archives*)

32 The reduced 'invasion stripe' markings (lower fuselage only), introduced at the end of December 1944, are well illustrated in this view of an L-4H (44-79914: 74-M) of the 180th FA Battalion, 26th Infantry Battalion. (*P. E. Cunha*)

33 An 8th Infantry Division L-4, crewed by Capt. Cecil C. Ellzey (pilot) and Lt Paul Dumas (observer), on a snowbound strip near Stolberg, a few miles east of Aachen on the edge of the Hurtgen Forest in January 1945. (*C. E. Ellzey*)

Above left: 34 The L-5B (44-16731: 63-B) received by the Ninth Army HQ Air Section on 9 February 1945, with (left to right) Lt Col. Robert M. Leich (Artillery Air Officer, Ninth US Army), Maj. Bryce Wilson (Artillery Air Officer, First US Army) and Maj. Charles 'Chuck' Lefever (Artillery Air Officer at HQ 12th Army Group). (*R. M. Leich*)

Above right: 35 Two mechanics of the 50th MR&RS about to start the engine of an L-4H (43-30314: 45-A) of the 35th Infantry Division. (*R. Haynes*)

Above left: 36 From November 1944 there were occasional reports by ground units of 'enemy Cubs' operating over the front. It was presumed that these were L-4s that had fallen into German hands, and this was subsequently proved to be correct. One such aircraft is seen here after it had been 'recaptured' by GIs who added the words 'Don't shoot! – U.S.A.' to its Luftwaffe markings. (*R. Haynes*)

Above right: 37 This L-4H (44-80298: 49-M) was a replacement for 44-79768, an aircraft of the 696th FA Battalion attached to the 2nd Armored Division that was damaged by bombs during the night of 24 February 1945. (*R. Haynes*)

Above left: 38 A rare photograph of an L-4 directing artillery fire, with numerous shell bursts and white phosphorus clouds streaming north on a moderate wind. The L-4 (coded 76-K) belonged to the Ninth US Army, and the photo was taken during the approach to the west bank of the Rhine near Cologne on 8 March 1945. (*US National Archives*)

Above right: 39 Lt Robert W. Miller confers with Cpl Stanley Jackson before making a reconnaissance flight over the Rhine in 87-G, an L-4 of the 84th Infantry Division, 20 March 1945. (*R. M. Leich*)

40 Mechanics of the
50th MR&RS working
on a Ninth Army L-4
at München-Gladbach,
Germany. (*R. Haynes*)

41 The Plexiglas
'eyebrows' and one-
piece windshield
modifications carried
out by the 50th MR&RS
can be seen in this view
of Cpl Dick Licherean
in the cockpit of an L-4.
(*R. Haynes*)

42 Seen here on a strip
near Krefeld, Germany,
1/Lt Charles W. Clayton
Jr, pilot, and Sgt Thomas
J. Johnson, observer,
are applying symbols
on their L-4J of the
325th FA Battalion, 84th
Infantry Division, to
indicate the completion
of fifty missions,
24 March 1945.
(*R. M. Leich*)

43 The L-5B (44-17190) of the HQ Air Section, Ninth US Army, at München-Gladbach on 8 April 1945. (*R. M. Leich*)

44, 45, 46 Three photographs showing a crash crew of the 50th MR&RS at work recovering an L-4H (44-80575: 98-H) of the 219th FA Group. This aircraft, flown by Lt Kreuzberry, crashed while taking off from a short strip on a hot day with no wind. (*R. Haynes*)

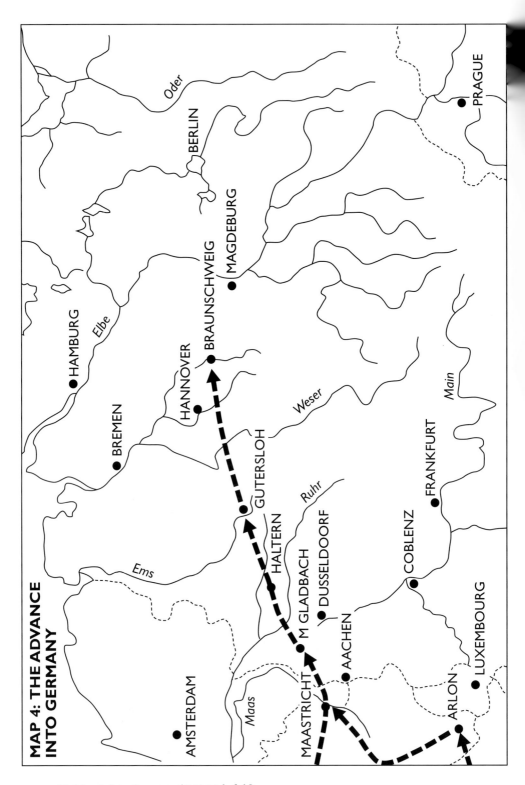

MAP 4: THE ADVANCE INTO GERMANY

PRAGUE

Oder

BERLIN

HAMBURG

Elbe

MAGDEBURG

BREMEN

HANNOVER

BRAUNSCHWEIG

Weser

GUTERSLOH

Main

FRANKFURT

Ruhr

HALTERN

COBLENZ

M GLADBACH

Ems

DUSSELDOORF

AACHEN

AMSTERDAM

Maas

MAASTRICHT

LUXEMBOURG

ARLON

47 Map 4: Into Germany. (*P. V. Wakefield*)

48, 49, 50 While taking evasive action from an attacking German fighter on 15 April 1945, Lt Montgomery of the 5th Armored Division crashed into a haystack. The second photo is a close-up of the wrecked L-4H (44-80603: 54-F), with men of the 5th Armored Division pulling the aircraft backwards to free the cockpit area, while the third shows Lt Montgomery being removed from the wreck. He sustained a broken leg and arm, but his observer was uninjured. (*W. Kyle*)

Above left: 51 During a presentation ceremony in Brunswick, Germany, Col. Laurence H. Hanley presents the Bronze Star to Lt Col. Robert M. Leich, Artillery Air Officer, Ninth US Army. (*R. M. Leich*)

Above right: 52 S/Sgt Herbert G. Moore of the 153rd LS removing the mailbag from his L-5 on a strip near Weimar, Germany, after completing a scheduled mail run to the HQ of VIII Corps, Ninth US Army, on 30 May 1945. (*R. M. Leich*)

53 This aircraft was one of the early L-4As returned to the Piper factory for overhaul and then reissued to meet a shortage of later L-4Hs and L-4Js. On arriving in Europe, 43-10537 was issued to VII Corps, and is seen here in May 1945 with the markings 26-U of 188th FA Group. It has been modified to include the 'turtledeck' cockpit canopy. (*R. Haynes*)

54 A post-war casualty. This 2nd Infantry Division L-5 (44-17323: 74-Z) was damaged on take-off from a strip at Kruma, Czechoslovakia, on 30 May 1945. (*P. E. Cunha*)

CHAPTER 8

Into Germany, February 1945

The first of many changes affecting the Ninth Army took place on 3 February with the transfer of 8th Infantry Division to the First Army. In addition, the zone occupied by the Ninth's XIX Corps was taken over by the First Army's VII Corps, with XIX Corps then taking over part of the XIII Corps zone and its troops. At the same time the newly operational XVI Corps took over some of the British 2nd Army's zone, together with command of the American 35th Infantry Division and the British 7th Armoured and US 8th Armored Divisions. These and other changes eventually resulted in an enlarged NUSA, which by mid-February comprised three Corps (XIII, XVI and XIX) with three Armored Divisions (the 2nd, 5th and 8th), nine Infantry Divisions (29th, 30th, 35th, 75th, 79th, 83rd, 84th, 95th and 102nd) and, for a short period only, the 7th British Armoured Division. Together with the Air OPs of attached FA Groups and non-divisional FA battalions, the 'Conquer Air Force' now comprised some 230 aircraft.

Allied plans for a renewed offensive were disrupted on 9 February when the Roer dams were blown by the Germans, causing the river to overflow and flood adjacent areas. This made it impossible for NUSA to continue its advance into Germany until 23 February, when an attack was launched across the Roer by XIII, XVI and XIX Corps. Despite stiff enemy resistance, intensely cold weather and extremely muddy conditions, the Ninth then advanced 53 miles in the next two weeks, reaching the Rhine at Wesel and clearing 34 miles of the west bank. From Wesel the Ninth pushed on to Düsseldorf, taking 30,000 prisoners along the way, but throughout this period increased German fighter aircraft activity was experienced against Air OPs in the Ninth Army's sector. To counter this threat, consideration was given to providing fighter cover, but the only available fighters were Republic P-47 Thunderbolts of XXIX Tactical Air Command and these were needed for higher priority fighter-bomber strikes. Accordingly, to give Air OPs a degree of protection, a plan was evolved for intended P-47 fighter-bomber strikes to be pre-advised to the FA so that any Air OP missions planned for that area might be flown at the same time, but in practice this proved difficult to implement. Fortunately, although heavier than of late, FA aircraft losses were not serious.

One of the XVI Corps units participating in the action across the Roer was the 407th FA Group, the HQ and HQ Battery of which moved from Stolberg to Laffeld on 1 February, on which date it fired its first mission of the war, providing reinforcing fire for the 35th Infantry Division and the British 52nd FA Brigade. At this time, enemy troops were no more than 2,000 yards from Laffeld, with only 50-60 British infantrymen in between. The three FA battalions attached to the Group – the 211th, 754th and 758th – had similarly moved, taking up positions in the vicinity of Schleiden, Bruggelschen and Schiefenduhl respectively. The Air OP activity of these units was co-ordinated by the Group Air Officer, sorties being flown from a Group airstrip in close proximity to the 407th's command post. Patrols by single L-4s, augmented by additional aircraft when the tactical situation warranted it, were flown throughout the hours of daylight, weather conditions permitting. These were mainly for the direction of artillery fire, but in addition the Group S-2 (Intelligence Officer) flew for at least an hour each day to gain first-hand knowledge of the terrain and to update situation and intelligence maps, daily periodic overlays of which were sent to the Group's battalions.

Every effort was made to provide Air OP support for all the Group's firing activity, which was controlled by the XVI Corps Artillery Fire Direction Center, with intelligence gathering an important additional function. However, the poor weather that prevailed for much of the month hampered operations. The Group HQ also suffered its first Air Section casualties at this time. This occurred on 28 February, when an L-4 flown by Lt William M. Smith was shot down by enemy small arms fire. The L-4 crashed about 1,000 yards behind enemy lines, but Lt Smith and his observer, Capt. Edwin B. Buttery (Assistant S-3), were rescued, both seriously wounded. A replacement pilot arrived on 1 March, but Lt Smith made a good recovery and returned to duty on 16 April.

The advance to the Rhine, known as Operation *Grenade*, involved the Ninth Army very actively as the southern prong of a pincer attack co-ordinated with the Canadian First Army's Operation *Veritable*. Nevertheless, the 407th FA Group's after action report for the month includes an item on less warlike matters, reporting that the Special Service Organisation had functioned well during this difficult period, providing movies twice weekly and Red Cross 'Donut Wagons' once weekly. In addition, the SSO drew Post Exchange (PX) supplies weekly for the Group HQ and its attached battalions, with the PX Officer also obtaining Coca-Cola from Brussels for the entire organisation. Special Service personnel also processed orders for flowers and other gifts for delivery in the United States. However, the report continued, the morale value of the PX contribution is doubtful in view of the scanty supplies received, adding that the readily available American Red Cross kit was 'ample to satisfy the needs of men for candy, cigarettes, razor blades, etc., without the Post Exchange'. The report concluded: 'Considering the drain on time, manpower and transportation in securing meagre PX supplies and Coca-Cola from distant supply depots, it is questionable whether these activities should be carried on during combat'.

Extracts from the HQ NUSA Air Journal for 1-28 February 1945, compiled by Lt Col. R. M. Leich (Army Headquarters at Maastricht)

February 1

(1) Twelfth Army Gp, Maj. Lefever, reported:

(a) Reinforcement pilots. Out of 60 arriving in the next 15 days, NUSA will get 12.

(b) Controllable pitch props. Action will be taken to obtain enough to equip all L-4Js shipped to the Theater. The J is different to the H in that it is especially adapted for the ready installation of the controllable pitch prop. [In fact the L-4J was manufactured with the Roby R002 variable pitch propeller installed, but this proved unsatisfactory in service and was replaced with the Sensenich 72C42 fixed pitch propeller used on the L-4H and earlier models. Most L-4Js were so fitted before delivery to units.]

(c) L-5B. This version of the L-5 cannot be modified by USSTAF. Any changes required to make it adaptable to FA use will have to be made by the MR&RS. ETOUSA has requested USSTAF to send one to this Army immediately for test. One solution to the poor visibility feature of this model is to exchange as many L-5Bs as possible with Liaison Squadrons for their L-5Es (not too good an idea because the aircraft of these squadrons have about 3-400 hours on them).

(d) Three AAF Air Depot Units are headed for this Theater. These have four officers and 54 enlisted men and were designed to do the job now being done by the MR&RSs. In Seventh Army one such unit, composed of Arty personnel transferred to the Air Forces, has been handling a load of over 400 aircraft. Its CO is recommending that their TO&E be changed to provide an additional officer and 15 additional men. (An MR&RS has 9 officers and 180 EM).

(2) XIX Corps Arty Air Officer, Capt. Reed, furnished further details of the crashed L-4 of 119th FA Gp (see January 30 entry). This aircraft, 43-29770 (32-I) of the 203rd FA Bn, pilot Lt Kuhn, received major damage in a forced landing. A replacement is required. Wreckage is pretty close to the front lines. Lt Zicard is to arrange for a crash crew pick-up on a day of limited visibility, and prepare 44-80188 as a replacement.

(3) Maj. Lever called concerning K-20 cameras. He advised that two are still at Burtonwood for pick-up by XVI Corps, but these were already picked up by the XVI's Arty Air Officer, Maj. Hallstein. If they are still confused, have the cameras shipped to the 50th MR&RS and we'll issue them to another unit.

(4) Pilot status for January: Number of pilots authorised, 177; Number on hand, 188. Number of pilots lost in January, 5 (LaRue, Badura, King, Promar and Earle).

(5) XIX Corps Arty Air Officer, Capt. Reed, reported that one of the two aircraft picked up by 78th Inf Div 'in error' (see Air Journal for January 30) was in 'terrible shape' and would be returned. Comment: That's why it had not been assigned to the Division and why the matter was brought up by this office.

(6) 35th Inf Div pilots Lts Yates and Deancast, with observers Lts Venable and Fitzgerald, arrived at Arty strip en route to join their unit. Remained overnight. The other pilots are at Luxembourg and will probably arrive tomorrow. Lt Yates reported that the Division was short of two pilots and one airplane. Called Third Army Asst Arty Air Officer, Lt Yorkaman, who stated that Third Army could not replace either the pilots or the aircraft.

February 2.

(1) Lt Collins flew Capt. Cole, Engineer Section, on a round trip to Y-10 Le Culot. Winds were 25-30 mph with gusts up to 40 mph.

(2) XIX Corps Asst Arty Air Officer (Lt Johnson) was informed that L-4H 43-30051 at 50th MR&RS for repair would be ready for pick-up tomorrow.

(3) L-pilots of this Section flew 133 hours during the month of January.

(4) Arty Air Officer of the 35th Inf Div (Maj. Davidson), with 4 other pilots and 5 observers arrived at the strip en route to join their unit. All airplanes of the unit upon arrival here

are grounded pending further instructions, for security reasons. Maj. Davidson requested assignment of a replacement L-4 (45-A) to replace one short in the unit and the assignment of two pilots. Action: Two pilots and an airplane (44-80200) will be assigned.

(5) XIII Corps Arty Air Officer, Maj. Smith, reported damage in a landing accident to L-4 44-80201 (82-KK), pilot Lt Wilhelm, 261st FA Bn. No personnel injuries. A replacement aircraft is required. Lt Zicard to arrange for pick-up of the wreck at 202nd FA Gp Arty airstrip and the preparation of 44-80235 as a replacement.

(6) Lt Zicard reported that a crash crew was unable to pick up the wrecked L-4 (43-29770) of the 203rd FA Bn since it was too close to enemy lines and a truck could not approach within ½-mile.

(7) Called 12th Army Gp and requested Major (since yesterday) Lawton to indicate to Arty Air Officer (Maj. Lefever) a requirement for 12 replacement L-4s. This figure should be reduced only by the number of L-5s to be furnished us and should provide a 10% reserve in the Army.

February 3

(1) XIX Corps Arty Air Officer, Capt. Reed, called to ask if repairs had been completed on 44-80188 of the 203rd FA Bn. He was told it was ready to be collected.

(2) XIII Corps Arty Air Officer, Maj. Smith, reported the operational loss of 43-30529 (68-O) of the 207th FA Bn at 196th Gp strip. Pilot, Lt Gilbert, who was flying alone, was hospitalized with minor injuries. A replacement L-4 is required. Lt Zicard will arrange for pick-up of wreck and preparation of 44-79950 for assignment as replacement.

(3) Information obtained from a PoW captured on January 31 indicates that he saw what appears to be the crash of the 690th FA Bn Air OP on detached service (DS) with the 771st Tank Destroyer Bn on January 26.

February 4

(1) Orders requested for the return of 690th FA Bn from Detached Service with 771st TD Bn to parent unit.

(2) L-4s 44-80240 and 44-79938 were turned in by 690th FA Bn Air Section. FUSA Arty Air Officer, Maj. Bristol, informally concurred with the return of this Air Section to its parent unit without aircraft and short of one pilot (Lt Badura, MIA).

(3) XIX Corps Arty Air Officer, Capt. Reed, requested that wrecked L-4 44-79689 be picked up at Corps strip, repaired and returned to unit.

(4) Maj. Lefever reported that our requirement for 12 replacement aircraft had been passed to the Air Forces.

(5) 2nd Armd Div Asst Arty Air Officer, Lt Kistler, arrived at Arty strip with 16 pilots and observers and remained overnight. (The Div Arty Air Officer is on leave in Paris.) He was given one of our aircraft to visit XIX Corps. He stated that they were glad to be back in NUSA.

(6) 35th Inf Div Asst Arty Air Officer, Capt. Hasselbach, visited CP. He stated that his Air OP Sections would depart our strip on return of the Div Arty Air Officer from a visit to XVI Corps (probably today).

February 5

(1) Lt Zicard reported that L-4 43-30529 of the 207th FA Bn, which received major damage in an operational accident, was beyond economical repair and would be salvaged by 50th MR&RS.

(2) Information received from 84th Inf Div indicates that the two pilots who collided in mid-air when the unit was with FUSA were Lts Vanderveer and Bonnett. Both, together with their observers, were killed.

(3) Arty Air Officers of XIX Corps, 29th, 30th and 83rd Divs were requested to submit informal memoranda to this office concerning their experiences in the operation of L-5 aircraft.

February 6

XVI Corps Asst Arty Air Officer, Lt Williamson, visited Arty strip to turn in surplus L-4H 44-79954.

February 7

(1) FUSA Arty Air Officer, Maj. Bristol, stated that Maj. Lefever would visit us soon to discuss co-ordination between armies in answering Lt Col. Wolf's letter concerning L-5s. He further stated that the CG ETOUSA had awarded Cpl Streeper (the 29th Inf Div FA mechanic who first devised Plexiglas eyebrows) the Legion of Merit.

(2) Maj. Lefever called concerning L-5Bs: 'Will notify you later today (probably) when you can pick up an L-5B at Denain. We were able to get only two out of Air Force stocks and are giving these to Third and Ninth Armies.'

(3) 9th Air Force Liaison Officer, Col. Sprague, called to ask whether we were having airplanes delivered to us at A-92 St Trond. It appears that St Trond has had some admin troubles with the allocation of light aircraft. Answer: No. Our airplanes have been coming to us through A-93 Liège.

(4) Signal Section reported 176 light-weight cases for the SCR 610 radios used in FA aircraft were on hand at Signal Depot No. 3. They will release them to us and we will place them with Tech Supply, 50th MR&RS, for issue.

(5) Lt Helms visited VII Corps Arty and 8th Div Arty to check on a wrecked L-4 of the 203rd FA Bn which has not been picked up due to its proximity to front lines. He had not returned by dark.

(6) 84th Inf Div Arty Air Officer, Capt. Paschall, visited CP to discuss Air OP matters. He has two aircraft in 23rd MR&RS undergoing repairs. Told him to pick them up there. They are glad to be back in NUSA.

February 8

(1) XIX Corps Arty Air Officer, Capt. Reed, requested information on availability of one-piece windshields. Informed 'we are out' and can't get a promise of early delivery.

(2) Called FUSA Arty Air Officer, Maj. Bristol, to request that the appropriate VII Corps unit keep an eye on L-4 43-29770, wrecked by 203rd FA Bn but too close to enemy front lines for pick-up. He stated that he would furnish 84th Div two airplanes (which they were short of upon arrival here).

(3) Reconnaissance of A-93 Liège revealed no newly arrived replacement L-4s for NUSA.

(4) Lt Montgomery assumed duties of Ops Officer at the Arty Air Strip (relinquished by Lt Helms).

(5) Information received from Maj. Lefever indicates that AAF Regulations 35-37, dated Nov 29, 1944, lifted the horsepower restriction (190) on Liaison Pilots, authorising them to fly any Liaison type aircraft. This adds only the L-1 to the list of airplanes which may be flown, but there is no telling what it might do in the future (after all, what does the Arty/R P-51 do?).

(6) At approximately 1645 hrs an AT-6 buzzing the Arty airstrip in not too drastic a manner was probably mistaken for an Fw 190 and was fired upon by AA. The pilot hit the deck to avoid the flak and, apparently untouched, headed westward.

(7) A 50th MR&RS mechanic, taxying a XIX Corps L-4 which had been in for repairs, hit a boundary marker, thereby causing damage requiring more repairs.

February 9

(1) Twelfth Army Gp, Sgt Hogan, reported that one L-5B (44-16731) was ready to be picked up at A-83 Denain. With time being 'of the essence', 125th LS Ops Officer, Capt. O'Brien was requested to pick up the airplane for us today, which he did!

(2) 21st Weather Detachment, Capt. (since yesterday) Whitney, reported a long-shot prediction of 40 mph surface winds before morning. Arty airstrip, 34th Bgde and XVI Corps notified (the XIII and XIX Corps have their own weather service).

(3) 349th FA Gp pilot, Capt. Pfeiffer, visited Arty strip to obtain repairs to his L-4, which had been damaged (while in flight) by enemy MGs.

(4) Maj. Lefever called concerning:

(a) Plexiglas. 'Enclosures, windshields, and eyebrows are being made up in modification kits in the UK. What are your requirements?' Answer: 250 enclosures, 25 windshields, 50 eyebrows.

(b) Wings. 'The MR&RSs have been complaining that because of lack of facilities and good 'dope and fabric men', they have been unable to get out wings, thereby holding up release of aircraft to units. Yet 20 sets are in stock at 10th ADG and not a single MR&RS requisition has been received. Can you check the 50th?'

(c) Tailwheel springs. 'There are 40 pairs of tailwheel springs at A-83. Will you pick them up when you get the L-5 and see if FUSA can use half of them?' Answer: Yes.

(d) Squadron code markings. 'If any units come to you without any, do you have enough of your own left to start assigning them?' Answer: Yes.

February 10

(1) FUSA Arty Air Officer, Maj. Bristol, was requested to release (in our name) five of eight replacement L-4s (delivered to A-93 Liège for us yesterday) to Seventh Army pilots. This was because of shortages in their units of 27 aircraft. Serial Nos 44-80672, -80203, -80567, -80613 and -80143 were reported to Maj. Lefever, who will arrange for their replacement to us. Three aircraft will be picked up tomorrow and brought to the Arty airstrip.

(2) XIII Corps Asst Arty Air Officer, Lt Roark, reported that the Corps Arty Air Officer, Maj. Smith, had had a landing accident (gusty winds, hit a telephone pole at Corps strip), was in hospital (48th Field Hosp) and that L-4 43-30396 (68-A) was washed out. Passenger,

Maj. Windget, Engineer Section, was not injured. Lt Zicard to have wreck picked up. It will not be replaced as it was an 'extra'.

(3) 17 one-piece windshields were received at 50th MR&RS today.

February 11

(1) Visited XIII Corps Arty Air Officer, Maj. Smith, at 41st Evac Hosp. He had not been injured as seriously as first believed when he was carried from his crashed airplane on a stretcher, and expects to be out of the hospital in a few days. His wrecked L-4, picked up by the 50th MR&RS, is also considered repairable.

(2) Squadron code marking 63-A was painted on our new L-5B (named 'The Skipper'). A cabin heater was also installed.

(3) Capt. Mathews reconnoitered landing strip near 41st Evac Hosp. Found one which should be satisfactory for an L-5.

(4) About five heavy caliber shells landed between the 349th strip and XVI Corps strip. Shell fragments caused minor damage to three aircraft.

(5) Visit from Capt. C. M. G. Murphy (Air OP Officer, attached to 2nd British Army, pilot for Gen. Dempsey) and Squadron Leader M. Tyou, HQ Belgian Air Force, to discuss Air OP operations, equipment, organization, aircraft, etc. Each was given a little Cub dual instruction by Capt. Mathews (still a frustrated Fort Sill instructor). S/L Tyou is charged with setting up Air OPs in the Belgian Army.

(6) Lts Zicard, Lekfe and Morgan and T/3 Roehrich visited A-93 to check airplanes received there for NUSA. Six were there: 44-80597, -80603, -80212, -80577, -80591 and -80347. The last two were picked up; the balance will be collected tomorrow.

February 12

(1) Maj. Lefever reported that 19 reinforcement pilots departed the UK five days ago, all headed for NUSA.

(2) Visited XIII Corps Arty Air Officer, Maj. Smith, at 41st Evac Hosp. Looks like his absence from duty will be approximately two weeks, returning to full duty in about two months.

February 13

(1) All pilots of the Section participated in ferrying five replacement aircraft from A-93 Liège: Serial Nos 44-80577, -80212, -80603, -80597, -80186. Present airplane status is:

	L-5	L-4
Army Air Sub-Section	1	2
Army Pool – flyable	0	12
Undergoing repairs	0	11
On order	0	5

(2) An AAF pilot, who was lost, almost delivered an L-1 for the 153rd LS (FUSA) to the Arty air strip. He landed in an adjacent field, out of gas. We will arrange to deliver it in due course to its proper destination. The pilot was flown to A-93 Liège by Capt. Mathews.

(3) XVI Corps Arty Air Officer, Maj. Hallstein, reported wreck of L-4 44-79731 (82-I) of 407th Gp at the Gp Arty airstrip. Airplane went over on its back (seemingly European

custom) while taxying in strong gusty wind. No personnel injuries. Lt Zicard to arrange for pick-up of wreck and preparation of 44-79960 as replacement.

(4) Twelfth Army Gp Arty Air Officer, Maj. Lefever, reported that he was visiting ETOUSA tomorrow in an attempt to put through some sort of policy which would permit the return to the USA of a limited number of FA Air Observers to receive pilot training at Fort Sill. Agreed that this might be a good source of pilots (a) if consistent with rotation policy, (b) if other sources in US have dried up, and (c) if physical requirements are met, etc.

February 14

(1) 265th FA Bn pilot, Lt Nelms, visited Arty strip to obtain repairs to his L-4. On February 13, on his 13th mission since his return from hospital, his airplane picked up enemy ground fire which cut two drag wires in his left wing.

(2) Called Maj. Bristol, FUSA Arty Air Officer, and told him that the 153rd LS could come and collect their L-1 at our strip. We're through with it and will stick to L-4s and L-5s.

February 15

(1) An AAF Liaison pilot has been assigned to the 50th MR&RS. He reported today. This is a waste of time and money, since we will have to continue to test fly aircraft before accepting them for delivery to units.

(2) Called XIX Corps Air Officer, Capt. Reed, concerning radio cases. He also stated that the wrecked airplane seen by Maj. Dwyer near the 29th Inf Div strip belonged to the 104th Div. The aircraft hit wires and the pilot is hospitalized.

February 16

(1) Lt Zicard was checked out in the L-5.

(2) 153rd LS (FUSA) picked up the L-1 at the Arty air strip.

February 17

(1) Maj. Smith (XIII Corps) has been moved (on February 13) from the 41st Evacuation Hospital to the 15th General Hospital at Liège.

(2) Lts Oliver and McKierman, 95th Inf Div pilot and observer, who made an emergency landing 12 miles south of Maastricht on account of weather, visited the CP and were given transportation to return to their unit. The airplane, 66-H, was not damaged.

(3) Capt. Pinnerton, Flying Control, XXIX TAC, called concerning complaints received from Y-32 Ophoven that a pilot was disturbing the operational traffic at the strip by shooting landings and paying no attention to the tower. Since the airplane turned out to be an L-1 (S/N 111), it was suggested that he call the 125th LS since we have no L-1s.

(4) 35th Inf Div Asst Arty Air Officer reported the wreck of L-4 43-30454 (68-EE) by Lt Cozina, 692nd Bn pilot. Lt Cozina took off and fog closed in over the field behind him. In attempting to land he stalled the ship and dropped it in, causing considerable minor damage. 44-79781 is being assigned as a replacement and Lt Zicard has been requested to send a crash crew to pick up the wreck.

(5) XVI Corps Arty Air Officer, Maj. Hallstein, called to report that the 548th FA Bn, a new unit coming to XVI Corps, was short of two airplanes that had been cracked up and left

at their last strip. He requested that squadron code markings 82-K and 82-L be put on the replacement aircraft. Action withheld pending further information from 12th Army Group.

February 18

(1) XIX Corps Arty Executive Officer, Col. Winn, requested that our L-5 be given to 30th Div Arty for their use in checking out their pilots. This is the third attempt by the unit to obtain the airplane, but each time for a different reason. Explained that it could not be done. 30th Div has four competent L-5 pilots already, which is probably more than all of the rest combined in the Army. Our L-5 is needed here for a variety of obvious reasons.

(2) Maj. Lefever called concerning:

(a) Replacement airplanes, 548th Bn: 'The understanding is that Fifteenth Army will forward units to you complete with squadron code markings already assigned to aircraft. Will check to get story on two planes short in this unit, including data on Air OP Loss Reports, Forms 14, and pick-up of wrecks.'

(b) L-5s: 'No more information on expected arrival date.'

(c) Reinforcement pilots: 'Your 19 left Paris on February 13.'

(3) XVI Corps Arty Air Officer, Maj. Hallstein, was informed that L-4s 44-80162 and 44-80954 would be assigned to the 548th Bn, which unit, upon losing two aircraft when a hangar blew down, was informed by Fifteenth Army that NUSA would furnish replacements.

(4) XIII Corps Arty Air Officer, Maj. Smith, called. He returned from the 15th General Hospital to his unit today, with his broken throttle hand in a cast and sling and his shoulder bound up, but ready for duty.

(5) Arty air units with NUSA currently as follows:

XIII, XVI and XIX Corps; 34th FA Brigade; 2nd and 5th Armd Divs; 29th, 30th, 35th, 75th, 79th, 83rd, 84th, 95th and 102nd Inf Divs.

(6) Maj. Lefever: 'Our recommendation of 8 December to CG ETOUSA that K-20 cameras be furnished to all Div and Corps Arty HQs, and reproducing equipment to Corps Arty HQ, is still bogged down in USSTAF pending availability of necessary equipment. We have almost given up hope of getting it through before the next war.'

(7) Comment by Maj. Liston on the use of K-20 cameras by FA units. 'The 125th LS is capable of taking all required pictures with K-22 cameras and of delivering rush prints (9"x9") to units within 4-6 hours (and is now doing so for two Corps and a Brigade). This is, of course, subject to weather, availability of paper, chemicals, etc.'

February 19

(1) From Maj. Lefever: '75th Inf Div Arty Air Officer, Maj. Wolff, is here with all of his airplanes and pilots. Will dispatch him to Arty air strip as soon as the weather breaks.'

(2) Maj. Morrison, 40th FA Gp, requested that Gp Air Officer, Maj. Sugg, who is en route to Maastricht for Metz with two aircraft, be dispatched, on arrival, to 34th FA Brigade air strip.

(3) 548th FA Bn pilots, Lts Carrigg and Brume, visited Arty strip to pick up two aircraft to replace two which received major damage in England.

(4) 75th Inf Div Arty Air Officer, Maj. Wolff, together with three other pilots and four aircraft, arrived at Arty strip from Verdun en route to join their unit. Remained overnight. Five pilots and aircraft that remained overnight at Liège, and one pilot and aircraft that had not left Verdun yet, should arrive tomorrow. Need one K-20 camera, 10 one-piece windshields and nine sets of eyebrows.

(5) 70th FA Bn pilot, Lt Black, visited Arty strip to obtain repairs on his airplane. Remained overnight.

(6) Status Report as of this date:

	Pilots	Aircraft L-4s L-5s	K-20 cameras	
Authorized	263	209	27	*17
On hand	269	260	1	9
On requisition	19	5	7	2
Excess	25	56	26 deficit	6 deficit

Not authorized but required.

February 20

(1) 75th Inf Div Arty Air Officer, Maj. Wolff, reported that his five airplanes and pilots had arrived from Liège, that he had reconnoitered a strip, and that the entire group would depart to join their unit on Feb 21. Remained overnight.

(2) XVI Corps Arty Air Officer, Maj. Hallstein, reported that the 79th Inf Div Arty Air Officer, Maj. Lawrence, had checked in at his CP, that their aircraft are en route, that the unit is OK on pilots but short of one airplane. The 8th Armd Div and 35th Inf Div had shied away from his offer of providing K-20 cameras to them. Lt Zicard is to prepare 43-30523 (46-(??)) for assignment to fill shortage in 79th Inf Div Arty.

(3) L-4 43-30454, wrecked by 692nd Bn, was repaired and returned to the unit (Lt Cozina) and the assignment of 44-79681 as a replacement was canceled. The latter airplane was returned to the 50th MR&RS for major repairs which are required and which were overlooked.

(4) Lt Zicard reported that two units (32 men) of the 50th MR&RS, which had been transferred as a cadre to start an MR&RS for Fifteenth Army, had been returned completely.

(5) FUSA Arty Air Officer, Maj. Bristol, reported that the 75th Inf Div Arty pilot, Lt Lytle, was remaining overnight at Spa and would proceed to Maastricht tomorrow. Asked him to check on L-4 43-29770 to see if it had been picked up by the 23rd MR&RS.

(6) Maj. Lefever stated that he would arrive at Maastricht tomorrow afternoon. He is staying over in Spa tonight to have a new engine installed in his L-5 by 23rd MR&RS.

February 21

(1) Maj. Bristol, FUSA Arty Air Officer, reported that L-4 43-29770, wrecked by 203rd FA Bn too close to enemy lines to be picked up, was picked up Feb 20 by 23rd MR&RS. It will now be relieved from assignment to the unit.

(2) 75th Inf Div pilot Lt Lytle arrived at Arty strip and was dispatched to join his unit. The other pilots of this Division proceeded to their new strip in the British area.

(3) 40th FA Gp Arty Air Officer, Maj. Sugg, and pilot Lt Stewart arrived at Arty strip. They were dispatched to 34th FA Bgde strip.

(4) Nine of the 19 expected reinforcement pilots arrived (Beck, Stevenson, Dean, Dekey, Linder, Byers, Sanders, Sperrin and Tuel).

(5) XIII Corps Arty Air Officer, Maj. Smith, reported forced landing of 102nd Div L-4 44-80124 (76-E) due to enemy ground action. Lt Guerra, pilot, escaped without injury, though the aircraft was brought under heavy mortar fire after it landed. A replacement is required. An attempt will be made to rescue the wreck. Lt Zicard is to prepare 44-80037 as a replacement, which the Div Arty Air Officer, Capt. Dobbs, will pick up today.

(6) Lt Col. Bradshaw, AAF observer, visited Section and Arty strip, departing at 1300 hrs for Alsdorf in L-4 63-C to visit units. He returned at 1900.

(7) Distribution to units of tie-down rings (for installation in aircraft) was started today.

February 22

(1) Lt Col. Kenney telephoned to say that he had had a slight accident and was at an Engineer unit just outside of Liège. He requested that Lt Col. Leich send two L-4s to the nearest airfield so that he and Capt. Robinson could proceed with their trip. Arrangements were made for two pilots to pick them up at A-93 Liège. A later telephone call confirmed that the two officers reached their destination safely.

(2) Capt. George Smith, XVIII A/B Corps, called to report arrival of Lts Leefe and Andrews with Lt Col. Kenney and Capt. Robinson as passengers. Remained overnight.

(3) Maj. Lefever flew L-5B 63-A to 83rd Inf Div Arty strip.

February 23

(1) Lts Leefe and Andrews returned from XVIII A/B Corps with Lt Col. Kenney and Capt. Robinson as passengers.

(2) The Arty Air Officers of the following units reported a good show today, with no known losses or casualties: XIX Corps, XVI Corps, XIII Corps and 34th FA Brigade.

(3) Twelfth Army Gp Arty Air Officer, Maj. Lefever, returned from Verdun, using our L-5B (63-B).

(4) FUSA Arty Air Officer, Maj. Bristol, reported that our 63-B, flown by Maj. Lefever, was at his strip and that he would return it to us. Told him that we would come and get it.

February 24

(1) XIII Corps Arty Air Officer, Lt Lester, hit some wires while being chased by Me 109s. No injuries to him or his observer. His L-4, 44-80239 (76-C) is at Map Ref 977616 and will have to be replaced. Lt Zicard will have wreck picked up and is to prepare 44-80292 as replacement.

(2) XIX Corps Arty Air Officer, Capt. Reed, reported that Lt Patton, 666th Bn pilot (on his second combat mission) had, between 0830 and 0900, been pounced upon by seven Me 109s at an altitude of 1,500ft and had successfully evaded all but one, which got in some hits from behind and below. Though injured (in his feet) by the explosion of a shell, Lt Patton made a successful forced landing (on account of shots into engine) and was evacuated.

The observer was unhurt. Lt Zicard is to pick up the wrecked L-4 44-80350 (which was inspected by Lt Col. Leich and appears to be repairable) at 258th FA Gp strip, and to prepare 44-79938 (32-RR) as a replacement. A reinforcement pilot will be sent attached unassigned to 258th Gp, remaining in this status pending determination of Lt Heath, convalescent pilot formerly with the unit.

(3) 252nd FA Gp Arty Air Officer, Capt. Skelly, departed to join his unit. His pilots, Lts Hutton and Belleiu, were dispatched to XVI Corps Arty airstrip after having squadron code markings (82-O and 82-P) applied to their L-4s.

(4) Lts Andrews and Sanders carried M. Balbaud (French) and Mr Maxted (British), war correspondents, to XIII Corps Arty strip.

(5) Maj. Smith (XIII Corps) is recovering from his recent accident and hopes to fly tomorrow. He is very interested in the L-5, thinks it will be very useful for administrative missions, but is wary of it on very small fields.

February 25

(1) XIX Corps Arty Air Officer, Capt. Reed, reported that 238th Gp L-4 43-29731 (32-E) had been shot down across the Roer River, the pilot, Lt Thompson, having a leg broken, the observer being uninjured. Replacement required. The wreck is presently inaccessible. Lt Zicard to prepare 44-80597 as a replacement. Lt Andrews will be sent to the unit to replace Lt Thompson, reporting at the Corps airstrip with the new airplane.

(2) XIII Corps Asst Arty Air Officer, Lt Roark, reported that two L-4s of the 5th Armd Div had collided in mid-air, killing one pilot, 1st Lt W. M. Patrick, and slightly injuring the other. No observers were carried. The accident occurred in the vicinity of the Div Arty airstrip. L-4 43-30016 (54-F) was burned when fuel tank exploded after hitting the ground. L-4 43-30104 (54-C) had one wing torn off. Lt Zicard to send a new wing for the repair of one ship, to pick up the burned ship and to prepare 44-80603 as a replacement. Lt Montgomery will be sent as a replacement for Lt Patrick.

(3) 2nd Armd Div Asst Arty Air Officer, Lt Kistler, reported that Ju 87s strafed their strip and dropped anti-personnel bombs between 2100-2200 hrs last night, damaging two L-4s but injuring no personnel. Damaged airplanes were 43-49768 (49-M) and 44-80558 (33-F), belonging to the attached 696th FA Bn. He requested replacement of 43-49768. Lt Zicard is to pick up this damaged L-4 and prepare 44-80298 for assignment as replacement. Additional info will be furnished concerning the flyability of the 696th FA Bn L-4 before action can be taken.

(4) Maj. Zimmerman gave the Roer River battleground the once-over from the L-5, flown by Capt. Mathews.

(5) XIII Corps reported that 44-80233 (63-J) (Lt Badura, 690th FA Bn) listed as missing in action, was now accessible at Map Ref 958703. Lt Zicard to have it picked up.

(6) Lt Col. Leich, accompanied by Lt Stevenson, visited A-93 Liège and spotted five replacement L-4s. Lt Montgomery and T/3 Tye checked them over and determined that they were for NUSA and could be flown out (will do on 26 Feb). Their serial numbers are 44-80220, -80223, -80582, -80629 and -80669.

February 26

(1) Lt Stevenson assumed responsibilities of Operations Officer at the airstrip in place of Lt Montgomery, transferred.

(2) Capt. Mathews and nine other pilots in five airplanes visited A 93 Liège for the purpose of ferrying in five replacement L-4Js (see entry for Feb 25).

(3) XIX Corps Arty Air Officer, Capt. Reed, was asked to follow up on L-4 44-80558 of 696th Armd FA Bn, alleged to be unflyable. He stated that no action should be taken for a few days to pick up wrecked 43-29731 because of heavy traffic on Roer River bridges (Item 1 of February 25 refers).

(4) Lt Zicard searched the area in which Lt Beck is reported to have had a forced landing yesterday, but to no avail. His last known location and the markings and serial number of his aircraft (63-F and -347) were reported to FUSA Arty Air Officer, Maj. Bristol, who was asked to have his units check. Also reported to 125th LS (Lt Williams) and XXIX TAC Flying Control (Sgt Sperry).

February 27

(1) Lts Zicard and Tuel visited 2nd Armd Div Arty airstrip and picked up 44-80558 of 696th Armd FA Bn (damaged by strafing). Airplane was flown back to Arty strip and 44-80186 assigned to the unit as a replacement.

(2) 50th MR&RS was requested to pick up wrecked aircraft 43-29731 and 44-80233, hitherto inaccessible. Both were spotted from the air by Capt. Mathews (Items 1 and 4 of Feb 25 refer).

(3) Lt Montgomery, now a 5th Armd Div pilot, picked up L-4 54-F, which was at Arty airstrip.

(4) Airstrips of all units are in a 'fluid' condition, i.e., they are moving. Lt Col. Leich, Maj. Knoche (Engr), Capt. Lenczyk (125th LS) and Lt Zicard reconnoitered and located a suitable strip, which can be occupied immediately, but which will be prepared with 30ftx1000ft Sommerfeld matting by March 3.

(5) An 84th Div pilot, Lt Miller, sketchily reported the loss of two aircraft, 87-D and 87-(?). Both were badly shot up and will have to be replaced. One observer was killed and one pilot (Lt Martinez) injured. Lt Zicard to pick up wrecks and to provide replacement aircraft.

(6) Lt Col. Leich and Lt Zicard made another aerial search of the vicinity of Olne for Lt Beck (and airplane) who has been missing. No luck today. (Later: Message received from FUSA, signed by Lt Beck, at 1440 today. He stated that he and the airplane were OK, had been forced down by weather and would return when weather permits.)

(7) Conference with Maj. Buchanan, Quartermaster Section, concerning distribution of 73 octane fuel. We recommended that it be handled through Corps POL Dumps with measures initiated to safeguard it from being issued for other than aviation use. Agreed to furnish him an informal memo outlining our ideas on the subject. Also indicated future fuel requirements, to be confirmed in writing. Present monthly requirements approx 60-70,000 gals.

February 28

(1) On February 26 four L-1s were delivered to the Army strip. The pilots departed hurriedly. Investigation discloses that they are for the 153rd LS (FUSA), which is at Spa. When notified of their location by the 50th MR&RS, the 153rd stated they didn't want them.

(2) 29th Inf Div Arty Air Officer, Maj. Swenson, reported location of his new strip as of March 1, and also crash of 43-30078 (43-H). Lt Norton, pilot, ran out of fuel on return to his strip and crashed trying to stretch his glide. He requires minor repairs, his L-4 major repairs. Lt Zicard to pick up the wreck and to prepare 44-80240 for assignment to unit.

(3) L-4s 43-30207 and 44-80223 were furnished to 84th Inf Div as replacements for two wrecked aircraft (43-30362 and 44-80774).

(4) XVI Corps Arty Air Officer, Maj. Hallstein, reported loss of 407th FA Gp airplane 44-79960 (82-I) when hit by enemy 20-mm flak at 1,500ft. The L-4 crashed 1,000 yards behind enemy lines, but the pilot, Lt Smith, and observer, Capt. Buttery, were rescued, both seriously injured. The airplane burned and is presently inaccessible. He requested a replacement L-4 but will notify us later concerning requirement for a new pilot.

(5) Lt Col. Leich, Tec 3 Roehrich, Pfc Van Slyke and nine pilots visited the new strip.

(6) Pilot status as of 28 Feb, as reported to Twelfth Army Gp, is as follows:

Authorized	269
On hand	281 (includes 12 in Army Pool)
Losses in February	8

Killed	Wounded
Patrick (8th Armd Div)	Whaley (30th Div)
	Thompson (258th Gp)
	Martinez (84th Div)
	Prather (959th Bn)
	Smith (407th Gp)

Airplane status as of 28 Feb, furnished to 50th MR&RS as follows:

	L-4	L-5
Authorized	191	60
On hand	252	1
Operational	251	1
Undergoing repairs in army unit	1	0
Army Pool	6	0
Undergoing repairs in MR&RS	17	0
L-4s missing in action (listed below)	3	0

Serial No.	Unit	Location (last known Map Ref)
43-29731	228th FA Group	(028620)
44-79960	407th FA Group	(933857)
43-30215	959th FA Bn	(190807)

CHAPTER 9

Attack on the Rhine, March 1945

The Allied advance into the Germany continued, with München-Gladbach falling to the Ninth Army's XIX Corps on 1 March. The following day, two Divisions, the 83rd Infantry and 2nd Armored, reached the Rhine at Neuss and, on 3 March, Krefeld was cleared by XIII Corps. A few days later, the Rhine had been reached in all sectors of the Ninth Army's front, and by 10 March XVI Corps had wiped out the last organised resistance west of the river.

Keeping up with the offensive, HQ NUSA moved its command post to München-Gladbach on 10 March, and ten days later the HQ's rear echelon opened at Rheydt. The three Corps attached to NUSA at this time were exercising control over three Armored Divisions (2nd, 5th and 8th), nine Infantry Divisions (29th, 30th, 35th, 75th, 79th, 83rd, 84th, 95th and 102nd), and a number of attached units including the 407th and 411th FA Groups. As usual, HQ NUSA's moves throughout this period were closely followed by the 125th Liaison Squadron, which arrived at München-Gladbach on 9 March, but three Flights remained on detached service with the Army's Corps HQs. Shortly before this, on 7 March, a Maastricht-based L-5 (42-99303) of the 125th, flown by Lt Charles P. McBride, was damaged in an accident at Vlyringen, Belgium.

Unusual at this time was the assignment to the Ninth Army of an FA Battalion manned by black enlisted men with a mixture of white and black officers. This was the 351st, which arrived in the UK in December 1944 with the 350th FA Battalion to form the 350th FA Group (Colored). The two battalions, with six black officer liaison pilots in their Air Sections, re-equipped under the auspices of 15th US Army and in February departed Southampton for Le Havre, en route to Camp Twenty Grand at Yvetot. On 6 March, the 351st, equipped with 155 mm howitzers, was reassigned to the Ninth Army and moved to Alsdorf, Germany. This was followed, on 10 March, by a move to Neuss, near Düsseldorf, where the battalion, now attached to the 407th FA Group, went into action for the first time.

While on patrol on 24 March, the pilots of two L-4s of the 959th FA Battalion saw the crash of a B-24 Liberator and, hoping they might be able to aid the bomber's crew, decided to land alongside. This they accomplished safely, but after they landed the B-24 exploded, badly damaging both L-4s. Luckily there were no personnel injuries. Another unusual incident occurred that day when a horse ran onto the road on which an L-4 of the 75th Infantry Division was landing. The pilot was unable to avoid hitting the horse, which then ran off, seemingly unhurt, but repairs to the L-4 included replacement of its badly damaged left wing.

That same day, 24 March, NUSA launched an assault crossing of the Rhine by XVI Corps (30th and 79th Infantry Divisions) while XIII Corps carried out a feint operation. This was followed on 30 March by XIX Corps attacking eastwards towards Münster and Hamm, but the main offensive was entrusted to XVI Corps which, having established bridgeheads across the river, pushed to the south and south-east towards the Ruhr. This quickly developed into an enormous pocket containing German Army Group B. The 35th Infantry, which took part in this action after crossing the river in the Rheinberg area, was one of five Divisions attached to XVI Corps, the strength of which included fifty-four FA battalions operating 108 Air OPs. Overall, the Ninth Army was now operating 300 L-4s, but nineteen were lost during the month, eight of them being destroyed by enemy fighter aircraft.

One such engagement was experienced on 30 March by Lts Joseph F. Gordon and Anders Hansen, respectively the pilot and observer of an L-4 of the 65th Armored FA Battalion. While on patrol over the town of Haltern they were attacked by one of two Fw 190s that had been strafing tanks of the 2nd Armored Division, to which their battalion was attached. Joe Gordon took immediate evasive action, but a single burst from the enemy fighter shattered the L-4's propeller and caused other damage. In the crash landing in the built-up area that followed, the Cub went onto its nose in a vegetable garden, but both crew members escaped unharmed. Fortunately the aircraft's radio was still working and about an hour later, following a call to base, Sgt Lester Weeks and Cpl Haval of the 65th's ground crew arrived in a half-track laden with spare parts and tools. With a new propeller installed, patches covering bullet holes in its fabric covering, and other repairs completed, the L-4 was towed to a field that Joe Gordon assessed was just adequate for a take-off with only a pilot on board. And so it proved, but very marginally, and after a precarious climb-out Gordon was on his way back to the 65th's airstrip, with Anders Hansen and the two mechanics following in the half-track.

Like a number of other rapidly advancing Ninth Army units, the 407th FA Group displaced seven times during March. After departing Gangelt on the 2nd, its Air Sections subsequently operated from airstrips at Arsbeck, Sael Huysen, Kamp, Friedrichsfeld, Hinxe, Nothelle and Polsum. In the course of these moves it became apparent that a recent change in standard operating procedures was proving beneficial. Instead of accompanying the HQ column, Air Section ground personnel now moved independently, enabling them to take more direct routes to new airstrips. Despite the disruption caused by so many moves, the L-4s of the 407th Group, including those of the attached 758th, 211th and 351st FA Battalions, flew missions on twenty-seven days in March. Operating under a central Group control, these comprised 112 combat patrols, twenty-nine adjustments of fire, fourteen reconnaissance missions and twenty-four administrative flights.

Extracts from the HQ NUSA Air Journal for 1-31 March 1945, compiled by Lt Col. R. M. Leich (Ninth Army HQ at Maastricht)

March 1
(1) XVI Corps Asst Arty Air Officer, Capt. Welter, requested that a pilot be assigned to replace Lt Smith, 407th FA Gp, who was hospitalized after being shot down. Lt Sherrill

was dispatched to XVI Corps Arty strip in a replacement L-4 (44-80208) and arrived there before lunch.

(2) L-4 44-80201 was assigned from the Army Pool as a replacement to 959th FA Bn.

(3) FUSA Arty Air Officer, Maj. Bristol, reported that Lt Baldwin, 743rd Bn pilot en route to join his unit in XVI Corps, was weathered in at Spa. The Battalion's other pilot, who made a forced landing on running out of fuel, was somewhere in the vicinity. Both would be dispatched to Maastricht but remained overnight at Spa. Maj. Bristol, fed up with lost pilots, called later and said he would hold the 743rd pilots at his strip until we send for them. It seems that one, already lost once, took off in soupy weather and became lost again. A 'bell-boy pilot' will be sent to the FUSA strip when the weather permits, to take the wanderers in tow.

(4) Lt Zicard, accompanied by Lt Newbury, Engineer Officer, 50th MR&RS, visited XIII Corps Arty strip to locate remains of the wrecked but hitherto inaccessible L-4 44-80233. Saw München-Gladbach and almost the Rhine by mistake.

(5) 5th Armd Div pilot, Lt Trachtenberg, reported that L-4 43-30249 (54-D) flown by Lt Chiacon, was shot down by enemy ground fire, the pilot receiving leg wounds. The aircraft is repairable; requires the installation of a new right wing. A replacement pilot is also needed. Lt Trachtenberg also reported the landing accident of 43-30061 (54-C), pilot unknown, which went over on its back. A replacement aircraft is required. The unit will call here for a pilot and aircraft tomorrow. Lt Zicard is to find (at the MR&RS) an aircraft which can be supplied, deliver a new wing to the site of the damaged aircraft, and pick up the wreck.

(6) Twelfth Army Gp Arty Air Officer, Maj. Lefever, unable to withstand the wrath of two Army Arty Officers and two Army Arty Air Officers, succeeded in borrowing from the Air Forces an L-5B on which modification experiments will be undertaken at 45th ADG.

March 2

(1) Lts Sanders and Tuel flew to Spa to lead in Lts Baldwin and Grantzenberg, 743rd FA Bn pilots. Since no squadron code markings were on their aircraft, XVI Corps Arty Air Officer, Maj. Hallstein, was called. He assigned markings 82-II and 82-JJ and stated that a pilot of 252nd Gp would come here to lead the pilots forward to join their unit.

(2) 5th Armd Div Asst Arty Air Officer, Lt Trachtenberg, visited the Arty strip to pick up Lt Dean and L-4 44-80669, both furnished as replacements.

(3) The four unwanted L-1s were flown away today (see entry for February 28).

(4) Lts Linder and Beck delivered a replacement L-4 to the 29th Inf Div, and Lts Wimberley and Crouser delivered one to the 84th Inf Div.

March 3

(1) Maj. Lefever called concerning L-5B modification. 'Would like to borrow yours.' OK, if we can borrow one from the 125th LS (OK'd by Lt Col. Art Miller and Capt. Fred Lenczyk). Will deliver 'The Skipper' on March 4 to A-83 Denain/Valenciennes.

(2) Lt Zicard reported that the following L-4s, missing in action (MIA), have been picked up and are as indicated:

Serial No.	Unit	Date MIA	Status
43-29731	228th Gp	25 Feb	Salvaged
44-80233	690th FA Bn	27 Jan	Salvaged
43-30061	5th Armd Div	1 Mar	Repairable

(3) Capt. Mathews visited XVI Corps strip and XIII Corps Fire Direction Control strip, where supply of 72 octane gasoline was discussed with XIII Corps Asst Arty Air Officer (Lt Hanchey). Lt Hanchey was told a supply of 73 octane gas was to be maintained in the Corps Class IV DPs. Lt Hanchey reported no losses of aircraft or pilots for today.

(4) A visit was paid to XIX Corps FDC strip by Capt. Mathews and a discussion with the Asst Arty Air Officer, Lt Johnson, revealed the loss of 44-80095 (82-C) by the 25th FA Bn. He requested a replacement aircraft and that the old one be picked up. Action: Lt Zicard to pick up wreck and assign 44-79731 as a replacement.

(5) Lt Gens Spaatz and Doolittle landed at the Arty air strip.

(6) Col. Hanley and Capt. Mathews have determined that an L-5 will not work out of soft fields where an L-4 will work easily.

March 4

(1) Lt Zicard reported that 50th MR&RS had been unable to pick up the following aircraft MIA:

Serial No.	Unit	Location (Map Ref)	Reason
(a) 43-30215 2	5th FA Bn	190807	Unable to locate
(b) 44-79960	407th FA Gp	933857	Mines

Action: (a) XIX Corps Arty Air Officer, Capt. Reed, reported vicinity 145795 as the location of wreck. The MR&RS was requested to check again. (b) XVI Corps Arty AO, Maj. Hallstein, was out of range of communications, but the matter will be taken up with him.

(2) XVI Corps Arty Air Officer (Maj. Hallstein) asked that if 788th FA Bn aircraft arrived without squadron code markings, to give them 82-KK and 82-LL.

(3) 34th FA Bgde Asst Arty Air Officer (Lt Feldt) visited the CP (bringing Maj. Young).

(4) 261st FA Bn pilot, Lt Wilhelm, visited the Arty air strip to obtain repairs to his airplane. Remained overnight on account of weather.

(5) Lt Col. Leich and Capt. Mathews visited airstrips of 30th Inf Div, XIX Corps Arty (moved strip – could not locate), XIII Corps Arty and 557th FA Bn Arty.

(6) 30th Inf Div Arty Air Officer, Maj. Blohm, reported the total loss by fire and explosion (believed caused by saboteurs) of two L-4s, 44-80157 and 43-29791, at his old strip near Rodingen. CIC is investigating. Action: Lt Zicard to prepare 43-30396 and 44-80582 as replacements (44-E and 44-F). The unit will call for them on March 5.

(7) XIII Corps Arty Air Officer, Maj. Smith, stated that on March 5 he would move his strip from Anrath to Mors. He allocated 68-QQ and on down the alphabet as open squadron code markings which we can assign to XIII Corps units arriving without them.

March 5

(1) Lt Zicard reported that wrecked L-4s 43-30215 (see March 4 report) and 44-80095 (see March 3) were picked up and are repairable.

(2) Capt. Mathews completed arrangements with CO, 125th LS, Capt. Lenczyk, and CO 50th MR&RS, Maj. Davis, to 'go over' the München-Gladbach airfield on March 6. Capt. Lenczyk has determined that the fighter group no longer has intentions of occupying the field.

(3) Lt Col. Leich attempted to deliver the L-5B to A-83 Denain, but turned back 40 miles out due to fog. An accompanying L-5 from the 125th LS followed that life saving maneuver, the 180 degree turn.

(4) Called Col. Fagg, G-3 Air, with regard to reported request from XIX Corps for all-day fighter cover for Air OPs, four of which were alleged to have been shot down today by Me 109s flying off airfield F3198, with these personnel losses: 1 pilot missing, 1 pilot and observer injured. Col. Fagg questioned necessity of cover since the Arty wasn't doing much firing, etc. Explained that Air OPs fly from dawn to dusk on patrol, etc. No other facts were available from G-3 Air (Maj. Crawford) but a call to the Corps produced the following loss report by Capt. Reed, XIX Corps Arty Air Officer:

Unit	Aircraft	Cause	Results
959th Bn	32-W (43-30296)	N/A	Lt Koons, pilot, and observer hospitalized.

(One replacement aircraft and one pilot wanted, attached unassigned to 258th FA Gp).

| 978th Bn | 32-R (43-30282) | N/A | Lt Trautman, pilot, and observer to duty. |

(One replacement aircraft needed)

| 95th Div | 66-J (43-36776) | N/A | Pilot and observer to duty. |

(One replacement aircraft needed)

| 95th Div | 66-F (44-79676) | N/A | Pilot (Lt Nichols) and observer killed. |

(One replacement aircraft needed; one pilot wanted for assignment to unit).

Lt Zicard to arrange pick-up of wrecks and the preparation of replacement aircraft.

(5) 34th FA Brigade Arty Air Officer, Maj. Keating, authorised release of squadron code markings 69-NN and on down the alphabet for aircraft of units arriving without markings.

March 6

(1) G-3 Air, Maj. Crawford, reported that plans had been made today to provide one armed recce sortie every hour of daylight in the Army Zone, instead of full-time fighter cover for Air OPs as requested by XIX Corps. 'It's a waste of money to use a $15,000 fighter to protect a $1,000 Cub.' The plan was for today only. (Comment: weather probably stopped even that.)

(2) The following assignments of replacement L-4s were made:

Unit	Squadron code markings	Serial No.
959th Bn	32-W	44-80350
978th Bn	32-R	44-80232
95th Inf Div	66-F	44-79681
95th Inf Div	66-J	44-80629

(3) 30th Inf Div Arty Air Officer, Maj. Blohm, and 13 pilots visited the CP for lunch. Unit is en route to a new location at Echt, Holland. Weathered in, so remained overnight.

(4) Called XIX Corps Arty Air Officer, Capt. Reed, concerning locations of airstrips of 2nd Armd Div and 95th Inf Div, both of which appear to be within range of enemy mortar and

artillery fire. He was already aware of this and said he would see if something could be done. It was explained that a critical shortage of aircraft would not permit any large scale replacement of losses.

(5) Maj. Lefever stated that only five replacement L-4s could be supplied on our orders for ten; should the situation get too tough we may be able to borrow some from FUSA.

March 7

(1) 2nd Armd Div Asst Arty Air Officer, Lt Kistler, requested permission to bring in an aircraft which had been combat damaged (hole in spar) in exchange for 44 80558, formerly assigned to 696th Armd FA Bn (attached). Reply: OK. Lt Kistler recommended that instructions be issued to non-armored units participating in Air OP operations with Armd Bns (a good idea, which we will work on after finding out more about it).

(2) Lt Zicard reported that L-4 43-30296 (32-W) of 959th FA Bn had been picked up and, not being repairable, would be salvaged.

(3) Lt Sanders flew replacement L-4 (82-C) to 25th FA Bn, to which unit he will be attached by Corps.

(4) Lts Beck and Dewey visited A-93 Liège to see if any replacement aircraft had arrived. Couldn't even see the field through the fog.

(5) Capt. Mathews and the CO of 125th LS, Capt. Lenczyk, made a reconnaissance in the vicinity of München-Gladbach for an airstrip for the LS and the MR&RS. A strip was located and plans made to occupy it immediately. An extensive search of the area had not produced a more convenient or practical location. 50th MR&RS CO, Maj. Davis, will be taken to the strip tomorrow to make plans for the movement of his unit.

March 8

(1) T/3 Roehrich and T/3 Tye moved to München-Gladbach to establish the necessary facilities for the operation of our new strip.

(2) Added to the list of nicknames for the L-4 (Puddlejumper, Piperschmitt, Giant, Sewing-Machine, Maytag Messerschmitt, Cubbersnipe, First Sergeant, etc.) is that introduced by the Dutch: 'The So-Sad-One'.

(3) XVI Corps Arty Air Officer, Maj. Hallstein, called to report that the 788th FA Bn had arrived from Fifteenth Army short of one aircraft, and that an Air OP Loss Report was being filed. An L-4 that arrived on his strip had no squadron code markings and as the pilot had not been instructed to check in at the Army Arty airstrip at Maastricht, he had wandered around the Army zone looking for the Corps. Requested Corps to have the unit's two pilots fly in their own aircraft to have squadron code markings applied and to pick up a replacement (which should have been furnished before the unit arrived here). Lt Zicard will prepare 44-80220 as replacement. Squadron code markings 82-K and 82-L were assigned.

(4) 8th Armd Div Arty Air Officer, Maj. Cross, visited the strip to turn in his excess aircraft 43-30546 (21-A). He thanked us for assigning Lt Linder as a replacement pilot and said that Linder had been assigned to the 405th Armd Bn (his old Bn) with everyone happy about it.

(5) XIX Corps Arty Air Officer, Capt. Reed, reported the loss, and complete destruction by our artillery fire, of 422nd FA Gp aircraft 44-80027 (28-X), flown by Capt. Kerrigan with

an NCO observer. The pilot, who crossed the Channel from the UK with me on August 27, and observer were both killed. Replacement pilot and aircraft will be required. Lt Zicard will prepare 44-80645 for replacement and Lt Stevenson will be transferred to the unit, effective March 10.

(6) Notified 34th FA Brigde Arty Air Officer, Maj. Keating, of the move of our airstrip and that 547th FA Bn pilots were at Liège, awaiting good flying weather before heading this way.

March 10

(Ninth Army Command Post opened at München-Gladbach, Germany)

(1) Army Air Section (less Lt Zicard) moved to München-Gladbach airstrip carrying following passengers: Majs Linton and Hazen, and Sgts Skinner, Kersh, Hamilton and Collins.

(2) The following arrived at Maastricht strip en route from Fifteenth US Army to join their units. The code markings shown here were applied to their aircraft and the pilots were led to München-Gladbach by Lt Zicard.

Unit	Pilot	Aircraft S/No.	Squadron code markings
XIII Corps Units:			
411th Gp	Capt. ?	44-80373	68-UU
	Capt. Phillip	44-80248	68-VV
	Lt Erikson 44-80535	(See Note 1)	
787th Bn	Lt ?	44-80665	68-SS
	Lt ?	44-80405	68-TT
349th Bn (Note 2)	Lt ?	44-80175	68-QQ
	Lt ?	44-80163	68-RR
34th FA Brigade Units:			
547th Bn	Lt ?	44-80340	69-NN
	Lt Becker	44-80344	69-OO
549th Bn	Lt Phillips	44-80548	69-PP
	Lt ?	44-80564	69-QQ

Note 1. Spare aircraft 44-80535 obtained in UK by unknown methods, turned in for reassignment by Army.

Note 2. These pilots did not arrive at München-Gladbach but remained overnight at Maastricht.

(3) Lt Stevenson departed to join 422nd FA Gp (in replacement aircraft 44-80546) with XIX Corps Arty pilot Lt Moran, who left his aircraft at the strip for necessary repairs due to having taxied into a 'dud' on strip.

(4) XIII Corps and 34th FA Bgde sent 'guides' to lead pilots to join 411th Gp and 787th, 349th, 547th and 549th FA Bns.

(5) Requested XIX Corps Arty Air Officer, Capt. Reed, to supply squadron code markings for two aircraft of 361st Bn. Assigned 32-BB and 32-CC.

(6) Lt Zicard will remain at rear echelon strip of Air Sub-Section (Maastricht) until 50th MR&RS completes its move to München-Gladbach, at which time he will move forward. A small detachment of the 50th has already moved up.

(7) To correct an error in the Journal for March 8, the passenger in the aircraft piloted by Capt. Kerrigan (destroyed in flight, allegedly by one of our own shells) was not an NCO observer but the CO of 422nd FA Gp, Lt Col. Higgie.

March 11

(1) Squadron code markings 82-MM and 82-NN were obtained from XVI Cops for 351st FA Bn aircraft (change 1). Pilots flew their aircraft back to Maastricht for the application of these markings and tail serial numbers. XVI Corps Arty Air Officer sent a 407th Gp pilot to Maastricht to lead pilots forward. (CO of the 50th MR&RS gratuitously offered the information to Lt Zicard that he could not feed supper to the pilots of this unit.)

(2) 102nd Inf Div Arty Air Officer, Capt. Dobbs, reported that three Me 109s had attacked L-4 44-80145 (76-J) flown by Lt Boileau with Lt Scarborough, observer. Each 109 made two passes at the Air OP, starting at 1,000ft and quitting below the tree tops. One put a hit in the Cub's engine, causing it to make a crash landing, which wrapped it up pretty well but neither pilot nor observer were hurt. Lt Newbury, Engnr Officer 50th MR&RS, will be requested to pick up the wreck and to prepare an aircraft for assignment as replacement. The unit will send a pilot to the Arty airstrip on March 12.

(3) Lts Myers, Beck, Hammarstrom and Zicard ferried two Pool aircraft from the old to the new Arty airstrip. Of ten aircraft remaining at Maastricht, nine are presently flyable and will be ferried to München-Gladbach on March 12 by XVI Corps Arty pilots, whose services were offered by Maj. Hallstein.

(4) XVI Corps Arty Air Officer, Maj. Hallstein, reported that 252nd Arty Air Officer, Capt. Skelly, flying as observer, and Lt Huttlin, pilot, had been shot down at 1400 hrs today by three Me 109s which attacked them at about 1,000ft and worked the Air OP over right down to the deck. Neither was killed, but both received MG wounds and a few assorted broken bones and were evacuated. In attempting evasive maneuvers the pilot dug one wing into the ground and cart-wheeled the aircraft. Someone had the presence of mind to cut the switch and there was no fire. A replacement aircraft and two replacement pilots are required (one aircraft and one pilot for immediate replacement; one pilot in a few days, pending some transfers to be made by the Corps Arty Commander). Lt Newbury, Engineer Officer, 50th MR&RS, will be requested to pick up the wreck of 44-80745 (82-P) and to prepare a replacement aircraft.

(5) FUSA Arty Air Officer, Maj. Bristol, called to say that he was flying back to the USA for 30 days temporary duty in HQ AAF (probably to give advice on the military specification of the ideal liaison aircraft). Capt. Stevenson, his Assistant, will carry on in his place during his absence.

(6) XIX Corps Arty Air Officer, Capt. Reed, reported that 258th FA Gp Asst Arty Air Officer, Lt Gasser, with Capt. Kirk as observer, had been shot down at 1550 hrs by four Me 109s, their aircraft burning and neither pilot nor observer getting out. Air OP was at about 500ft, estimated by ground observers. All the enemy fighters came in shooting, two attacking from underneath. Gp Arty Air Officer, Maj. Banigan, does not immediately want a replacement pilot since Lt Heath is expected to be returned to the unit. They can wait a few days for a replacement aircraft. Lt Newbury, Engnr Officer, 50th MR&RS, will be requested to check the location of the wreckage of 43-29638 (59-FF) and to prepare a replacement.

March 12

(1) Capt. Mathews flew our L-5B to 45th ADG at Denain and returned via 125th LS.

(2) Lt Col. Leich visited the Air OP Rest Center (Hotel Derlon, Maastricht). Officer in charge, Capt. Turman, is ready to start on March 13. He was informed that 20 pilots and observers would arrive there by 1500 hrs on that date. Lt Zicard will visit the Center for the first evening meal.

(3) Called Maj. Lefever concerning replacement aircraft and was told: 'We can transfer eight to you from the FUSA Pool. Pick them up at 23rd MR&RS (near Liège). Will check with ETOUSA to see what has happened to your eight replacement pilots. If they don't turn up we can transfer some from Third Army, where there are 24 excess pilots.'

(4) CO 125th LS, Capt. Lenczyk, requested that we give him information concerning the shooting down of liaison aircraft by enemy aircraft, so that he can pass it on to his pilots.

(5) L-4 44-80535 (76-J) was supplied as a replacement to 102nd Inf Div. Picked up by Lt Boileau, who lost his L-4 yesterday.

(6) Pilots from XVI Corps flew in eight Pool aircraft from Maastricht. Two remain there, pending completion of repairs.

March 13

(1) XVI Corps pilots, lent to Army, ferried in eight replacement L 4s (-497, -004, -200, -778, -022, -487 and -547) from 3rd MR&RS (FUSA), near Liège. [In full, these serial numbers were most probably 43-30497, 44-80004, 43-30200, 44-79778, 44-80022, 44-80487 and 44-80547.]

(2) 252nd FA Gp Arty Air Officer, Capt. Skelly, who was shot down by enemy aircraft on March 11, died of his injuries the same day. He was the second old friend 'original grasshopper' who has been lost (both in the same manner).

(3) XVI Corps Arty Air Officer, Maj. Hallstein, reported that his assistant, Capt. Welter, would be transferred to 252nd Gp as Arty Air Officer vice Capt. Skelly, and that a vacancy will be held in the Corps Arty Air Section until he had selected a successor.

(4) Lt Beck and L-4 -774 [most probably 44-79774], assigned to 252nd FA Gp, departed to join the unit.

(5) Notified Maj. Lefever that our L-5B had been delivered on March 12 to 45th ADG Engnr Officer, Capt. Cregar.

March 14

(1) Status of excess L-4H aircraft in the Army is as follows:

Immediately available for assignment: 4

Undergoing minor repairs: 14

Undergoing major repairs: 4

Inaccessible for recovery (probable salvage): 2

(2) AAA Section, Capt. Pattenberg, checked to determine whether a Cat 1 Certificate should be given to the Cub pilot who was supposed to have crowded an Me 109 to the ground (XIII Corps G-2 Periodic Report). After careful investigation by XIII Corps and XVI Corps Arty Air Officers, it was determined that someone's imagination had gotten the better of him

concerning this incident in which an enemy aircraft had definitely been shot down by AA immediately after having attacked a XVI Corps Air OP.

(3) Lt Zicard moved up from the rear echelon to the Arty airstrip to assume his usual duties of liaison with 50th MR&RS.

(4) Maj. Lefever stated that he will ask 45th ADG to continue to deliver replacement aircraft to A-93 Liège until such time that the large München-Gladbach airfield is ready to receive traffic. He later called to report that two L-4s were delivered to Liège today. He will notify us as soon as delivery is made of the balance of our present order (three L-4s).

(5) Lts Goodspeed and Radney, pilots with the 745th FA Bn, called at Arty strip en route from Rouen to join their unit in XVI Corps. Squadron code markings 82-OO and 82-PP assigned and XVI Corps Arty Air Officer asked to pick them up and lead forward.

March 16

(1) Conversation with XVI Corps Arty Air Officer, Maj. Hallstein, concerning an L-4A in the 79th Div. 'We've noticed this listed in the February report and would like to have the unit turn it in for a newer model H or J. Will you check and let us know if Capt. Lawrence thinks it necessary.'

(2) Maj. Yewell, 46th ADG Depot Supply Officer, reported that production of one-piece Lucite windshields is under way and that deliveries should start around March 23.

(3) Lts Myers and Hammarstrom ferried in two L-4Hs (44-80377 and 44-80395) from A-93 Liège.

(4) 95th Div Arty Air Officer, Maj. Blaha, reported correction in the serial number of the L-4 turned in. The correct number is 44-79716.

(5) Maj. Lefever reported that eight replacement pilots were leaving 11th RD on March 16, en route to NUSA and that 5-10 more might be shifted from First and Third Armies. Also, modifications on our L-5B would be complete on March 19, on which date he expected to pick it up and bring it back, via First and Third Armies.

(6) XVI Corps Arty Air Officer, Maj. Hallstein, reported that he had visited the Air OP Rest Center and that it was a 'good deal' with excellent food, etc., and that all the pilots there were very happy.

March 17

(1) Lts Hammarstrom and Myers ferried in replacement L-4H 44-79669 (with experimental side blisters) from A-93 Liège.

(2) Lt Hammarstrom flew Pvt. Angelo Tework to Maastricht and then proceeded to Liège (with a Liaison Squadron pilot) to pick up a replacement L-4, which he flew to the old strip. It will be picked up and brought in tomorrow.

(3) 2nd Armd Div Arty Air Officer, Capt. Mahon, reported loss of 43-29667 (49-R), shot down by six Me 109s at 1440 hrs today. Pilot, Lt Reid, 78th Armd Bn, and observer, Lt Middleton, were both hospitalized, with fair and good chances respectively for recovery. Aircraft burned. Three enemy fighters attacked from the rear and three from one flank, driving the Air OP to 15ft altitude, where explosive shells took effect. Though seriously injured, the pilot maintained sufficient control to make a crash landing. A replacement

L-4 and pilot required. Lt Zicard to check on crash and to prepare a replacement aircraft.

(4) Lt Zicard returned L-4 -061 [most probably 43-30061] to 50th MR&RS for additional work, having found 20 separate items (without flying the aircraft) which made it unacceptable. Reported the facts to the 50th MR&RS Test Pilot and Tech Inspector (Lt Ciabattoni), who was disinterested, then to Engineer Officer, Lt Newbury.

(5) Fifteenth Army Arty Air Officer, Maj. Thornton, called and stated that he expected to straighten out the situation at Rouen, from where pilots of units are dispatched forward, since 61st FA Brgde Arty Air Officer, Capt. Hertzmark, who had the dispatching job, was transferred to the Air Force (as Engineering Officer of an assembly unit). We requested him to dispatch pilots in future to Y-56 München-Gladbach which, according to XXIX TAC Opns Officer, Lt Mackenzie, will become operational on March 22. This is the field where one taxi strip is used as our Arty air strip.

(6) 83rd Inf Div Arty Air Officer, Maj. Bird, reported at 1700 hrs, that an Air OP had been shot down in the vicinity of Map Ref 280980. Later, Lt Duffy, XXIX TAC, Flying Control, called at 1830 hrs and stated that he had received a report from a Capt. Friedman of 'Diablo Blue' (probably a subordinate unit of 'Diablo', the 11th Cavalry Gp, which is in XIII Corps), that an Air OP was shot down in the vicinity of 281998, when attacked by an enemy jet fighter, and that the aircraft and crew were burned beyond recognition.

(7) Called XIII Corps, Capt. Weir, who knows only that one of 5th Armd Div's ships was shot down this afternoon.

(8) Called 5th Armd Div Arty Air Officer, Maj. Boughton, who reported that 10 Me 109s sneaked over the Rhine, two of them making a pass from behind and below 43-30104 (54-A) being flown on a 'Horsefly' training mission by Div Arty pilot Lt Lund, with Lt Steele, an Ordnance Officer, acting as observer. Both were killed and the aircraft completely burned. Lt Zicard is to prepare a replacement aircraft and Lt Myers will fill the vacancy.

March 18

(1) Fifteenth Army Arty Air Officer, Maj. Thornton, called to report that pilots of 210th FA Gp (Maj. Magruder and Capt. Phipps) and 219th FA Gp (Capt. Ray and Lt Kreuzaberg) had left Rouen on March 17 bound for A-93 Liège. He provided squadron code markings (96-F and 96-FF and 96-H and 96-HH respectively) for the units and stated that these had not been applied before departure. Both units reported arrival at Liège, and Lt Moran, XIX Corps Asst Arty Air Officer, borrowed for the occasion, went there to pick them up and to notify A-93 Flying Control to dispatch any other FA pilots looking for NUSA to Y-56 München-Gladbach. 34th FA Brigde and XVI Corps Arty Air Officers were notified of these arrivals at the Arty strip and were asked to send guides for them on March 19.

(2) L-4 44-80347 was assigned as replacement to 5th Armd Div. Lt Myers departed to join the unit by Jeep, on account of bad weather, and will return to pick up the aircraft on March 19.

(3) L-4 44-80591 was assigned as replacement for 2nd Armd Div. Lt Hammarstrom departed in it, to join the unit, in tow of Capt. Mahon (Div Arty Air Officer) and Lt Kistler.

(4) Replacement aircraft 44-80335 was flown in from Maastricht by Lt Myers.

(5) An interesting mystery exists in the finding of a 'high order burst' shell fragment from a Jerry 150 (identified by Ordnance) in the wing leading edge of 63-D at the Arty air strip, although the ship has not flown for four days. Nor was the shell fragment seen by mechanics performing its last Daily Flight Inspection four days ago.

(6) XIII Corps Arty Air Officer, Maj. Smith, reported that the AAA spotter who saw 5th Armd Div's aircraft shot down on March 17 had been unable to broadcast an enemy aircraft warning because of transmitter trouble at the time. Maj. Smith proposes using a low flying (rearward) enemy aircraft warning plane, etc. He requested data on Air OP losses of all Armies from various causes since D-Day (for Col. Williams). Will request statistics, etc., from Maj. Lefever.

March 19

(1) Called XVI Corps Arty Air Officer, Maj. Hallstein, to report arrival of 219th FA Gp pilots.

(2) Maj. Lefever called to report: 'The L-5B modifications are completed on "The Skipper", which I will fly back on March 19. There is now so much visibility that the passenger feels that he is falling out.'

(3) Maj. Lefever returned our modified L-5B. Remained overnight. This was a false alarm! 45th ADG had not completed making drawings of the modification, which is excellent, so he is returning it there. Just wanted to show us before putting on final touches. It will be ready in two days.

March 20

(Rear echelon of Ninth Army Headquarters opened at Rheydt, Germany)

(1) Maj. Lefever accompanied by his mechanic, T/Sgt Hogan, departed for A-83 Denain in 'The Skipper' (the L-5B), to turn it over for finishing touches to modifications at 45th ADG. He was requested to provide comparative statistics for Air OP losses since D-Day and stated that he would mention it to ETOUSA. (So that kills that!)

(2) Futile attempts were made to notify FUSA Acting Arty Air Officer, Capt. Stevenson, that we would trade him the 'Pregnant Princess' (the experimental blister job L-4) for a conventional L-4.

(3) An L-4 was lent to Maj. Haydock, for his use while Sgts Tye and Roehrich changed a tire on his L-5.

(4) Lt Helms flew Maj. Buchanan, QM Section, on a recce for possible POL Dumps.

(5) 472nd FA Gp Arty Air Officer, Maj. Halter, visited the CP. Reported his airstrip location.

(6) XVI Corps Arty Air Officer, Maj. Hallstein, reported that 35th Inf Div pilot, Lt Yates, had been hospitalized on account of illness and requested that we have Lt Pitts, excess pilot in 79th Inf Div, transferred to fill the vacancy.

March 21

(1) The 50th MR&RS has a codename, at last – 'Goldfish'.

(2) FUSA Acting Arty Air Officer, Capt. Stevenson, sent Lt Farwell to pick up the 'Pregnant Princess' and replaced her with a conventional L-4 (44-80110).

(3) Squadron code markings 63-O have been reserved for Maj. Haydock's aircraft.

(4) 95th Inf Div Arty Air Officer, Maj. Blaha, reported crash landing due to engine failure of L-4H 44-79554 (66-G). No personnel injuries and no replacement required, but repair and return of aircraft requested. Lt Zicard will pick up the wrecked aircraft and see it through repair facilities for early return to unit.

(5) XIII Corps Arty Air Officer, Maj. Smith, reported an unidentified L-5 flying in Corps area with no squadron code markings and having invasion stripes under wings and fuselage. Reporting unit expressed fear that it might have been operated by the enemy. Called 125th LS and asked them to warn any L-5s operating in the Army zone to stay away from forward areas if they did not have squadron code markings.

March 22

(1) Maj. Lefever reported that the modified L-5B will be ready at A-83 Denain on the 22nd at 1400 hrs. 125th LS will send a pilot to pick it up for us.

(2) Propellers. Maj. Lefever: 'Critically short, none on the Continent. 45th ADG has A1 priority for air shipment of 200. Understand they're not available in the USA.'

March 23

(1) Lt Thompson, 79th Inf Div pilot, turned in L-4A 42-36504 (46-WW) in exchange for L-4J 44-80232.

(2) Lt Zicard reported receipt by 50th MR&RS of 15 one-piece windshields (sorely needed) from 45th ADG, but all unserviceable due to intransit handling damage.

(3) 258th FA Gp and 258th FA Bn pilots visited strip to have squadron code markings changed on their ships.

(4) XIII Corps Arty Air Officer, Maj. Smith, reported landing accident to 102nd Div aircraft 44-80535 (76-J). Lt Boileau, pilot, and Lt Scarborough, observer, were uninjured. Replacement aircraft is required. Lt Zicard to pick up damaged aircraft and to prepare 43-30215 as a replacement.

March 24

XVI Corps Arty Air Officer, Maj. Hallstein, reported that L-4s 44-80201 (32-X of 959th FA Bn) and 43-30528 (33-DD) were damaged when the pilots saw a B-24 crash and landed to give aid. After they landed, the B-24 exploded, damaging both L-4s. Personnel uninjured. Replacement aircraft required. Lt Zicard to pick up wrecks and prepare two replacement aircraft.

March 25

(1) XVIII Abn Corps Arty Air Officer, Maj. Haydock, reported that a 17th Abn Div aircraft, 44-80525 (73-(?)) was shot down by enemy ground fire, resulting in complete loss of the aircraft (possible salvage of engine), but not even scratching pilot or observer. Replacement is required. Lt Zicard will prepare replacement for pick-up before noon on March 26, with squadron code markings 73 (no letter). Action to pick up wreckage will be delayed pending clarification of its location.

(2) 75th Inf Div Asst Arty Air Officer, Capt. Nelson, reported that an aircraft of the unit, in making a road landing, hit a horse which ran onto a road (then off) and damaged the left wing. He requested a new wing, complete with aileron, be delivered to Div Arty strip. Lt Zicard will take necessary action.

(3) L-4 44-80377 (32-X) released to 959th FA Bn as a replacement; 43-29778 (33-DD) was released to 695th FA Bn.

(4) Maj. Lefever reported that 'as an emergency measure 56 L-4As and Bs had been shipped. Your next batch will be these. The L-4H landing gear vee will fit, but the brakes, connector hoses and instruments are different and will present a supply problem since no spares are available. As soon as Hs and Js are available (and 350 are expected through May), we'll want to return the As and Bs to the Air Forces.'

March 26

17th Abn Div pilots Lts Breithouft and Sawyer visited the Section to pick up a replacement L-4 (43-30497) and report circumstances in which Lt Breithouft was shot down. A bypassed 20 mm AA gun did it. The gun and crew were captured immediately after the incident.

March 28

97th Div Arty Air Officer, Capt. Low, and ten pilots arrived at the CP en route to join their unit. Remained overnight. They will be forwarded to XXII Corps on March 29, after tail serial numbers have been applied to their aircraft.

March 29

Maj. Lefever reported 'some L-5s should be ready to go from Rouen now. Yours will be delivered to Y-56 München-Gladbach. Please keep in touch with them.'

March 30

One L-4H (44-80009) and nine L-4As (43-29082, -29095, -29115, -29126, -29130, -29185, -29195, -29286 and -36168) were delivered from A-83 Denain to Y-56 by AAF ferry pilots (under Capt. Hester), and transferred across the road to our strip by our pilots.
[43–36168 is incorrect – it was not an L-4; also, 43–29286 was an L-4H, not an L-4A.]

March 31

(1) 2nd Armd Div Asst Arty Air Officer, Lt Kistler, reported the requirement for an aircraft to replace 44-80556 (49-L) recently assigned to the unit, but found to have an engine improperly assembled. The engine failed in flight and the aircraft was damaged in the resultant landing. Lt Zicard will pick up the wreck, arrange for the filing of a report on its engine through the 50th MR&RS, and prepare 43-30022 as a replacement. Lt Kistler also requested that an aircraft and pilot be sent to the 2nd Armd Div on temporary duty to perform certain courier missions. Lt Lynch will be picked up at our advance strip on April 1 by Lt Kistler. Aircraft 44-80577 (63-J) will be used by Lt Lynch.

(2) Army Air Section pilots flew 315 hours during March.

(3) XVI Corps Asst Arty Air Officer, Lt Williamson, called about props. He was told that if he had any aircraft grounded because of prop problems, we would remove some from our Pool aircraft and forward them to him, but with no supply in Europe, we could not fill requests from units for spares.

(4) Lts Helms, Sharp, Sword, Zicard and Daniels flew 50th MR&RS detachment personnel to advance strip. Lt Zicard remained there.

(5) 97th Inf Div pilots departed to their Div Arty strip. Lts Parker and Smith and Capt. McGuire returned at dusk and remained overnight.

(6) XIII Corps Arty Air Officer, Maj. Smith, called concerning report received from a 102nd Div unit that two bodies had been found. One had been identified by the tags as that of Capt. Curran (258th FA Gp observer, killed March 11) but the other lacked identification except for a pair of 'L' pilot's wings and a parachute. The location was close to the spot at which the aircraft was shot down, and since the bodies were found together, it is assumed that the one not identified is that of Lt Gasser (?), 258th FA Gp Asst Arty Air Officer (which fact was reported to Maj. Smith). The aircraft wreck was picked up by the 50th MR&RS a few days after the accident.

(7) Three Pool L-4s will be lent to the 125th LS for an indefinite period to enable their 12 new pilots to get in a little flying practice. Capt. O'Brien agreed to take care of the maintenance required, in accordance with our inspection form requirements.

(8) Maj. Lefever called concerning:

(a) New ADG. '45th ADG has been given another mission and will be relieved immediately from backing up the MR&RSs. 16th ADG (moving to Y-56 München-Gladbach on April 3) will take over the responsibility.'

(b) Pilots. 'Don't expect any more from the States before June 1. In a few days we will transfer five or six to NUSA from the surplus in other Armies, to even the distribution up a little.'

(c) L-5s. 'Six are ready now, ten more in a few days. Some of these are for air force units, but start looking for a couple, maybe tomorrow.'

CHAPTER 10

Victory, April–May 1945

By the beginning of April there was no doubt that Hitler's promised 'Thousand Year Reich' was coming to a premature end. On the first day of the month, the Ninth and First US Armies made contact at Lippstadt to complete the encirclement of the Ruhr Valley and its industrial area, with the Ninth's XIII Corps pushing on eastwards from the Rhine to take Münster on 3 April. That same day an L-4 of the 2nd Armored Division was shot down by three Bf 109s, seriously wounding the observer, Lt Morton, but the pilot, Lt Hammarstrom, escaped injury. An L-5 of the 125th Liaison Squadron was also shot down on the 3rd, but fortunately its pilot, T/Sgt Ray E. Davis, survived the crash and then spent a couple of days with 'Ground Pounders' fighting to take a nearby town. When this was achieved he returned to his squadron and went on to complete seventy-two combat missions before hostilities ceased.

NUSA's attachment to the British 21st Army Group was terminated on 4 April when it returned to General Bradley's 12th Army Group. That same day the Weser River was reached by XIII and XIX Corps, with Hamm then cleared by XIX Corps. Keeping up with these spectacular advances, HQ NUSA moved its command post to Haltern, but the drive continued unabated. By 11 April, the 2nd Armored Division had reached the Elbe, Hanover was taken by XIII Corps, and Essen had fallen to XVI Corps. The following day the 2nd Armored Division (XIX Corps) established a bridgehead over the Elbe, Brunswick was cleared, and HQ NUSA moved yet again, opening its command post at Gütersloh. On 13 April, the 83rd Infantry Division, under XIX Corps, established a second bridgehead over the Elbe while Duisburg was taken by XVI Corps, but the day was notable for a remarkable advance by the 5th Armored Division. In what was probably the fastest single spurt in the history of armoured warfare, the 'Hell on Wheels' Division covered 60 miles in less than 24 hours to reach Tangermünde, a small town situated on the Elbe some 35 miles downriver from Magdeburg. The American front on the Elbe was now 100 miles long, and on the east side of the river troops were within 52 miles of the German capital, Berlin.

During the first two weeks of April there were five attacks on Ninth Army Air OPs by enemy fighters, resulting in major damage to four of them, with four pilots and one observer injured and admitted to hospital. Enemy ground fire caused major damage to two more L-4s, with the pilot of one being hospitalised. In addition, one pilot was killed in action on the ground and another was unavailable due to illness. In the same period there were twelve operational accidents (four on take-off, three on landing, four caused by weather, and one by the onset of darkness), but there were no serious injuries to personnel. Replacement aircraft were supplied to units as necessary to maintain strength, but three units were short of one pilot each pending the arrival of reinforcements.

Although the mechanics of the 65th Armored FA Battalion had done well in repairing 'in the field' the L-4 43-30495 (59-I) shot down over Haltern on 30 March, its pilot, Lt Joe Gordon, soon found that its handling characteristics had been adversely affected by the crash landing. This was due to airframe distortion, and as the aircraft was also due for an engine change, arrangements were made for the necessary work to be carried out by the 50th MR&RS. Accordingly, on 11 April, Lt Gordon flew 43-30495, minus its radio, from his strip near the village of Grasdorf to the new *Conquer* airstrip at Gütersloh, near Bielefeld. However, as the 50th was unable to start work on the aircraft until the next day, he was given a replacement L-4H (43-29487).

While waiting for the squadron markings 59-I to be applied to his new aircraft, Joe Gordon met Capt. George W. Parker, a USAAF B-26 Marauder medium bomber pilot who had just been appointed Air Liaison Officer at HQ XIX Corps. Capt. Parker was en route by Jeep to that Headquarters, which happened to be situated close to Joe Gordon's strip, and on discovering this, the Cub pilot offered to give the Air Force officer a lift to his new station. This was gladly accepted, and after marking the position of the Grasdorf strip on the Jeep driver's map, so he could meet up again with Capt. Parker, the two officers took off. However, on arrival at Grasdorf they found the strip deserted, the 65th FA Battalion having moved on. Without radio the L-4 pilot was unable to contact his unit, and a search along the route it had possibly taken met with no success. By now very low on fuel, Joe Gordon decided to land beside a truck column that was stationary on a main road, and after a successful landing he approached the driver of a two-and-a-half ton truck to request his spare 5-gallon can of petroleum. This was willingly given, and after refuelling his L-4 Gordon took off again in search of his unit. But by now it was dusk, and in the failing light Gordon decided to land beside a column of tanks, hoping to use the radio in one of them to contact the 2nd Armored Division's Artillery HQ. After a low pass, to check the suitability of the proposed landing field, he turned onto final approach. The next thing he recalls was regaining consciousness in a field hospital, with a broken leg and other serious injuries. Capt. Parker was also in hospital, less seriously hurt, but neither officer had any recollection of the crash and events preceding it. Only some time after the war did Joe Gordon discover Ninth Army reports (see the journal entry for 11 April) that indicated he had probably been shot down by ground fire, examination of the crashed L-4 revealing it had 'a belly full of buckshot and what appear to be rifle bullet holes in the gas tank'. However, Joe Gordon still thinks it more likely that 'a Fw 190 or Me 109 caught us unawares as I was concentrating on other things rather than keeping the usual lookout for enemy aircraft'. Fortunately he made a good recovery and survived the war, after which he resumed work as an architect in Dallas, Texas, and has since written a book on his experiences as an L-4 pilot, *Flying Low* (published by Southfarm Press, ISBN 0-913337-43-9). The book covers much of his life, but is mainly an excellent account of his time as an L-4 pilot with the Field Artillery.

In addition to its three Armored and nine Infantry Divisions, NUSA was now temporarily exercising command over the 17th Airborne Division, adding another ten L-4s to its establishment of Air OPs. However, by 14 April, the end of the war in Europe was clearly in sight, with XVI Corps, along with the newly arrived Fifteenth Army, clearing the last resistance in the Ruhr pocket. In the south, General Patton's Third Army continued its advance towards Czechoslovakia, but hardening resistance stemmed the First Army's lightning charge across Germany while an unexpected counter-attack in the Ninth Army zone forced the 2nd Armored Division to withdraw from its bridgehead over the Elbe. Three battalions of the 2nd returned before a bridge built by engineers was destroyed by German artillery fire, leaving three battalions cut off on the east side of the river. DUKW amphibious vehicles came to the rescue, but some personnel were forced to swim across.

The Ninth Army's XIX Corps took Magdeburg on 18 April, on which day the Army Headquarters arrived at Münster. By now the British were only 20 miles from Hamburg, the Seventh US Army had practically completed the encirclement of Nuremberg, the Third US Army had crossed into Czechoslovakia, and the Russians were closing in on Berlin. The end seemed imminent, but despite this the German counter-attack on the Ninth Army front gained more ground. On 19 April, a strong force of enemy infantry and armour attacked the Ninth's northern flank in a determined attempt to break through and join up with SS units holding out in the Harz Mountains, but by 21 April the Harz area was cleared by XIX Corps while XIII Corps launched an attack to clear an additional portion of the west bank of the Elbe.

In line with the Ninth Army's advance, the attached 125th LS moved to Haltern on 4 April, but eight days later continued to Gütersloh, where it remained until 24 April, when yet another move placed the squadron at Brunswick. A week later, on 1 May, an L-5 (42-993050) on a mission from here was involved in an accident at Signy-le-Petit, France, but within days the war was over and operational flying came to an end.

Throughout its time with HQ NUSA, the 125th had Flights, and sometimes even single aircraft on detached service with units, but perhaps the experience of Sgt John H. Miller was unique. From the time the 5th Armored Division crossed the Rhine River until the end of the war, Sgt Miller served on detached duty as personal pilot to the Division Commander, Maj. Gen. Lunceford E. Oliver, and not even his own squadron knew precisely where he was or what he was doing.

As with several other units of Ninth Army, the second half of April brought a significant change in role for the 407th FA Group and its attached 758th, 211th and 666th FA Battalions. During the period 1-15 April, the Group had fired 6,722 rounds of ammunition, many of them Air OP directed, but from the 18th onwards the 407th was engaged on duties of a security and military government nature. The Group experienced four more displacements in April, these being to Stucken, Soginden, Laerfeld and finally to Lemgo, from where its Air Sections continued to operate under the same centralised control but now engaged on air patrols to supplement vehicles on road patrols. Battalion aircraft were also made available for courier and other work, and in one case, where Group HQ and a Battalion command post were far apart, one aircraft was sent to the Battalion CP daily to act as a message carrier. To facilitate similar messenger, courier and inspection flights between Battalion HQs and their Battery CPs, three auxiliary landing strips were established in each Battalion sector. This changed role for the Group is well illustrated in its summary of activity for April, which reveals that 137 operational missions (25 adjustments of fire, 28 combat patrols and 84 reconnaissance missions) were outnumbered by 224 administrative flights.

On 23 April, HQ NUSA opened a new command post at Brunswick, and then came another period of many unit changes. The 5th Infantry Division was transferred to the Third Army, while the 8th Infantry returned to the Ninth, as did VII and VIII Corps (and their divisions), which returned from the First Army on 6 May. The end – Victory in Europe – came two days later, making 8 May a day to be remembered for all time as VE Day. Throughout its nine months and ten days of combat, the Ninth Army had fought magnificently. *Conquer* had truly conquered.

Extracts from the HQ NUSA Air Journal for 1 April-8 May 1945, compiled by Lt Col. R. M. Leich (Army Command Post at München-Gladbach, Germany)

April 1

(1) One L-5B (44-17184) was received from 45th Air Depot Group. XIX Corps Arty Air Officer, Capt. Reed, was notified to bring in an L-4 in exchange. L-4H 43-29647 (32-C) was brought in and put in the Pool. The squadron code markings 32-A were applied to the new L-5, which was flown away by Capt. Reed.

(2) The CO of the 125th LS (Capt. O'Brien) reported that Engineers under Capt. Gilbert would complete the laying of 200ft of matting on the airstrip at Haltern at 1400 hrs on 2nd. Strip is about 900ft long with clear approaches and adequate aircraft dispersal area.

(3) 2nd Armd Div Arty Air Officer, Lt Kistler, reported that Lt Emerick, pilot, and Capt. Mahon, observer, were forced down on the afternoon of March 31 when six Fw 190s jumped them. The enemy aircraft came out of cloud (approx 1,400ft) and split up into three elements of two and attacked in three directions. Lt Kistler went down to ground level in an attempt to evade the enemy aircraft, but hooked his wing on a hedgerow and wrecked his L-4 49-W (44-80116). The enemy aircraft then strafed the wreck. Personnel uninjured except for being a bit stiff. Lt Kistler has already seen Lt Zicard, who is furnishing a replacement (new squadron code markings 49-E on replacement).

(4) Lt Lynch departed in 63-J for advanced 50th MR&RS strip to join 2nd Armd Div on temporary duty.

(5) Three L-4As (42-29093, 42-29126 and 42-36166) were turned over to the 125th LS for their temporary local use. Five airplanes in the Pool are AOG because props have been removed to supply units requiring them.

April 2

(1) Preparations were carried out for moving the Arty Air Section. Movement will be possible in a couple of hours.

(2) Lt Zicard reported that 44-80145 had been delivered as a replacement to 2nd Armd Div (Item 3 of April 1 refers).

(3) Maj. Lefever called: 'Two L-5s (44-17184 and 44-17169) were shipped to you on April 1. About six more are due any day now.' (44-17184 was given to XIX Corps, 44-17169 has not been received, but 44-80202 came in on April 3 and will be given to 2nd Armd Div).

(4) L-5 modifications will probably be done by 16th Air Depot Group.

April 3

(1) 2nd Armd Div Asst Arty Air Officer, Lt Kistler, visited forward strip and reported that three Me 109s had forced down an Air OP piloted by Lt Hammarstrom, who crash landed his damaged airplane. One pass was made from above and behind, the 109s having dived out of cloud. Pilot was only shaken up, but observer Lt Morton was very seriously wounded with only a slight chance of recovery. Lt Zicard arranged to provide a replacement L 4 and deliver it to the unit. (The last time Lt Zicard delivered an aircraft to this unit he rode the spearhead of the Armored column until it reached the 3rd Armd Div to close the pocket, then landed and turned the aircraft over to the 2nd Armored pilot.) The wreck will be picked up.

(2) L-5 44-17202 was delivered from 45th Air Depot Group minus records and clock. Ferry pilot agreed to forward missing items with next delivery. Remained overnight. Squadron code markings 49-C (obtained from 2nd Armd Div) will be applied to this aircraft, which will be delivered to 2nd Armd after one of their pilots has been given some transition training and been checked out.

(3) Lt Col. Leich and Capt. Mathews visited forward 50th MR&RS strip and Lts Zicard and Limme. Remained for lunch. Discussed moving closer 'to the sound of guns'. Also visited *Conquer New* airstrip at Haltern. Work is under way on the strip and should be completed by the 4th.

(4) XIX Corps Arty Air Officer, Capt. Reed, will visit *Conquer New* on April 5 to discuss moving '50th Forward' forward. He provided 44-J as squadron code markings to be applied to the next L-5 which arrives and which will be assigned to the 30th Inf Div. Capt. Reed also reported that 742nd FA Bn pilot Lt Hasen had put an aircraft over on its back on landing in gusty wind, without injuries to himself or observer. Replacement aircraft is required. 258th FA Gp Arty Air Officer was instructed to send back to Lt Zicard at 50th Forward strip for replacement.

(5) VI Corps Arty Air Officer, Maj. Hallstein, reported that L-4 44-80337 (85-J) of the 75th Inf Div had crashed, injuring Lt Mann and S/Sgt O'Hara. The accident was caused by an error of judgment by the pilot, who, hampered by a soft field, tangled with a telephone line and pole. Both pilot and observer were hospitalized and Maj. Hallstein requested that a replacement pilot and aircraft be sent to the Division at its present location at the earliest possible time.

April 4

(Ninth Army Command Post opened at Haltern, Germany)

(1) Air Section moved to the *Conquer New* strip at Haltern today, with Lt Helms and Sgt Boerner remaining at the *Conquer Old* strip at München-Gladbach to maintain liaison with the main body of 50th MR&RS. Seven pilots made flights from München-Gladbach to Haltern, transporting six officers (two colonels, two lieutenant colonels, two majors) and T/3 Roehrich (Air Section mechanic).

(2) First claims for enemy prisoners captured by an Air Section were entered by Lts Sinex and Lynch on April 2. While out making a ground run for a wrecked Air OP, they flushed out seven German soldiers, disarmed them and turned them in.

(3) 8th Armd Div Arty Air Officer reported take-off accident to L-4 44-80479 (21-C) on April 2. The pilot, Lt Stone, and observer were uninjured. Lt Zicard picked up the wreckage, which may be repairable, and replaced it with 43-30282.

April 5

(1) Maj. Lefever called to report: 'L-5B 44-17169 was damaged at A-93 Liège while being ferried to you and will be delivered when repairs are completed. Also, can you send an informal break-down of flying time on NUSA aircraft, in 50 hour blocks. The question has arisen in connection with a proposal to crate and ship aircraft elsewhere.'

Records covering all flying time on 233 aircraft in the Army, as of February 28, was as follows:

Hours	No. of Aircraft
Below 50	28
51-100	39
101-150	30
151-200	31
201-250	25
251-300	22
301-350	11
351-400	10
401-450	14
451-500	7
501-550	4
551-600	3
601-650	6
700-750	2
800-900	1
Over 1000	1

It is estimated that reports of flying time for March will average 45 hours per airplane.

(2) 95th Inf Div pilot, Lt Stricklin, reported that one of their L-4s, 44-79554 (66-G), was shot up and requested that crash pick-up crew stop at Div Arty strip. No other details provided.

(3) 84th Inf Div Asst Arty Air Officer, Capt. Auld, reported that he had been shot down from 2,000ft by flak, with no injuries. His L-4, 44-80241 (87-A), which was damaged, can be picked up. Unit will collect a replacement from the 50th MR&RS Forward strip.

(4) 83rd Inf Div reported (via Capt. Reed) the loss of an L-4 due to flak and requested a replacement. No further particulars were provided. Later reported that the aircraft is not too seriously damaged. A new right wing will be provided by Lt Zicard.

April 6

(1) 50th MR&RS Forward echelon and main body are moving to Gütersloh, the former on April 7 and the latter eventually.

(2) A pilot of the 125th LS ferried L-5B 44-17202 (earmarked for 2nd Armd Div) to *Conquer New* airstrip.

(3) Capt. Mathews and Capt. O'Brien (125th LS) reconnoitered Gütersloh airfield and on the recommendation of Col. Sprague the 50th MR&RS will be established there.

(4) Lts Sharp and Sword ferried a replacement L-4 from München-Gladbach to 50th MR&RS Forward strip.

(5) Report received from Message Center concerning garbled oral message about the crash of L-4 68-B, one mile from Venlo. The pilot made the report so is evidently uninjured. Called XIII Corps (Col. Eaton) who stated that their 68-B was OK and on the field. (68-BB is assigned to 211th Gp, a FUSA unit). A pilot will be sent to Y-55 Venlo on April 7 to investigate.

April 7

(1) 2nd Armd Div Arty pilot, Lt Emerick, called to pick up new L-5B 44-17202. He requested that the squadron code markings 49-E be applied to it. He turned in L-4 44-80145 (49-E).

(2) Lt Sword, investigating the reported crash of 68-B at Y-55 Venlo, found only that an L-5 of the 125th LS had broken a prop in a forced landing there.

(3) Lt Carrell, 8th Armd Div pilot, flew in L-4 44-80449 (21-B) for repairs. Told him to pick it up at Gütersloh on April 9. We will deliver it there for repairs by Lt Zicard's 50th Forward unit, which started its move from Dorsten today. Lt Carrell also reported an accident to his own L-4 (44-80487: 21-D) when he hit wires while making a forced landing due to weather. Replacement required; no personnel injuries. Lt Col. Leich flew him to Dorsten where he obtained 44-80095 as a replacement. Lt Zicard will pick up the wreck.

(4) Lt Helton, 95th Inf Div Arty pilot, flew in Lt Jordan, a 351st FA Bn pilot, who reported a take-off accident to his L-4 44-80153 (82-M) at the 95th Inf Div's strip. A replacement is required, but there were no personnel injuries. Told them to collect a replacement (43-30004) at Gütersloh late on April 8. Lt Zicard will pick up the wreck.

April 8

(1) Maj. Lefever reported that there would be eight L-5Bs for us today at Y-56 München-Gladbach (16th Air Depot Group). Made following allocation, in priority order: 30th Inf Div, NUSA Arty Air Section, 83rd Inf Div, XVI Arty, 34th FA Bgde, XIII Corps Arty, 5th Armd Div, 8th Armd Div.

(2) Notified 30th Inf Div that L-5B 44-17200 (44-J) is assigned to them, to be picked up by Maj. Blohm, Arty Air Officer. An L-4 will be turned in to Gütersloh.

(3) Lt Col. Leich picked up NUSA L-5B 44-17190 (to receive squadron code markings 63-B)

(4) XIX Corps Asst Arty Air Officer, Lt Johnson, was requested to notify 83rd Inf Div Arty Air Officer to pick up his L-5 from Lt Helms at München-Gladbach, and to turn in an L-4 at Gütersloh.

(5) XVI Corps Arty Air Officer, Maj. Hallstein, is to pick up his L-5 (code markings 82-A requested) from Lt Helms and turn in an L-4 at Gütersloh. He remained overnight.

(6) XIII Corps Acting Arty Air Officer, Lt Hanchey, was notified to pick up his L-5 at the Army Arty airstrip (where he will be checked out) and to turn in an L-4 at Gütersloh. He was also asked to notify 5th Armd Div to do the same.

April 9

(1) XIII Corps Asst Arty Air Officer, Lt Roark, reported an attack on his L-4 on March 8 (believe this should be April 8) in the vicinity of Hannover by six Fw 190s. He was flying at

400ft above an armored column and noticed personnel of the column seeking cover. He hit the deck and was jumped from the rear. Each enemy aircraft 'took a burst' as it went past and two returned for a second pass. Ground personnel opened fire on the enemy aircraft, so they left without having damaged the Air OP or injured its personnel.

(2) Capt. Mathews and Lt Col. Leich visited the new Army Arty airstrip at Gütersloh, the 30th Inf Div Arty Air Officer (Maj. Blohm), and a German airfield near Orlinghausen. Action has been initiated to make minor repairs to a Gotha 105 found there, and perhaps move it to Gütersloh.

(3) XIII Corps Asst Arty Air Officer, Lt Roark, visited the Army strip with aircraft mechanic T/Sgt Perry. Lt Roark was flown to München-Gladbach by Lt Hogan to be checked out and take delivery of an L-5. He turned in L-4 44-79717 (68-B). The new L-5 will bear the squadron code markings 68-A. Sgt Perry is to work with our mechanics to become familiar with the L-5.

(4) Arrangements were made with the 125th LS to use M/Sgt Kauitzsch (pronounced Couch) to check out NUSA pilots on L-5s at München-Gladbach.

(5) XVI Corps Arty Air Officer, Maj. Hallstein, took delivery of L-5 44-17173 (82-A) at München-Gladbach today. He will turn in an L-4 at Gütersloh 'one of these days', permission having been granted to hang on to it until we need it or until his pilots, Lts Williamson and Ball, have been checked out on the L-5.

(6) 34th FA Bgde Arty Air Officer, Maj. Keating, visited the Army strip today. He will check in at München-Gladbach with Lt Helms on April 10 to pick up an L-5 and be checked out on it.

(7) Maj. Lefever reported that we could expect a windfall of ten replacement pilots from the USA in a few days.

(8) TLX message sent to Corps, Brigade and 29th Inf Div concerning new location of 50th MR&RS (two miles NE of Gütersloh).

April 10

(1) The 50th MR&RS was requested to move to a German airfield in the vicinity of Bielefeld. Two hangars, barracks and one twin-engine Gotha were immediately available.

(2) 5th Armd Div Asst Arty Air Officer, Lt Trachtenberg, reported the loss of an L-4 in an operational accident. As details are not known at present, Lt Zicard is prepared to supply 44-79717 as a replacement.

(3) 84th Inf Div Arty Air Officer, Maj. Paschall, and his Assistant, Lt Durant, visited Arty airstrip en route to Maastricht. Lent them 63-E to complete their trip, which started from Hannover in a Jeep (they will return it to Gütersloh strip). They reported two incidents:

(a) While on patrol on April 8, Lt Vanmeter, pilot, and Lt Ruzicka, observer, were attacked by eight Me 109s and forced down. Aircraft 44-80127 (63-E) was a total wreck, pilot and observer hospitalized. A replacement aircraft and pilot were required. Lt Zicard is to have wreck picked up and a replacement aircraft prepared.

(b) At 0850 on April 8, Lt Young (280th FA Bn pilot), with an E M War Correspondent, Pvt. Shank, were caught by weather (low ceiling) while flying to *Conquer* Press Camp and while trying to turn back crashed into trees on a ridge. No personnel injuries. L-4H 44-79889 was a total loss. Lt Zicard is to prepare a replacement. Maj. Paschall was requested to pick up replacements at Gütersloh on April 13.

(4) Major Lefever called: 'As requested, will ask AAF to deliver replacement airplanes to Y 99 Gütersloh after April 13. Let me know if you need any more L-4s as a few are now on hand in the Theater Pool.'

(5) Lt Helms has problems in taking care of Fifteenth Army pilots, taking care of our dog 'Tie-Down', assisting units taking delivery of L-5s, and ferrying 17 L-4s (plus his own) to the new 50th MR&RS strip.

(6) XVI Corps Arty Air Officer, Maj. Hallstein, reported that the correct serial number of his L-5 is 44-17193. On 11 April he will send 10 pilots in five airplanes to München-Gladbach to ferry aircraft for Lt Helms.

(7) XIII Corps Asst Arty Air Officer, Lt Roark, returned from München-Gladbach in their new L-5 (44-17176), picked up T/Sgt Perry and proceeded to Gütersloh to lead Lt Sinex to the new Corps strip.

April 12

(HQ Ninth Army Command Post opened at Gütersloh, Germany)

(1) 8th Armd Div Arty Air Officer, Maj. Cross, came in to the new strip to pick up L-4 44-80217, which had been repaired.

(2) 959th FA Bn pilot, Lt Kimberley, visited Arty strip with a bent lift strut after being told he couldn't get it repaired by 50th MR&RS at Bielefeld. He wanted to know if we could get it fixed. We managed to get both the lift strut and the prop changed.

(3) 65th Armd Div pilot, Lt Gordon, came in with an L-4 needing an engine change and 1st and 2nd echelon repair. As 50th MR&RS could not take care of it until noon on April 12, he was given a new aircraft, 43-29487 (59-I), and we took in the old one (43-30495).

(4) Messages sent to units and other HQs concerning the locations of the new Arty strip at Gütersloh and that of the 50th MR&RS strip at Bielefeld.

(5) Nine Pool aircraft were ferried from München-Gladbach to Bielefeld.

(6) 16th Air Depot Group (Aircraft Allocations Section) stated that three more L-5s had arrived for NUSA units. These will go to 8th Armd, 83rd Inf Div and 29th Inf Div.

(7) Fifty complete kits to modify L-4s (including one-piece Lucite windshields, eyebrows, turtledecks, side windows, etc.) have finally arrived at 50th MR&RS.

(8) 17th Abn Div pilot, Lt Sawyer, reported two wrecked aircraft:

(a) On April 11, 1st Lt Kauner was caught out by ground fog, tried to land and hooked tail of aircraft on a fence, washing out 44-79786 (73-(?)).

(b) On April 11, 1st Lt Gonger, also caught by ground fog, tried to land but stalled in and completely washed out 44-80393 (73-G). Lt Zicard notified 50th MR&RS to pick up wrecks and arrange to have replacement aircraft ready.

April 13

(1) XIX Corps Arty Air Officer, Capt. Reed, was asked to inform 83rd Inf Div that we have an L-5 for them to collect. Capt. Reed was also told that L-5s are placarded at 120 mph because of rear spar failures.

(2) 8th Armd Div Arty Air Officer, Maj. Cross, visited Gütersloh Arty strip and was asked to visit München-Gladbach to pick up an L-5 from Lt Helms and turn in an L-4 at 50th MR&RS.

(3) 29th Inf Div pilot, Lt Kenney, stopped in at Haltern Arty strip. He was requested to inform Div Arty Air Officer, Maj. Swenson, that an L-5 was awaiting him at München-Gladbach and that upon taking delivery of it to turn in an L-4 at 50th MR&RS.

(4) Maj. Lefever arrived for a short visit and discussed:

(a) Replacement L-4s – we want at least 25 in the Army Pool at a time; ordered ten more to be delivered to 50th MR&RS.

(b) Roby controllable pitch props – we have no knowledge of any L-4s in our units fitted with these, but will be alert to possible wearing of gears (reported by Fifteenth Army).

(c) Service of westernmost NUSA units by 27th MR&RS (Fifteenth US Army) located at Neuss. We will give them the details of which units are to receive certain services, including crash pick-ups, but aircraft replacement will be by 50th MR&RS. We will notify 27th MR&RS of locations of wrecks to be picked up. We will also collect some tailwheel springs at 50th MR&RS and deliver them to the 27th to help them out.

(5) 29th Inf Div Arty Air Officer, Maj. Swenson, reported that he had picked up L-5 44-17177 at München-Gladbach and was turning in L-4 43-30010 to the 50th MR&RS at Bielefeld.

(6) Lt Moyer, 2nd Armd Div 'Air' (probably air support or something, but not FA) reported the crash of an L-4 (probably 59-I) of 65th Armd FA Bn, pilot unknown (we believe it was Lt Gordon) at an unknown location, cause unknown. Pilot's leg was broken. Replacement pilot and aircraft required. Replacement aircraft and Lt Daniels, pilot, were dispatched to join the unit and Lt Daniels was requested to send back needed data via Lt Sharp. Lt Moyer also reported the wreck of L-5B 44-17202 (49-E), being piloted by Lt Emerick when forced down by four Me 109s. The aircraft was damaged on landing but the pilot took off again and wrapped it up without injury to himself. An L-4 was requested (on loan) until the L-5 has been repaired. Lt Zicard is to prepare a replacement aircraft for delivery by Lt Sharp and to arrange for the pick-up of the wreck.

(7) 219th FA Gp Arty Air Officer, Maj. Hume, visited Arty strip at Gütersloh to report take-off crash of L-4 44-80575 (98-H) piloted by Lt Kreuzberry. Causes: hot day, no wind, short strip. No personnel injuries. Maj. Hume was sent to 50th MR&RS to obtain replacement L-4 (44-80395) from Lt Zicard, who reported the location of the wrecked aircraft to 50th MR&RS.

(8) Two incidents (both in 748th FA Bn) were reported by 258th FA Gp:

(a) 44-80536 (12-H) flown by Lt Norman was hit by enemy ground fire (20 mm AA) while on a registration mission. Pilot was shot through his leg, behind the knee. Field repairs were made and the aircraft flown to 50th MR&RS. Pilot replacement only needed. (No action by Army – no pilots available.)

(b) 44-80335 (12-HH) flown by Lt Hansen was also hit by enemy ground fire and forced down. No personnel injuries, but a replacement L-4 is required and 43-29195 was so assigned. Wreckage will be picked up by 50th MR&RS.

(9) 34th FA Bgde turned in L-4 43-30401 (69-A), having taken delivery of L-5B 44-17337. The following accidents were reported:

(a) 349th FA Gp reported wreck of 44-80583 (83-P of the 745th FA Bn). Pilot Lt Radney and observer uninjured. Pilot overshot field after dark. Lt Lynch was requested to deliver a replacement aircraft to Lt Radney.

(b) 5th Armd Div reported wreck of 44-30358 (54-H). Pilot, Lt Nicol, and observer uninjured. Landing accident on a road in a cross-wind because of 'weak brake'. Replacement aircraft required. Lt Zicard was requested to arrange for pick-up of wreckage and to provide a replacement aircraft to Lt Nicol.

(c) 557th FA Bn (attached to 5th Armd Div) L-4 44-79672 (24-X) flown by Lt Abercrombie. No personnel injuries. Take-off accident due to soft ground. Aircraft hit tree tops at the end of the strip. Lt Zicard is to arrange crash pick-up and to furnish a replacement aircraft to Lt Abercrombie.

(10) 5th Armd Div pilot, Lt Francis, and observer, Lt Martin, emptied three clips of .45 ammo at a German Air OP (Storch), getting in some hits. The German aircraft crashed while attempting an evasive maneuver. The pilot tried to evade capture by the Cub's crew, who landed at the scene. The German observer had a bullet wound in his foot. Both became captives.

(11) The Air Sub-Section's twin engine Gotha 105 was test hopped today by Capt. Mathews, who checked himself out at 50th MR&RS strip. This was accomplished notwithstanding the aroused suspicions of two P-51s who gave chase, unsuccessfully.

(12) Lt Lynon, serving as a courier pilot for the 55th AAA Bgde, departed in 63-C, having wrapped up 63-J near Rheinberg in a hot-day short field landing. He was directed to report location of damaged L-4 (44-80577) to 27th MR&RS, NW of Neuss, so that they could pick it up for repairs. Incident reported to AAA Section Exec, who apologized for causing trouble.

April 14

(1) 258th FA Gp Asst Arty Air Officer, Lt Heath, reported another wreck (No. 11). L-4 44-80377 (32-X), flown by Lt Wimberley, crashed on take-off in a cross wind. Only slight injuries to pilot and none to observer. Sent Lts Heath & Wimberley to 50th MR&RS strip with a request to Lt Zicard that a replacement aircraft (43-30252) be provided.

(2) XVI Corps Arty Air Officer, Maj. Hallstein, called and stated that he would send 10 pilots in five airplanes to München-Gladbach on April 15 to ferry five airplanes to 50th MR&RS strip.

April 15

(1) Maj. Hallstein (XVI Corps) reported that two wrecked L-4s of 258th Gp units and one of 219th FA Gp were left in situ when the units moved. Told him that these were to be picked up by 27th MR&RS, but didn't know what they planned to do about it. We will also relay request to 34th Bgde to send two airplanes and two pilots to this HQ on Temporary Duty for about ten days to work as courier pilots with the 125th LS.

(2) 5th Armd Div Arty Air Officer, Maj. Boughton, reported an attack by an Fw 190 on L-4 44-80603 (54-F) flown by Lt Montgomery (our ex Operations Officer) on April 12. The pilot was hospitalized as a result of injuries (broken leg and arm, etc.) received when his evasive action took his aircraft into a haystack. His observer was uninjured. The aircraft is a total wreck and a replacement is required. Lts Helms or Zicard to arrange for the pick-up of wreck and to prepare an aircraft for delivery to unit. No replacement pilot is immediately available.

(3) Lt Helms visited the CP. He reported the following aircraft at München-Gladbach awaiting ferrying: L-5Bs 44-17189, 44-17205; L-4Bs 43-891, 43-968, 43-1313, 43-1314, 43-1428; L-4As 42-36442, 43-29052, 43-29132, 43-29161; L-4J 45-4543. Plus 63-G. The 326th Ferrying Squadron will ferry the above L-4s to Bielefeld. We will ferry one L-5 and carry back a 125th LS pilot to get the other. At least five of the following Pool aircraft were started on their way by XVI Corps pilots today – 44-80110, 44-80535, 43-29647, 43-29130, 43-29082, and 42-15286 (two of these arrived at the 50th strip).

(4) Lt Sharp returned from ferry trip to 2nd Armd Div. Lt Kistler, the 2nd Abn Div pilot who flew him back, gave additional details concerning the crash of an L-4 of the 65th Armd FA Bn (see April 12). It appears that the aircraft was found to be a complete wreck, with the appearance of having spun in with a possible bullet hole in the fuel tank and 20-mm fragments here and there. Little more is known, but it is believed that the pilot, Lt Gordon, was shot down as he returned from ferrying the aircraft from the 50th MR&RS strip. Lt Zicard will pick up wreck. Replacement aircraft and pilot have already been provided. Lt Kistler also reported the injury from enemy rifle fire of Lt Jeffries, observer, who was riding with Lt Failing, pilot, who was unhurt.

April 16

(1) Distribution of Air Sub-Section personnel and equipment is as follows (München-Gladbach abandoned April 16):

Gütersloh	Bielefeld	Brunswick
CP:	50th MR&RS:	Lt Zicard
Lt Col. Leich	Lt Helms	Lt Sharp
Capt. Mathews	1 L-4 (63-G)	1 L-4 (63-B)
T/5 Hamblen		1 L-5 (63-CC)
Airstrip:		
T/3 Roehrich		
T/3 Tye		
Sgt Boerner	Temporary Duty	
T/5 Van Slyke	XIII Corps Arty – Lt Sinex	
'Tie-down' (pet dog)	785th FA Bn – Lt Hogan	
2 L-5s (63-AA and 63-B)	55th AAA Brigade – Lt Lynch	
1 L-4 (63-A)	1 L-4 (63-C)	
1 Gotha 150		
1¾-ton truck		
V-3 II		

(2) 5th Armd Div pilot, Lt Myers, visited CP. Asked him to inform his unit that a replacement aircraft (54-F) and pilot would be dispatched to our Braunschweig [Brunswick] echelon (Lt Zicard) as soon as the pilot becomes available.

(3) 84th Inf Div Arty Air Officer, Maj. Paschall, turned into the Pool L-4 43-29419 (87-I) and picked up L-5B 44-17205 (87-A). He also reported that L-4 44-80010 (87-G), piloted by Lt Atkins, had been forced down by three Fw 190s which attacked it at 500ft. The Air OP hit the ground when the pilot looked over his shoulder. No personnel injuries, but a

replacement aircraft is required. Lt Sharp will ferry replacement to the forward strip on April 17 and will arrange for crash pick-up.

(4) All Pool aircraft at München-Gladbach have been ferried to Bielefeld. Action will be taken to have the ten L-4s at 16th Air Depot Group ferried by 326th Ferrying Gp to 50th MR&RS forward strip at Braunschweig.

(5) Capt. Eaton, CO 27th MR&RS, reported that his unit had picked up 44-80583 and 44-80577 for repair and the following aircraft will be picked up today: 44-80335, 44-80377, 44-80575, plus another one reported. He will notify us when the aircraft are ready for flyaway.

(6) Lt Helms ferried L-5B 44-17189 to Bielefeld. It will be assigned to NUSA for use by Lt Zicard and bear squadron code markings 63-GG.

(7) Visited 50th Forward echelon at Braunschweig and gave Lt Zicard instructions to move to the airstrip on the south edge of town. It is a smaller field and there will be less chance of being thrown out of it by the Air Corps. Lt Zicard reported that by April 17 they would be able to service aircraft in the new location. This is the same location to be occupied by the 125th LS and the Arty Air section.

April 17

(1) Capt. Mathews, with a Staff Sgt pilot from the 125th LS, flew to Y-56 München-Gladbach to pick up L-5B 44-17190. En route he visited 27th MR&RS (Fifteenth US Army) and the new Army Arty Air Officer, Maj. Thornton. The CO of the 27th (Capt. Ratom) seemed happy to have the opportunity to serve the keenest and freshest Army on the Western Front by picking up and repairing our Rhine River vicinity crashes. He will notify us through Fifteenth Army when they are ready.

(2) Arrangements were made with the Aircraft Allocations Section to deliver our replacement L-4s to Braunschweig air strip. Five were already headed for Bielefeld.

(3) Lt Col. Leich visited 50th MR&RS strip at Bielefeld. Met Capt. Hester, 335th Ferrying Squadron, who was readying to return ferry pilots to Y-56 in his UC-64 transport. Requested he have them continue to Braunschweig and provided him with maps and Captain's bars to pin on Lt Zicard.

(4) Capt. Zicard visited Arty strip (from Braunschweig with Lt Sharp) to ferry L-5B 44-17120 (63-CC), which he will use. He reported the arrival of Capt. Hester and five replacement L-4s at Braunschweig (L-4B 43-1428 and L-4As 43-21932, 43-29052, 43-29161 and 42-36442).

(5) XIX Corps Asst Arty Air Officer, Lt Johnson, visited Arty Air strip with Lt Trigg (30th Div pilot) to pick up L-5B 44-17199 (sponsored by Detroit Coca Cola Bottling works, according to the sign all over its cowling) for 83rd Div. In exchange, in a few days the unit will turn in an L-4 to Capt. Zicard.

(6) 29th Inf Div pilot, Lt Hollemann, visited strip to report his forced landing (on account of darkness) in L-4 43-30040 (45-C) at a location near Bartrup. No personnel injuries. Replacement aircraft required. Lt Helms to determine accurate location of wreck for crash pick-up and to issue a replacement aircraft (44-80110) to the unit.

April 18

(Rear echelon of Ninth Army Headquarters opened at Münster)

(1) Information was received that on April 17 a 30th Inf Div Arty aircraft mechanic and his helper were ambushed by the enemy while driving a ¾-ton truck loaded with fuel. The mechanic was killed when the truck was set on fire by a *Panzerfaust*. The helper was wounded and apparently escaped.

(2) The AAA Section Exec Officer reported that AA units had shot down four Storch aircraft (German Air OPs). It had been reported that Col. Hutton, 2nd Armd Div Arty Commder, had been flying one of this type of aircraft in forward areas. XIX Corps Arty Air Officer, Capt. Reed, said that the Corps was taking action to stop flights by US personnel in German liaison aircraft, for obvious reasons.

(3) CO 125th LS, Capt. O'Brien, reported that XXIX TAC had moved into 'our' Braunschweig airfield. He therefore decided to occupy a strip on the field north of the city.

(4) Dozens of missions were turned down today for lack of Pool pilots.

(5) A 695th Armd FA Bn pilot reported damage to his aircraft on April 17 when he dived for the ground to avoid an attack by an Me 109 about 15 miles NE of Klotar. He misjudged his speed and hit a tree with a wing in the pull out, but managed to get the L-4, 43-29622 (33-D), in for repairs.

April 19

(1) 30th Inf Div Assistant Arty Air Officer, Capt. Williamson, reported that 44-80120 (44-H) was completely wrecked by the wind when inadequate tie-downs were pulled loose.

(2) 269th FA Bn pilot, Lt Woody, reported an accident after getting lost near Paderborn while en route to Gütersloh and cracking a wing tip and bending longerons. He arrived at our strip and will be available on April 19 to fly Col. Smith.

(3) Capt. Zicard reported the arrival of five more aircraft (L-4Bs 43-1341, 43-986, 43-1313 and 43-891, and L-4J 45-4549) at our Braunschweig strip, completing the ten L-4s ordered.

(4) Capt. Zicard reported that the aircraft recently lost (on April 12) by the 65th Armd FA Bn, flown by Lt Gordon, was shot down by sniper fire. It was full of buckshot holes.

April 20

(1) Gen. Schabacker, 55th AAA Bgde, called to request that Lt Lynch, the pilot who has been serving him in a courier capacity, be allowed to continue the job for a while. Agreed, pending discussion of the matter with the CO of the AAA Section.

(2) 269th FA Bn pilot, Lt Woody, arrived at CP to fly a taxi mission for S-3 Section. Bucking a strong headwind while en route from 34th Bgde early this morning, he had to land in a small field. In so doing he damaged the airplane, but he managed to fly in and arrived at 1400 hrs. Agreed to lend him an aircraft while his L-4 is in the 50th MR&RS for repairs (should be ready in a couple of days). He remained overnight.

(3) Lt Stockwell, 777th FA Bn pilot, reported an incident that happened 'a few days ago'. When flying low over a Jeep on take-off he was fired upon by one of the occupants of the Jeep (cal .45 pistol). He did not know the names of the vehicle's passengers, one of whom was a Lt Col. and the other a Capt. (both FA). XVI Corps Arty Air Officer, Maj. Hallstein, will be requested to ask 349th FA Gp Arty Air Officer, Maj. Ricker, to furnish details of this incident (he's supposed to know them!).

(4) Nine reinforcement pilots (one, Lt Gettle, sick in hospital at GFRC) arrived from *Conquer Rear*, having been censoring mail in a GFRC unit at Münster for a week.

(5) 95th Inf Div Arty Air Officer, Maj. Blaha, turned in 44-79639 (66-N) to the Pool, having picked up a wreck (serial number not known) of one of our Battalions (unknown), had it repaired and retained it. An attempt will be made to straighten this out, somehow!

(6) L-4 aircraft are being modified (one-piece turtledecks, etc.), at rates indicated: At Braunschweig, one per day; at Bielefeld, one-half to one per day.

(7) L-4 43-29130 was lent to Lt Gary, a 751st Bn pilot, while his aircraft is undergoing repair at 50th MR&RS.

(8) Pet dog 'Tie-down' was buried at sundown. Incurably sick, she was put out of her misery by the Vet.

(9) Lt Col. Leich visited 16th Air Depot Group. The Aircraft Allocations Section reported receipt of four L-5s (three L-5Cs and one L-5E), the L-5Cs being 44-17325, 44-17359, 44-17362 and the L-5E 44-17460. Delivery of these aircraft will be to Braunschweig. We will retain the L-5E and allocate one of our L-5s (63-B possibly) and the other three to 102nd, 35th, 5th Armd and 79th Divs. Two more L-5s, expected shortly, will complete our requirements for all divisions.

(10) XIII Corps Asst Arty Air Officer, Lt Roark, visited CP. He stated that 102nd Div Arty Air Officer, Capt. Dobbs, did not want an L-5 at this time.

(11) Lt Col. Leich visited 27th MR&RS. The CO, Capt. Eaton, stated that they would modify the L-4s belonging to us which they are repairing and that these should be ready to fly away in about three days. The Engineer Officer requested that forms on wrecked airplanes -377 and -575 be sent to him.

(12) The L-4 in which 65th Armd FA Bn pilot Lt Gordon was shot down has a belly full of buckshot and what appears to be rifle bullet holes in the gas tank. Numerous reports have been heard of German civilians throwing bricks at low-flying Air OPs. XVI Corps Asst Arty Air Officer, Lt Ball, stated that he would be mortified indeed had a youngster succeeded in shooting him down with a sling shot.

(13) 35th Inf Div Arty Air Officer, Maj. Davidson, offered to trade a Luger pistol for an L-5! He also wanted to know when they could expect to get all their ships modified with the new topdecks. Answer: 'The 50th MR&RS is putting the modification into effect as fast as possible, but send an aircraft and mechanics back to learn how, and then do your own ships.'

April 21

(1) The following Loss Report was received today: On an attempted take-off on April 19, 102nd Div pilot Capt. Dobbs in 44-80083 (76-R) tried to avoid a collision with another aircraft which turned onto the runway. In so doing he turned down wind (wind speed 20-25 mph with strong gusts) and the L-4 went over on its back. No personnel injuries. Capt. Zicard arranged to pick up the wreck and replace it with 43-29768.

(2) 95th Inf Div Asst Air Officer, Capt. Marie (with Col. Clyburn, passenger) visited CP. He stated that the L-4 picked up by them (wrecked by 748th Bn) was 44-80335.

(3) Capt. Hertzmark (who assembles liaison aircraft at Rouen) called and asked how many L-5s we have (answer: 13, with four on the way from Y-56 München-Gladbach). He stated that many were being assembled and that we should expect to get quite a few more soon.

(4) Capt. Zicard visited CP. He reported that 50th MR&RS Forward echelon was going well and able to perform turtledeck modifications at the rate of two per day. The Forward echelon mechanics are not working union hours.

(5) Aircraft status of Army and Army Pool is as follows:

	L-4s	L-5s
Army	7	3
Temporary Duty with 55th AA Brigd	1	
Lent to 125th LS	2	
Undergoing repair at 27th MR&RS	4	
Undergoing major repair at 50th MR&RS	9	
Undergoing minor repair at 50th MR&RS	15	
Undergoing major repair, 50th MR&RS Forward	2	
Undergoing minor repair, 50th MR&RS Forward	8	
L-4s due in on exchange for L-5s	9	

(2nd Armd Div, 83rd Inf Div, XVI Corps, 8th Armd Div, 84th Inf Div, 102nd Inf Div, 35th Inf Div, 5th Armd Div, 79th Inf Div)

Totals:	57	3

April 22

Col. Fulton, Quartermaster, asked to have an aircraft (agreed by S-3 Section) pick him up daily at 1100 hrs at Gütersloh airstrip to go to Braunschweig, starting Wednesday, April 25.

April 23

(HQ Ninth Army Command Post opened at Braunschweig)

(1) Air Section moved to new Braunschweig location (airfield south of the city).

(2) Four L-5s (44-17325, -17359, -17362, -17460) were delivered to Braunschweig airfield by 326th Ferrying Group. L-5 44-17325 was delivered to 35th Inf Div pilot, Lt Johnson, who was checked out by Lt Lawrence.

(3) Two hailstorms did no damage to artillery aircraft at Braunschweig.

(4) L-5B -189 (63-CC) flown by Capt. Zicard, made a cross-wind forced landing due to carburettor ice and received damage to wing-tip and prop.

(5) Message from Maj. Lefever was dropped at Arty Air strip from a circling UC-64 (believed to belong to 16th Air Depot Group). It stated that they couldn't get into field (don't know why) and asked whether Lt Col. Leich could visit 50th MR&RS to see him (Lefever) and the Exec Officer 16th Air Depot Group and the CO of the 50th MR&RS (Maj. Davis). Capt. Mathews visited 50th MR&RS at Bielefeld and Majors Webster and Lefever came in later.

(6) Airstrip for Shuttle L-4s was established behind the CP, permission having been obtained from Deputy C/S, Col. Millener.

April 24

(1) Col. Miller stated that he was busy seeking a new strip for the 125th LS, which must move from their present (and third) location. It will probably complete the circle and end up at 'our' south field.

(2) Capt. Berry, 29th Div, reported:

(a) Lt Harry Simmons was attacked by two Fw 190s while flying at 800ft. The pilot hit the deck, but one enemy aircraft fired upon him, hitting his airplane's empennage. He landed the aircraft in a plowed field and took to the 'high timbers' unharmed. The aircraft (43-K) was flown in for repairs.

(b) Lt McNamara, after landing on the strip, was taxying his aircraft to a parking space between two houses when an Me 262 made a pass at him but couldn't get in a shot. The enemy aircraft turned for another attempt, but AA fire forced it away.

(3) Capt. Dobbs and another captain of the 108th Div picked up L-5 44-17369 (76-B) and turned in L-4 4329756 (or -758?) in exchange.

(4) Lts Durant, Barnes and Miller (83rd Inf Div) reported:

(a) Aircraft 44-80107 (87-H), piloted by Lt Miller, stalled out at 20ft when attempting to escape from four Me 109s. No personnel injuries. Crash crew dispatched by Capt. Zicard. L-4 43-28706 assigned as replacement.

(b) Lt J. S. Ford in 43-30207 (87-D) was forced down by enemy aircraft. An Me 109 came over at 200ft (after Air OP was on the ground) and strafed the plane. No personnel injuries. Damage to aircraft repaired by unit.

(c) Lt Barnes in 44-79933 was attacked by Me 109s. While attempting to land, stalled out and dropped in on one wing. Aircraft was flown in for repairs.

April 25

(1) 2nd Armd Div Asst Arty Air Officer, Lt Kistler, called concerning:

(a) the whereabouts of Lt Gordon, 65th Armd FA Bn pilot who was shot down and went to 119th Field Hospital. 'We should try to get in touch with him. Believe his story would be interesting.'

(b) Loan of an L-5 while their aircraft is being repaired by MR&RS.

(c) Flights in German gliders – is this OK? Answer 'No'.

(2) Lt Helms, Liaison Officer with the 50th MR&RS, visited the Section. Remained overnight. He reported the usual disagreeable situation existing there.

April 26

Capt. Zicard reported the following: L-4 43-30388 was turned in by the 83rd Inf Div in exchange for its L-5 (44-17464), delivered by ferry pilot (this L-5 is earmarked for the 79th Inf Div, whose Arty Air Officer is being requested to come and get checked out in it).

April 27

(1) 2nd Armd Div Asst Arty Air Officer, Lt Kistler, reported that word had been received that Lt Morton, Lt Hammarstrom's observer when he was shot down by enemy aircraft, had died of his wounds.

(2) Maj. Boughton, 5th Armd Div, visited the Arty Air strip to be checked out in L-5 44-17362, which is being assigned to him.

(3) 125th LS CO, Capt. O'Brien, called. He would like to retain the two L-4s which we lent him as they are serving the unit very usefully in its present 'very busy' state. He likewise

indicated that two pilots from the 34th FA Bgde (Swan and Gray) were being extensively used. Explained that their unit wanted them back and would let him know further about them.

(4) Maj. Lefever requested information concerning Major or Lt Ross, NUSA pilot who cracked up an airplane, turned it in to the 27th MR&RS and borrowed a replacement, then cracked up that one and went back to get crack-up No. 1. All of this was supposed to have happened on 26 April. No more details known.

(5) Received L-5B 44-17169 today. It is earmarked for 95th Inf Div Arty and action will be taken to so notify Maj. Blaha, Div Arty Air Officer. This will be the last L-5 which we can expect for a while. Deliveries have now been made to all Divisions except the 75th.

April 28

(1) Arranged with CO 125th LS, Capt. O'Brien, to release two pilots and airplanes of 34th FA Bgde units to their organizations and to provide the 125th with two L-4Bs from the Pool.

(2) 695th Armd FA Bn pilot, Lt Townes, reported major damage to his L-4, 43-28622 (33-O), when forced down by four enemy aircraft. No personnel injuries. Capt. Zicard to pick up wreck and assign 43-80120 as a replacement.

(3) XVI Corps Arty Air Officer, Maj. Hallstein, reported landing accident to 75th Inf Div L-4H 44-29607 (63-G), Lt Moran pilot. No personnel injuries. Lt Helms to arrange crash pick-up by 50th MR&RS and the release of a replacement aircraft.

(4) 95th Inf Div Asst Arty Air Officer, Capt. Marie, called to take delivery of L-5B 44-17169 (66-A) for the unit and agreed to bring in an L-4 in exchange in a few days.

(5) 35th Inf Div turned in L-4 43-29669 (45-C) in exchange for its L-5 already received.

(6) Maj. Rose, Asst Exec Ninth Army Rest Center, Heerlen, visited Section and reported following: Our pilot (Lt Harris) dispatched there on April 26, found an oil leak in his airplane, stopped at 27th MR&RS, left the ship for repairs and proceeded to Heerlen in a borrowed airplane. Overtaken by darkness, he attempted a forced landing two miles north of Heerlen, hitting a telephone pole and wires. He was taken to 32nd General Hospital (Aachen) and, although not seriously injured, will not be able to fly for a week or 10 days. Arrangements were made for 27th MR&RS to pick up the wrecked L-4 (44-80577) on April 28. Lt Kershaw was flown to 27th MR&RS by Lt Donnelly to pick up our repaired aircraft and then proceed to Heerlen to carry on in place of Lt Harris. Prior to receipt of this report, Capt. Zicard was dispatched to 27th MR&RS to see what this was all about.

(7) 79th Inf Div pilot, Lt Kangas, was notified that their L-5 was ready at Braunschweig and that they should pick it up and turn in an L-4.

(8) Code markings 63-Z and insignia will be placed on the captured Gotha II in a very low priority 'unless desired by the Arty Officer'.

April 29

(1) 125th LS released Lts Gray (210th FA Gp) and Dickson (256th FA Bn) from Temporary Duty with their XIX Corps flights. Pilots rejoined their units.

(2) WO Wilson, on behalf of Col. Miller, General Staff, requested that two more L-4s (making a total of six) be lent to the 125th LS in order for them to supplement their XIII

Corps flight. Told Col. Miller that a check would be made to determine whether or not we could do this (believe we can, in view of the extra large number of aircraft in our Pool).

(3) XVI Corps Arty Air Officer, Maj. Hallstein, called to report that the correct serial number of the L-4 cracked up by 75th Inf Div (reported yesterday) is 44-80276 (85-B). (Item 2, April 28 refers.)

(4) Capt. A. R. Hackbarth, 205th FA Gp Arty Air Officer (another of the original Grasshopper pilots and old friend) and three EM (including T/Sgt Rhodes, an original FA Airplane Mechanic) visited CP en route to the new location of their unit.

April 30

(1) Lt Sharp notified CO 125th LS that L-4s 43-986 and 43-29905 would be turned over to him today. WO Wilson, Office, General Staff, was notified.

(2) Lt Helms visited CP and reported:

(a) that 2nd Armd Div L-4 44-80042 is at Y-001/2 for modification.

(b) L-4 43-30013 released to 75th Inf Div as replacement for crashed 44-80276.

(3) 79th Inf Div Arty Air Officer, Maj. Lawrence, visited Arty air strip to pick up L-5E 44-17464 (46-A). He turned in L-4 44-80232 (46-B) in exchange. Capt. Mathews checked him out in the L-5.

(4) Maj. Swenson, 29th Div Arty Air Officer, called in. He will file an Air OP Loss Report on L-4 44-80240 (44-H or B?) into which a truck had backed and which had been brought in for major repairs.

May 2

(1) Four more L-4s were lent to the 125th LS (43-1428, 42-36442, 43-1341 and 43-29669), making the total ten.

(2) 326th Ferrying Group pilot, Lt Mahlstedt, visited the Arty Air strip and brought a copy of a message from 16th ADG requesting 125th LS to give up five L-5s (44-17176, -17179, -17188, -17207 and -17209) that were delivered to them in error. He also asked that they be turned over to us. Lt Short, Ops Officer, agreed to turn over four on 4 May and one (44-17179) on May 5.

(3) Capt. Zicard reported that 739th FA Bn had turned in L-4 43-29968 (32-W), which had 480 hours total time, and received 44-80083 in exchange. 95th Inf Div turned in 44-79681 in exchange for its L-5.

(4) Lt Helms reported 349th FA Gp L-4 44-80406 (82-F), damaged in landing accident, was flown by Lt Fields. No personnel injuries. Aircraft replaced by 44-79786. L-4 44-80276 of the 75th Inf Div was picked up by crash crew.

(5) XIII Corps Arty Exec, Col. Williams, called and reported incomplete details of two Air OP losses on May 2, both believed due to action by Russian aircraft:

(a) 196th FA Gp Arty Air Officer, Maj. Morrison, and Group Chaplain, on administrative flight. Two aircraft were after him. Aircraft burned, pilot evacuated to hospital, Chaplain severely burned.

(b) 84th Div aircraft – no one hurt. He requested that we check at Army Group level on action taken to keep Russian and our aircraft from tangling. Called Maj. Lefever ('old boy level') who stated that 'no-fly' lines had been established between Russians and ourselves at SHAEF levels.

(6) Five L-5s to be received from 125th LS will be allocated as follows: 44-17179 to 75th Inf Div, 44-17207 to XVI Corps Arty, 44-17176 to XIII Corps Arty, 44-17209 to 34th FA Bgde, 44-17188 to XIX Corps Arty.

(7) Capt. Zicard and Capt. Mathews made a recce in XVIII Corps sector for a new location for the forward echelon of the MR&RS. An airfield one mile NE of Hagenow, being used for PoW evacuation, was chosen. Complete unit moved, starting at noon, Capt. Zicard and Lt Sharp leading the way.

(9) Maj. Haydock, XVIII Corps Arty Air Officer, reported that the 407th FA Gp air sections, as well as other battalion air sections slated to work with the 6th British Airborne Div, were ready to operate and would do so as soon as they can catch up with the unit.

May 4

(1) Further information on 196th FA Gp's accident: Pilot, Maj. Morrison, 50-50 chance of living, 60% of his body with 3rd degree burns. Passenger, Gp Chaplain, Capt. Antunniccio, not much chance of pulling through. L-4 43-30385 (27-FF) burned. Replacement pilot not required until they get a replacement aircraft. Persons seeing the accident claim the markings on the ship were everything from Red stars to red circles. A check with aircraft spotters in the area shows that the only planes over the area were three LAG 3s (Russian single-engine fighters).

(2) 84th Div reported loss of L-4 43-29706 (87-H) – pilot Lt Miller hospitalized with a bullet wound in his hip. Replacement aircraft only required.

(3) Lt Hogan, on T/D with 788th FA Bn, visited Section on the first time he had flown this week. The Battalion's one pilot was being used on regular work, leaving Hogan on miscellaneous details, such as taking trucks on ration pick-up, etc. Request was made to relieve Hogan from duty with the 788th as we can use him to better advantage.

(4) In response to a query from them, XVIII A/B Corps Arty was told that 50th MR&RS Forward had left for Hagenow yesterday afternoon.

(5) Lt Col. Leich and Capt. Mathews visited 50th MR&RS Forward at Hagenow and XVIII A/B Corps Arty Air Officer, Maj. Haydock. Typical of this time, the following missions were flown by Arty Section pilots today:

Pilot	Passenger	Remarks
Lt Lawrence	Col. Smith	Visit to units.
Lt Lawrence	–	Westbound Ordnance run.
Lt Donnelly	–	Eastbound Ordnance run.
Lt Gerrish	–	Ferry aircraft to Hagenow.
Lt Isabell	Maj. Knoche (Engnr Sec)	To Heerlen. (Remained overnight)

(6) The following units picked up L-5s at Arty air strip: XIII Corps Arty, XVI Corps Arty, XIX Corps Arty, 34th FA Bgde.

(7) XVI Arty to turn in L-4 44-79954 at Bielefeld and will have 75th Inf Div pick up L-5 at Arty airstrip on May 6, turning in its exchange L-4 at Bielefeld.

(8) 210th FA Gp Arty Air Officer, Maj. Magruder, left drawing for cowling modification and asked about nearest point where he could get supplies and repairs. Was told we have already

completed the cowling mods and are putting them on airplanes. The Forward echelon of the MR&RS at Hagenow will handle all supply problems.

May 5

(1) Missions flown today by Arty Section pilots:

Pilot	Passenger	Remarks
Lt Lawrence	–	Eastbound Ordnance run.
Lt Gerrish	–	Westbound Ordnance run.
Lt Donnelly	Capt. L. (CML Section)	To FUSA – returned due weather.
Lt Isabell	Maj. Knoche (Engnr Sec)	In from Heerlen.
Lt Sharp	–	In from Hagenow, out to Bielefeld.
Lt Zicard	–	In from Hagenow. RON
Lt Helms	Sgt Roehrich	In from Maastricht.
Capt. Mathews	Lt Col. Fuge (Surgeon Sec)	To Maastricht. Remained overnight.

(2) Exec XIII Corps Arty, Col. Williams, requested to take action to see that:

(a) 84th Inf Div Arty submits survey on 44-80241, which was wrecked and 'misplaced' (requested several times).

(b) that 84th Inf Div Arty submit Loss Report on L-4 43-29706 (87-H), flown by Lt Miller. Lt Sharp to pick up crash.

(c) that 196th FA Gp submit Loss Report on L-4 43-30385, flown by Maj. Morrison and crashed and burned. Lt Sharp to check wreckage for salvage.

(3) Capt. Meehan, 102nd Inf Div Asst Arty Air Officer, reported crash of L-4 44-80149 (76-M), flown by Lt Lester. Operational accident (aircraft stalled on attempted take-off from soft field). No personnel injuries. Lt Sharp to pick up wreckage and to furnish 44-80232 as a replacement.

May 6

(1) On May 5 Sgt Sloan, Operations Sgt, 125th LS, reported receipt of information from the 9th AF Liaison Officer that L-4 44-80755 (98-F) of 210th FA Gp, flown by Lt Gray, had been shot down by Russian ground fire at 1020 hrs on the east bank of the Elbe River at Wittenberg, with apparently no injury to pilot and passenger. Lt Sharp to send a crash pick-up crew and to notify 210th FA Gp Arty Air Officer, Maj. Magruder (who was particularly interested as the payroll was supposedly on board). Coincidentally the pilot, Lt Gray, walked in and completed arrangements to ferry L-4 44-79681 from Braunschweig to Hagenow, where he would pick up 44-80388 from Lt Sharp as a replacement. (The payroll has not been picked up yet.)

(2) Lt Sharp at Hagenow reported the following:

(a) 7th Armd Div needs an L-5 prop for an AOG.

(b) Have four L-4s AOG on account of props.

(c) Russians won't let us get to the wreckage of 196th Gp aircraft which was shot down on May 2.

(3) 7th Armd Div Arty AO, Maj. Neal, requested an additional L-5, since the one received by the unit has been reserved by the Div Cmdr for his personal use, and cannot leave the ground without him on board. Answer: 'Too bad. How are you going to comply with instructions to check out your pilots, because we can't give you an extra L-5?'

(4) 84th Inf Div Asst Arty Air Officer, Capt. Auld, visited section to discuss wrecked L-4 44-80201 (which the unit is supposed to be surveying) because it could not be located by crash pick-up crew. We discovered that the Air OP Loss Report had given the wrong grid square. Lt Helms was notified of correct locations (66 miles from originally reported location).

(5) The following missions were scheduled for Arty Section pilots:

Pilot	Passenger	Remarks
Lt Col. Leich	Col. Thompson	Visit to FUSA, canceled due weather.
Lt Lynch	Maj. Nayden (Sig Sec)	Postponed until May 7.
Lt Lawrence	–	Westbound Ordnance run.
Lt Gerrish	–	Eastbound Ordnance run (did not arrive).
Capt. Mathews	Maj. Knoche	In from Heerlen.

13 visitors to CP during the day – everyone ate!

(6) FUSA acting Arty Air Officer, Capt. Stevenson called, among other things advising that Capt. Hill is taking the place of Capt. Bryant, 1st Inf Div Arty Air Officer. Didn't know if Bryant survived his crack-up on take-off in L-5. When he was evacuated, his chances did not look too good.

(7) FUSA Arty Air Officer, Capt. Stevenson, called, asking if we wanted to move the 27th MR&RS, which is at R-22, 20 miles east of Weimar.

May 7

(1) There have been 48 pilots attached-unassigned for periods of from one day to one month (or more) in this Section from November 1,1944, to May 1,1945. These, together with the assigned pilots of the Section, have flown approximately 1,600 hours during the period, or an average of 267 per month. Flying time during April totalled 525 hours.

(2) L-4 44-80585 (63-H) was left at 27th MR&RS for repairs (by Lt Kershaw) and 43-30061 (63-E) picked up.

(3) Lt Col. Leich and Capt. Mathews visited Arty Air Section FUSA and discussed future developments with Asst Arty Air Officer, Capt. (since 1 May) Farwell, CO 23rd MR&RS, Maj. Miller, and 12th Army Gp Arty Air Officer, Maj. Lefever. In general, the following was discussed (all plans based on the possible redeployment of 23rd MR&RS in near future):

(a) 23rd will turn over all flyable FUSA Pool aircraft to NUSA.

(b) NUSA will then ferry them from R-22 Jena.

(c) 23rd will turn over all non-flyable aircraft to 16th ADG – or salvage them.

(d) We will furnish a Liaison Officer to 23rd on May 8. He will be at Jena.

(e) 23rd will 'stay put' temporarily until its own redeployment and our own moving plans are known.

(f) Pending 'staying put', 23rd will service VII and VIII Corps and 32nd Brgde units.

(g) Upon confirmation of its redeployment, 23rd will turn over all stocks of spare parts etc. to 16th ADG and cancel all requisitions of units except for AOGs. All FUSA Corps and Divs (except the 78th, which cracked up their aircraft) and 32nd Bgde, 79th, 142nd, and 174th Gps, have been assigned L-5s.

(h) No more L-5s will be delivered for units, present crated aircraft being left crated for reshipment to the Pacific.

(4) 87th Inf Div Arty Air Officer, Maj. Schirmacher (formerly a civilian instructor of the original Grasshoppers) and 32nd FA Bgde Arty Air Officer, Maj. Townsend, were at FUSA CP and discussed various Air OP matters.

(5) VIII Corps Arty Air Officer, Maj. Houser (another original Grasshopper pilot), asked about Air Force supplies and possibility of getting more L-5s for Groups. Advised him that the 23rd MR&RS will continue to be his source of Air Force supplies, for a least a week. No more L-5s being assembled, but possible source might be units in process of redeployment.

(6) Lt Gerrish called from Buer, stating he had wrapped up his airplane. He wanted to know what to do with it and also how he was to get back. Told him to hold tight at Buer to see if Lt Lawrence came through, coming back on the Ordnance run and if he did, hook a ride with him. If Lt Lawrence doesn't pick him up, I made arrangements with Lt Isabell to see if Lt Helms could fly down and pick him up. Since the accident happened closer to the 27th MR&RS than to the 50th MR&RS, suggested Lt Gerrish try to get in touch with them to pick up the crash and repair it.

(7) Lt Brieden, 275th FA Bn, visited CP on routine courier run. Lt Isabell departed on the Ordnance run with Capt. Josephs as passenger.

(8) Lt Sinex, XIII Corps Arty, called and reported the following accident: 202nd FA Gp Arty Air Officer, Capt. Gee and his passenger, Capt. Johnson, were killed when the aircraft spun into the ground. (Capt. Gee succeeded Maj. Murrell as Air Officer when the latter was killed not long ago). Reports from witnesses state that the plane went into a spin at about 1,000ft and never came out. L-4 43-30046 (27-NN) was completely destroyed. Location is in the vicinity of Buetze. Time of accident 1100 hrs today. Hold up on replacement pilot. Lt Sharp to inspect wreckage for salvage.

(9) The field behind the CP had as many as four planes on it at one time. The only one I could recognise was 265th FA Bn. (The squadron code markings on two of them were 25-U and -V, which are V Corps markings.)

(10) Lt Sharp reported:

(a) 'Had slight mishap with the L-5 today. Coming in for a landing and motor conked out, had to land in a small field and nosed it up, damaging the prop and right wing tip.'

(b) L-4 44-80149 of 102nd Div picked up.

(c) Wrecked 210th FA Gp L-4 44-80755 picked up and 43-30388 assigned as replacement. Repairable. All instruments missing, probably to Russian GIs.

(d) Capt. Rawls, 404th FA Gp, turned in L-4 43-30341 for L-5 44-17209, turned over to Group by 34th FA Bgde.

(e) The following Pool L-4s are on hand at Hagenow: 43-29788, 43-30341, 44-79681.

May 8 – Victory in Europe (VE Day)

(1) Lt Col. Leich visited 50th MR&RS Rear at Bielefeld to discuss matters with Maj. Davis, to introduce new *Conquer* Liaison Officer, Lt Kershaw, and to dispatch Lt Helms to the 23rd MR&RS. It was a holiday, VE Day being celebrated with fireworks, venison, no work, etc.

(2) Ordnance Section, Maj. Blum, reported that the 876th ASP at Buer could be taken off the Ordnance courier run.

(3) 23rd MR&RS will continue to serve VII and VIII Corps in its present location, at least for the present. No more L-5s are being assembled.

CHAPTER 11

Return to Peace,
May–October 1945

The end of the war in Europe on 8 May did not see an end to casualties suffered by Air OP Sections of the Ninth Army. That very day Major Morrison, the 196th Group Arty Air Officer, died from the injuries he received when shot down some days previously, and two personnel died when an L-4 flown by a mechanic of the 6th Armored Division attempted to take off but crashed and caught fire. Another fatality occurred on 12 May, when an L-5 of the 79th FA Group crashed into a lake after striking a power line; the pilot survived but his passenger drowned. The next day an L-5 (42-99114) of the 125th Liaison Squadron, flown by S/Sgt Henry W. Lishaness and based at Brunswick-Waggum (R-37), was lost in a crash at Buchorst. This was followed by a further accident on 14 May, when both the pilot and observer of the 104th Infantry Division were killed when their L-4 crashed into a power line while flying very low along an autobahn. Nor were these the only Ninth Army aircraft and personnel losses at this time, as is revealed in the Air Journal extract which forms part of this chapter.

With the end of combat operations many changes took place in the organisation and disposition of Allied armies in the ETO. Some US units were to remain in Germany as part of the Army of Occupation, while others, including the Ninth Army, were to proceed via the US to the Pacific Theater of Operations (PTO) for the ongoing war against Japan. On 9 May, the Ninth comprised VII, VIII, XIII, XVI and XIX Corps, with fifteen Infantry Divisions (9th, 29th, 30th, 35th, 69th, 70th, 76th, 78th, 83rd, 84th, 87th, 89th, 95th, 102nd and 104th) and five Armored Divisions (2nd, 3rd, 5th, 6th and 8th). The Army reached a peak troop strength of over 650,000 on 20 May, by which time the rear echelon of the Army HQ was at Gütersloh, but it soon began reorganising and relinquishing many of its units. One of the first changes affected the 29th Infantry Division, which took over the Bremen-Bremerhaven Enclave Area from the British, the 29th then passing from XVI Corps to direct Ninth Army control. At the same time, British units began first relieving XIII Corps and then XVI Corps, while on 13 June, Russian units began taking over the VII Corps sector. Two days later the Ninth's active time in the ETO came to an end with the transfer of its remaining troops to the Seventh US Army. At the same time, units started handing in their aircraft to air depots for storage and eventual disposal, but prior to this an unusual incident was the theft, apparently by USAAF personnel, of four L-4s from NUSA's Maastricht airstrip (as reported in the Arty HQ Air Section Journal).

The 125th Liaison Squadron, which moved to Heidelberg on 10 June 1945, remained with HQ NUSA to the end, but on 25 July, on which date the squadron moved to Frankfurt-on-

Main, it was attached to the newly formed Headquarters Command, US Forces, European Theater. For administrative purposes the 125th had long been assigned to XXIX Tactical Air Command, but from 20 June until 15 December, on which date it completed its stay in Europe, it was reassigned to XII Tactical Air Command.

The first step in HQ NUSA's move back to the United States took place on 8 July 1945, when its command post at Brunswick closed and its personnel departed for Deauville, France. Shortly afterwards, the HQ Staff sailed from Le Havre on the liner *John Ericssen*, disembarked at New York on 6 August, and proceeded to Camp Shanks, New York State. But events in the Far East had taken a sudden turn following the dropping of atomic bombs on Japan, and plans to dispatch the Ninth Army to the PTO were cancelled. On 4 September, by which time Japan had surrendered, a Ninth Army command post opened at Fort Bragg, North Carolina, and inactivation followed on 10 October.

Extracts from the HQ NUSA Air Journal for 9 May-22 June 1945 compiled by Lt Col. R. M. Leich

May 9

(1) XVI Corps Arty Air Officer, Maj. Hallstein, called concerning a 35th Inf Div report that 'a single-engine, low wing, fixed gear, side-by-side monoplane, painted silver with American markings (squadron code markings 66-I) has been flown by this unit. Invited their attention to a Corps order against it, but Maj. Blaha said that the Division had permission (not given by Corps or Army). Later, a Major and a Captain flew to the strip in an L-4, allegedly marked 82-E (which is the number of Maj. Hallstein's L-5) and one climbed out and stole the German ship. Where it is now? No one knows.'

(2) Lt Sharp reported on the following L-4s:

Ready to go: 43-30341, 44-79681, 43-29768. Ready May 11: 44-80149, 44-80755.

Unfulfilled Obligations: One for 24th Inf Div, and one for 202nd FA Gp.

(3) FUSA Acting Arty Air Officer, Capt. Stevenson, called. He stated that VII Corps and the 3rd Armd Div each had one of the L-5s received when they hit Normandy. These are 'war wearies' and he asked what action should be taken to replace them. Answer: None (without taking new ones already allocated to other units), since we have now been told by Army Group not to expect any more L-5s.

(4) Called G-1, Capt. Burley, and reported the plan to relinquish on 27 May the hotel in Maastricht used as an Air OP Rest Center.

May 10

(1) XIII Corps Acting Arty Air Officer, Lt Henchet, reported that:

(a) the wreckage of the 202nd FA Gp aircraft (Capt. Gee's) had not been picked up, that it has no value, that the unit was moving and asked whether a guard should be left on it. Answer: No.

(b) the 196th FA Gp Arty Air Officer, Maj. Morrison, who was shot down several days ago, died of his injuries on May 8.

(2) Lt Helms reported from the 23rd MR&RS that there were about 14 L-4s on hand, six of which were ready for assignment, three were AOG requiring props, and five were under repair. Requested a complete list as soon as possible.

(3) VIII Corps Arty Air Officer, Maj. Houson, reported that a mechanic of 6th Armd Div attempted to take off from their strip with a passenger on 8 May. The aircraft crashed and burned, killing both occupants.

(4) 258th FA Gp reported an accident on May 9 to L-4 43-30152 (32-X) piloted by Lt Wimberley. No personnel injuries. Accident due to blown tire and damaged gear (caused by hitting obstruction on take-off) and nosing over of aircraft on landing. Apparently the unit is bringing the wreck to 50th MR&RS Rear. Lt Kershaw issued 43-29647 as a replacement.

(5) Lt Sharp, Liaison Officer with the 50th MR&RS Forward, made the following report:

(a) 202nd FA Gp aircraft (Capt. Gee's) was picked up and is being salvaged.

(b) 24th Inf Div aircraft (Lt Miller's) was picked up and is being salvaged.

(6) Lt Helms, Liaison Officer with the 23rd MR&RS at Jena, made the following report:

(a) Pool L-4s at 23rd MR&RS are:

Ready	AOG awaiting props	Minor Repair
43-1432	43-933	44-80325
44-80196	43-30464	44-80285
44-80503	43-30066	43-29657
43-30164		44-79924
44-80574		43-30178 (23-C)
43-30027		

(b) L-5s under repair:

44-16716 (R-8) (153rd LS)

42-99321* (R-8) (153rd LS)

43-99357* (23-B)

42-98520* (26-A)

[*These serial numbers, as given in the journal, are incorrect. No such 42- numbers appear in the USAAF 42- series list. Nor was -99357 either a 43- or 44- series aircraft.]

(c) 3rd Armd Div Arty Air Officer, Maj. Haney, asked for a new L-5, stating that he knew 50 new ones were at Nancy and that he would go there and get an exchange.

(d) L-4 44-80325 issued to 9th Inf Div in exchange for 43-29792, which was turned in after having been landed over a barrel.

(e) 23rd MR&RS turned in the following L-4s to16th ADG (all fly-aways): 43-29710, 43-30532, 43-30446, 43-29850, 43-30543 and 43-29503.

(7) Maj. Lefever asked if we would be prepared to turn in to 16th ADG about 15 'war-wearies' in exchange for new aircraft, if we can arrange it. Answer: Will do! The L-4s of re-deployed units will probably go direct to Air Forces (not MR&RSs), but L-5s will remain in ground forces.

(8) 102nd Inf Div Arty Air Officer, Capt. Meehan, reported the crack-up of an L-5 (-768) in close proximity to Ninth US Army Rear (Münster) when the engine cut in level flight. The carb heat was off when the engine quit. A landing was made in a rough field, but the ship hit a shell hole, going over onto its back. Capt. Meehan said he would wait at Ninth Army

Rear for the crash crew to lead them to the wreck. The ship might possibly be repaired with a new prop and some top enclosure pyralin, but the crash crew should be prepared to pick up the wreck and bring it in for repairs.

May 11

First US Army Arty Air Officer, Capt. Stevenson, called concerning request of 3rd Armd Div Arty Air Officer, Maj. Harky, that an extra airplane and pilot be authorized in each Armd FA Bn. Also asked whether this had been discussed in the Paris meeting of Arty Air Officers. Answer: 'No'.

May 12

(1) Lt Sinex assumed responsibilities of Operations Officer at the Arty Air strip.

(2) Traffic control tower, 125th LS, reported these violations:

(a) 63-E landing 90 degrees to runway.

(b) 59-P (Lt Vernon E. Wyvall, 531st FA Bn), landed against signals (second offence within ten days).

(3) Lt Donnelly, pilot, with Maj. Knoche, Engnr Section, landed on May 11 to inspect improvement to Gütersloh air strip and 'went over' in the high grass in L-4 43-30961 (63-E). No personnel injuries. Lt Kershaw to pick up aircraft at Gütersloh. L-4 44-80533 was supplied to Lt Donnelly to return to Braunschweig.

May 13

(1) A sketchy report was received concerning an accident to a 35th Inf Div aircraft which, while buzzing a river, hit a cable, resulting in the death of the passenger. No other details.

(2) FUSA Arty Air Officer, Capt. Stevenson, reported:

(a) The crash on May 12 of an L-5 of 79th FA Gp, piloted by 1st Lt William B. Larsen, who was injured. Passenger was drowned. The aircraft, while buzzing a lake, flew into a power line SE of Paderborn. No other details. Lt Kershaw to attempt to pick up the wreck. A replacement L-4 will be supplied to the unit.

(b) 23rd MR&RS will move out of Jena in 3-4 days and its services will not be available to us. Capt. Mathews visited CO 50th MR&RS to determine action to be taken by him to provide service to VII and VIII Corps and 32nd FA Bgde.

(3) XVI Corps Arty Air Officer, Maj. Hallstein, called concerning:

(a) Landing accident to L-4 44-80689 piloted by Lt Beck, 252nd FA Gp. No injuries to pilot. No passenger. Aircraft completely washed out. Lt Kershaw to see that the wreck is picked up and to issue a replacement aircraft when one becomes available.

(b) Take-off accident to L-4H 44-79741 of 754th FA Bn, piloted by Lt Dawe. Wheel knocked off on a fence, aircraft cracked up in crash landing. Lt Kershaw to have aircraft picked up and a replacement prepared for assignment.

(4) Call from Maj. Lefever: 'Re replacements for war weary aircraft. There are 14 for you at 16th ADG (München-Gladbach).'

May 14

(1) Col. Miller, General Staff, stated that there were 15 L-5s at 16th ADG, München-Gladbach (Y-56), earmarked for 'Army Arty'; and that the 125th and 153rd (formerly with FUSA, now under NUSA) LSs are short of 14 L-5s. Do we have a requirement for those at Y-56? Explained that 12th Army Gp had told us we would get no more L-5s, that those referred to might belong to another army, but if not, we would have a requirement for them in Arty units.

(2) Lt Helms reported that the 23rd MR&RS was planning on leaving Jena by May 15 and would not be responsible for aircraft there later than the 16th. He also reported the crash of a 104th Inf Div aircraft, L-4 44-80215 (97-(?)). The pilot, with his observer, crashed into a high power line while flying down the autobahn and zoomed to clear a bridge. Both occupants were killed. The aircraft was replaced with L-4B 43-1432.

(3) L-4 44-80196 was ferried in from 23rd MR&RS.

May 15

(Rear echelon of Ninth Army Headquarters opened at Gütersloh)

(1) Maj. Lefever reported that there were no L-5s at Y-56 München-Gladbach. The rumor that some were there was unfounded.

(2) Message (dated May 14) received from Capt. Turman, Air OP Rest Center, that four aircraft had been stolen from the airstrip by American officers. Their pilots are waiting here for instructions. An officer will be sent to Maastricht to check this situation.

(3) The following Arty Air Officers visited the CP to attend a conference or to discuss Air OP matters:

Unit	Name	Remarks
VII Corps	Maj. Miller	Conference
VIII Corps	Maj. Houser	"
XIII Corps	Lt Hanchey	"
XVI Corps	Maj. Hallstein	"
XIX Corps	Maj. Reed	"
32nd FA Bgde	Maj. Townsend	"
34th FA Bgde	Maj. Keating	"
78th Inf Div	Maj. Horne	Replacement of L-5
411th FA Gp	Maj. Shield	Routine
207th FA Bn	Lt Dranion	Routine
777th FA Bn	Lt ?	
280th FA Bn	Lt Young	To determine cost of Continental O-170-3 engine for survey.

(4) 32nd FA Bgde Arty Air Officer, Maj. Townsend, reported that no replacement is needed for the pilot of 79th FA Gp who flew their L-5 into a lake after hitting power lines. The aircraft is in 100ft of water and divers are presently attempting to remove from it the body of the passenger, a T/Sgt mechanic.

May 16

(1) Lt Sinex visited Maastricht to look into the theft (reported by Capt. Turman) of four
Arty L-4s, details of which are as follows:

Unit	Sq Codes	Serial No.	Pilot
29th Inf Div	43-D	43-30411	Lt (?)
777th FA Bn	6(8?)-L	44-79665	Lt Stockwell
8th Armd Div	54-G	44-80347	Lt Myers
84th Inf Div	87-E	44-80124	Lt Sword

At 1630 hrs, May 14, these aircraft were refuelled at Maastricht airstrip by three lieutenants
and one T/Sgt who arrived in a Jeep driven by a sergeant. All are believed to be Air Corps
personnel. Dutch guards stated that at least one was wearing pilot's wings. The four aircraft
were then flown away and the Jeep was driven away by the sergeant. Local MPs, airfields
at Liège, Brussels and Brimstone were notified. Action: This matter was reported to Flying
Control at XXIX TAC, Sgt Sperry, who stated that all TAC fields would be notified, as well
as Continental Flying Control, to apprehend the thieves and to grab the aircraft.

(2) At 1730 three pilots and their passengers visited the CP, having secured a lift from Y-58
Cologne, ate steak for supper, and then departed in aircraft (L-4s) lent from our Pool as
follows: 43-38006 to 29th Inf Div, 44-5033* to 777th FA Bn, 42-15286 to 8th Armd Div,
44-80778 (already assigned to 84th Inf Div but had not yet been picked up). Pilots returned
– couldn't find unit. Remained overnight. The pilots were to retain the aircraft lent to them
until further notice. [*This serial number, as given in the journal, is incorrect; 44-5033 was
not an L-4 serial number, nor could it have been 42-5033, which was a P-39 Airacobra that
went to Russia, while 43-5033 was a B-25 Mitchell. The only possibility is that it might have
been 45-5033, but there is no evidence to confirm that this L-4J came to the ETO.]

May 17

(1) Air OP Rest Center, Hotel Derlon, Maastricht, closed on May 15. During the two months in
which it operated, 316 pilots and observers visited there for 2-4 days each. The officer in charge,
Capt. Kevin D. Turman (20th Tank Destroyer Gp) and his assistant, Tec/5 William A. Barrs,
rejoined their unit on May 16, having been on temporary duty at the Rest Center since March 9.

(2) Lt Layton, 7th Armd Div pilot, visited CP to discuss turning in L-4 43-30002 as a 'war-weary' on
order of the Div Arty CO, Col. Martin, who said it was too noisy for him. The aircraft has 420 hours
and the engine 130 hours. Told Lt Layton to take the ship to 50th MR&RS for inspection by Lt Helms
or Lt Kershaw to determine whether or not the request is frivolous (in view of the pilot's report that he
considers the aircraft as being in good shape and giving perfect performance). If the ship is legitimate
war-weary, we will approve an exchange and notify the unit when it can pick up the new aircraft.

(3) Reported air section locations included two on airfields, the 8th Inf Div at Schweren
and 8th Armd Div at Göttingen. The 84th Inf Div was on a strip near Mehle.

May 18

(1) Lt Kershaw, Liaison Officer with the 50th MR&RS, reported the following:

(a) An L-5 of the 79th FA Gp, which is in 100ft of water in a lake south of Paderborn, will
probably not be recovered. Its serial number is not yet known.

(b) L-4 44-80393 (59-V) was picked up by 32nd FA Bgde for 79th FA Bn (to replace its L-5, still in the lake).

(c) L-4 44-80159 (62-G) was supplied to 252nd FA Gp as a replacement for 44-80609, wrecked May 12.

(d) L-4 44-80406 (62-E) was supplied to 754th FA Bn as a replacement for 44-79741, wrecked May 12.

(2) Maj. Lefever called concerning:

(a) Replacement aircraft. 'Can you let 15th Army have four to replace some blown away. The three NUSA crack-ups at their 27th MR&RS are not yet ready.' Answer: Yes. Have them pick them up at B-22 Jena from Lt Sharp.

(b) L-5s. Only 21 are still left on the Continent (in crates). ETOUSA says these will be assembled and divided between all armies.

(3) 102nd Inf Div Asst Arty Air Officer, Capt. Meehan, visited CP. He stated that 113th Evac Hospital had been placed 'Off Limits' to their pilots and a 500ft ceiling established in its vicinity. (This is the Hospital where the nurses 'provoked' the pilots into buzzing their quarters.)

(4) XXIX TAC (Lt Covert) visited our Operations trailer and informed us that XXIX TAC was 'taking over' at B-38 (our present field) and that only the main runway could be used for landing and taking off. This means we can't continue to use our own private little strip in front of our barn and that the larger strip which we have been using at times will become a taxi strip to the main runway.

May 19

(1) XIII Corps Arty Air Officer has issued an order calling for a weekly training schedule to be set up in all Air Sections. The schedule includes two hours of air work (stalls, spins, etc.), two hours of short field procedure, one hour power-off landings, and one cross-country flight not to exceed 100 miles.

(2) Maj. Thornton, Fifteenth Army Arty Air Officer, called. He doesn't need the four aircraft requested from us.

May 20

(1) 30th Div reported L-4 43-30498 (44-F) damaged by a wind storm on May 17. Lt Helms to pick up at R-99 [almost certainly this should be Y-99 (Gütersloh)] and prepare 43-30479 as a replacement.

(2) Lt Atkins, 84th Inf Div, reported a left wing damaged on an aircraft by high winds. Lt Helms to deliver a left wing to the 84th Inf Div strip.

(3) Lt Helms reported that L-4 44-79716 has been lent to 777th FA Bn while 44-80333 is being repaired.

(4) XXIX TAC Flying Control, Sgt Sperry, reported that some stolen Cubs had been located near A-92 St Trond, that they might be ours, and that we can obtain more detailed information from A-92. Lt Helms to visit A-92, find out details and notify units concerned to 'go get 'em' and to turn in the ones we lent them.

May 22

(1) Maj. Lefever called re:

(a) the 14 aircraft at Jena. Can we release them to Air Forces for their use? Will release 10 for them.

(b) Brodie Devices. 'There are two on the Continent. Construction crew won't arrive for another month. Is it OK with you if we don't give any to NUSA, but furnish them to Third and Seventh US Armies?' Answer: OK.

(2) XVI Corps Arty Air Officer, Maj. Hallstein, reported that all Air OP Sections which had been with the British had returned.

(3) 29th Inf Div pilot, Lt Fullerson, visited the CP. He stated that if his stolen aircraft is returned, he would still prefer to keep 42-15286, which we lent him as a replacement. Told him to see Lt Helms and that the transfer was OK with us, but we'd like him to assist us in returning the stolen aircraft from A-92 St Trond.

(4) 125th LS moved again (we've lost track of the score) from R-38 Brunswick (Broitzem), south of town, to R-37 Brunswick (Waggum), north of town. CO 125th, Capt. O'Brien, stated that 125th and 153rd LSs are operating a joint operation at R-37. He would like to retain the ten L-4s which we lent him, but agreed to ferry them to Y-56 München-Gladbach when he no longer needs them. He complained bitterly of lack of support by 50th MR&RS.

May 23

(1) Fifteenth Army Asst Air Officer asked if we could still let them have four L-4s from Jena. Told him that we had only two left here but we would release four at Bielefeld if he sent for them.

(2) 777th FA Bn pilot, Lt Schlacter, called to report that they would like to keep the aircraft lent to Lt Stockwell to replace the one stolen. Told him this was OK with us but he should check with Lt Helms to arrange the trade after having flown back the stolen aircraft (allegedly found at A-92 St Trond) to Bielefeld.

May 25

(1) Lt Sharp at Jena reported that the following L-4s were to be released to Air Forces: 44-79924, 43-30164, 43-29657, 43-30066, 43-29780, 43-30051, 43-29663, 44-80523, 44-80285, 43-933. L-4 43-30027 lent to 183rd Bn while 43-29809 is being repaired.

(2) The long-sought-after L-4 44-79949 (82-X) is believed to be at 27th MR&RS. Lt Helms will check with them.

May 26

(1) XVI Corps Arty Air O, Maj. Hallstein, reported that his assistant, Capt. Williamson, was accidentally killed on May 25 by his own pistol.

(2) Typical of missions carried out at this time by the NUSA Arty Air Section, the following were flown on May 26:

Pilot	Passenger	Remarks
Lt Kershaw	Sgt Marcus	To 104th Div, Halle.
Lt Donnelly	Pvt. Totell	To Maastricht – canceled.

Lt Isabell	T/5 Van Slyke	To Maastricht – remained overnight.
Capt. Zicard	–	To Breda.
Lt Col. Leich	Col. Hanley	To VIII Corps.
Lt Donnelly	Officer from HQ Cmdnt	To a destination not known.
Lt Col. Leich	Capt. Mathews	From Hildesheim.
Lt Lynch	Capt. Scannell	From Hildesheim.
Lt Sinex	Lt Sanders	From Hildesheim.

May 28

(1) 104th Inf Div Asst Arty Air Officer, Capt. Morris, and XIII Corps Asst Arty Air Officer, Lt Gerrish, asked about the disposition of their aircraft. Told to bring their L-5 here and to turn in L-4s to 16th ADG at Y-56 München-Gladbach, after letting Lt Helms check them (for completeness of records and condition) at 50th MR&RS, Bielefeld.

(2) 'Gypsy' Flying Control (XXIX TAC) reported that an L-4 had been seen by two British flyers on an airstrip 1.5 miles due east of the city of Magdeburg. The strip was guarded by the Russians and the L-4 in question had white markings on the side. No aircraft are known to be missing in this area.

(3) 548th FA Bn CO, Lt Col. Kerr, and pilot, Lt Carriog, visited the Section after landing downhill on the strip next to CP, ground looping 10 yards from the end of the strip to miss a man walking across the yard and wrapped the aircraft up between two trees. The pilot landed in spite of the fact that a red cross was on the field at the time, which he thought indicated a hospital. The wrecked L-4, 44-79954, was taken to our strip at Braunschweig to be picked up by the 50th MR&RS while Lt Carriog was given a new aircraft, 43-29082, to continue his trip to Third Army.

(4) 3rd Armd Div turned in L-5 42-98528, which was replaced by L-4 43-30178, as they had two L-5s. The L-5 will be turned over to the 119th Gp, XIX Corps, when it has received some minor repairs.

(5) 83rd Inf Div traded in war weary L-4s 44-80061, 43-29793, and 43-30287 at 16th ADG for new ships 45-4518, 42-15233 and 42-36787.

May 29

(1) XVI Corps Arty Air Officer, Maj. Hallstein, reported an accident in 219th FA Gp when Capt. Ray, while practicing stalls, had an engine failure and in the process of a forced landing nosed over, wrecking the aircraft. No further details known.

(2) Col. Miller, Sec C/S, asked if we could furnish an aircraft and pilot for a passenger run between Bad Nauheim and Coburg. No pilots available, but agreed to furnish 125th LS an L-4 if they would provide a pilot for the run. 125th LS, Capt. O'Brien, agreed to this and will pick up 43-30229 from our Pool here tomorrow.

(3) 76th Inf Div reported the loss of an aircraft, but no one injured. No other details known.

(4) 8th Armd Div turned in an excess L-4, 43-30282, which had been replaced by an L-5.

(5) L-5 42-98523 will be ready to assign 31 May and will go to 119th FA Gp, XIX Corps.

May 30

(1) Maj. Lefever called to inform us that the 50th MR&RS at Bielefeld is under the 42nd ADG at Ansbach, and for the moment all aircraft will be turned into the 50th.

(2) 236th Ferrying Squadron brought in five L-5Es. They will go to the 407th, 18th and 208th FA Gps and XIX Corps.

May 31

(1) Lt Helms was unable to find anyone in vicinity of Neckum knowing anything about reported wreck of an aircraft there. He also reported the exchange of the following war wearies and those issued as replacements for wrecks: ·

Unit	War weary and wrecked	Replacement
265th Bn	43-30044	44-1635*
763rd Bn	43-30287	43-36354
84th Div	44-30124 (stolen)	44-79639
351st Bn	43-30004	43-29163
637th Bn	43-29739	45-4520

(2) 79th Inf Div reported the loss of two aircraft, 43-89860* (46-R) and 43-30523, when one aircraft crashed into the other on the ground after the throttle had been opened as the pilots climbed into the planes. [*These serial numbers, as given in the journal, are incorrect; 43-89860 was actually a Republic P-47 and 44-1635 was allocated to a North American B-25 but not taken up as the order was cancelled.]

(3) 219th FA Gp reported wreck of 44-80395 caused when pilot failed to land in correct field after motor failed at 3500ft. The aircraft was replaced by 44-80388.

June 2

(1) Lt Helms, 50th MR&RS Rear, reported the crack up of L-4 43-30486 by 70th FA Bn, pilot Lt Valdez, when the aircraft, while being started, got away from the pilot and ran into a fence.

(2) Lt Sharp, 50th MR&RS Forward, reported bringing in the 76th Inf Div L-4 44-80503, to be salvaged.

(3) The 83rd Armd FA Bn replaced war weary aircraft 42-95114* with 43-29187 at Y-56 München-Gladbach. [*This serial number is incorrect; 42-95114 was actually a B-24H Liberator heavy bomber.]

(4) 95th FA Bn pilot, Lt Towner, reported cracking up L-4H 43-29776 when he landed in a field with tall grass that nosed him over. Lt Towner said he had not dragged the field before landing.

June 3

Message from SHAEF authorizing flights of Focke Wulf 44, Fieseler Storch and other German aircraft to substitute for shortage of liaison type aircraft. Suggested no action in view of Army order preventing use of these planes because of shortage of proper equipment and lack of experience and knowledge of Arty pilots.

June 4 [shown in the journal as June 3, presumably in error]

(1) Lt Helms, 50th Rear, reported crack-up of 84th Inf Div pilot Lt Clayton, when he landed in a field covered with high grass and aircraft went over on its back. Aircraft turned in to 27th MR&RS, but no further particulars known.

(2) The phantom wreck of the 84th Inf Div L-4 44-80241 which the MR&RS sent trucks to three locations and was unable to find and which was finally surveyed by the 84th Div, turned up many miles from any reported coordinates, and was in very small pieces.

(3) 265th FA Bn pilot, Lt Greer, called to report the crack up of L-4 43-30503 by Lt Morgan, the other pilot in the Bn, at the Hillersleben Proving Grounds. The engine quit while on an approach into the field, when the carb heat was applied suddenly. Only a few feet were needed to reach the field, but the aircraft cracked up on a rock pile and was completely wrecked.

June 6

(1) Lt Hogan, this Section, reported that he had cracked up 30 miles south of Jena on landing in a soft field, when he went over on his back. Lt Hogan was not hurt and said he would pick up the plane today with help of the 50th MR&RS and fly it back tomorrow.

(2) 50th MMR&RS reported five aircraft on the ground due lack of props. These aircraft are in the Army Pool. The 50th has been unable to get props from either the 16th or 42nd ADG.

June 7 [incorrectly shown in the journal as May 7]

(1) Six L-4s of the Arty Air Section were damaged by wind and hail in a storm that broke very suddenly yesterday afternoon. Damage as follows:

44-80107 – Ring worms on fuselage, flyable.

44-80196 –   ”   ”   ”

43-30401 –   ”   ”   ”

43-30373 (63-A) – Rudder, longerons, both wings, engine mounts damaged.

43-36504 (63-G) – Right wing, elevators, top pyralin, cabane V, damaged.

44-80535 (63-E) – Tail assembly, right wing, longerons, damaged.

Three aircraft were torn loose from their moorings by high winds when the ropes broke or the strut fittings were torn out of the wing spars. XXIX TAC Weather volunteered the information that they knew the wind was coming and were sorry they had not notified us.

(2) Lt Helms, 50th MR&RS Rear, reported 12 aircraft AOG at Bielefeld because of lack of props.

(3) 42nd ADG (Ansbach) reported that they would be unable to supply L-4 or L-5 parts for two to three weeks.

(4) XIX Corps Arty Air Officer, Maj. Reed, reported the location of wrecked aircraft 79-(E?) belonging to III Corps, Third Army.

(5) XXIX TAC, Maj. Childs, called to report more violations by Arty aircraft to traffic regulations at R-38 Brunswick. Asked Maj. Childs if anyone had anything to do at the field but check Arty aircraft as we had received reports of violations from at least five different sources and had yet to receive any written instructions on use of the field.

June 8

(1) 125th LS CO, Capt. O'Brien, reported squadron is leaving the HQ except for one flight and that Col. Miller, Sec C/S, would like to keep the eleven L-4s of ours they now have, using nine pilots assigned NUSA from 12th Army Gp to fly them.

(2) VII Corps Arty Air Officer, Maj. Miller, reported crack-up of 7th Armd Div L-5 44-17194. It was reportedly caused by engine failure. No injuries.

(3) XXIX Corps Asst Arty Air Officer, Lt Gerrish, asked about disposition of their aircraft. Told to turn them in to 50th MR&RS at Bielefeld.

(4) 50th MR&RS, Lt Sharp, reported that no L-4 props or gaskets were available for issue to units.

June 9

(1) VII Corps Arty Air Officer, Maj. Miller, asked about disposition of his aircraft and where he was to turn them in. He also wanted to know if he could take his L-5 to the departure port and then have a unit pilot come and get it. Told him to turn in aircraft to 50th MR&RS at Jena. L-5 should also be turned in to 50th at Jena before unit leaves present area.

(2) 125th LS CO, Capt. O'Brien and Lt Heineman, observer, visited Section to ask again about 11 L-4s with the squadron. Lt Heineman will maintain L-4s and then turn them in to the 50th MR&RS when and if HQ moves.

June 10

(1) 32nd FA Bgde Asst Arty Air Officer, Capt. Maxwell, reported that 79th FA Gp had picked up an L-5E from the airstrip at Marburg, where it had been abandoned supposedly by the XXIX TAC. The aircraft s/n was 42-99282. Told to turn in the L-5 to the 50th MR&RS at Bielefeld and we will try to find out who it belongs to.

(2) 95th Inf Div Arty Air Officer, Maj. Blaha, asked what to do with his aircraft as his G-4 had told him to turn them in to Y-56 München-Gladbach. Told him they should all go to 50th MR&RS at Bielefeld.

(3) Lt Col. R. M. Leich returned from a most eventful leave.

June 11

(1) 104th Inf Div pilot, Lt Potts, reported they were in process of turning in all their L-4 aircraft to the 50th MR&RS at Bielefeld and their L-5 to VII Corps (188th FA Gp). The Div pilots were then going to try to visit Paris en route to port.

(2) Lt Helms, 50th MR&RS Rear, reported that the 50th had received instructions from 9th Air Force that all aircraft were to be turned in to 50th MR&RS and then ferried by Arty pilots to 42nd ADG, Ansbach, and the Air Corps would furnish transportation for the ferry pilots. Lt Helms also reported that XXIX Corps and the 104th and 95th Divs had arrived at Bielefeld with all their aircraft to turn them in. Called 12th Army Gp, Maj. Lefever, and asked him to facilitate transfer of aircraft from 50th to 42nd ADG as we haven't any pilots available.

Assigned L-5 turned in by 95th Inf Div (44-17169) to 76 Inf Div. Requested Div to furnish five ferry pilots to ferry aircraft from Bielefeld to Ansbach.

(3) Lt Sharp, this HQ, reported the death of 326th Ferrying Group pilot, Capt. Hester, when he hit some high tension wires while flying an L-5 and crashed.

June 12

(1) L-5 42-99282 abandoned supposedly by XXIX TAC is assigned to 79th FA Gp, replacing the L-5 lost at the bottom of the lake.

(2) Lt Crockatt, 7th Armd Div, came in for the location of L-5 42-98520 (50th MR&RS) which is being lent to them.

(3) 87th Div Arty Air Officer, Maj. Schirmacher, one of the very original Grasshoppers, visited this section for the last time before going west.

June 13

(1) Told Lt Heineman, 125th LS, that we were assigning the 11 L-4s which were lent to the 125th. He does not want them, so the aircraft will be ferried to the 50th MR&RS as soon as the weather permits.

(2) Attempted to have planes ferried from Jena to Bielefeld, but weather interfered.

(3) 549th FA Bn pilot, Lt Phillips, reported -4 44-80548 damaged by hailstones. Aircraft replaced by 44-79423.

June 14

(1) Aircraft at Jena were flown to the main unit of the 50th MR&RS.

(2) CO of the Rest Center at Heerlen requested another L-4 and pilot for the purpose of shuttling CG of NUSA and his aide to Maastricht. Action: Lt Hogan will join Capt. Scannell at Heerlen on June 14.

(3) Lt Helms reported that 8th Inf Div has turned in its aircraft to the 50th MR&RS.

(4) VIII Corps Arty Air Officer, Maj. Houser, reported that the 87th Inf Div has turned in its aircraft to 42nd ADG and the assignment of L-5s as follows: 44-17481 to 203rd FA Gp; 44-17328 (turned in by 87th Inf Div) to 402nd FA Gp.

June 15

(1) Lt Col. Leich and Capt. Mathews returned from visits to XIX Cops Arty, HQ 12th Army Gp (Wiesbaden), Third Army (Bad Tolz), Seventh Army (Augsburg) and 42nd ADG (Ansbach), to discuss Air OP matters. The following decisions were made:

(a) That 50th MR&RS was no longer required by NUSA (or Third or Seventh Armies) and is available to IX AFSC, effective at once.

(b) That two L-5s of HQ NUSA Arty Section would be available to Seventh Army and two to XIX Corps, when we are ready.

(c) That Air Forces would be notified by 12th Army Gp to pick up flyable L-4s at 50th MR&RS, 125th LS and NUSA Arty Air strip.

(d) That Seventh Army Arty Air Officer (Lt Col. Shepherd) would notify us of disposition of excess pilots in NUSA HQ (Capt. Scannell and Lt Capps).

(2) Met 87th Inf Div Arty Air Officer, Maj. Schirmacher, at Y-44 (42nd ADG). He stated that 9 L-4s had been turned in to 42nd ADG there and that one L-5 had been turned over to VIII Corps Arty.

(3) 12th Army Gp Arty Air Officer, Maj. Lefever, was notified of 26 aircraft at 50th MR&RS, six aircraft at 125th LS, and five aircraft at NUSA, available for Air Forces to pick up.

(4) Capt. Johnson, XIX Corps Asst Arty Air Officer, reported the crack-up of 228th FA Gp's L-4 44-80597 at Spa, Belgium. Asked if 27th MR&RS would pick it up. Called Lt Col. Thornton, 15th US Army Arty Air Officer, who stated that the 27th MR&RS would do so.

June 16
(1) L-5 44-17361 assigned to 18th FA Gp.
(2) The following is a consolidated list of all accidents of the Ninth US Army during its period of operation:

Month	Hrs Flown	Take-off	Landing	Injured Pilot	Obs	Elements	E/A	Injured Pilot	Obs	Ground fire	Injured Pilot C	
Oct	3648						1					
Nov	4284	2	7				2					
Dec	3755		7	1						3	1	2
Jan	3906	4	5							2	2	
Feb	5768	5	3	1			1	1	1	8	3	1
Mar	9316	2 (Sabotage)	4				9	7	4	5	2	
April	15257	12	10	1	1	1	12	4	2		2	
May	19456	8	5	2	5		1			1		
June	?	3	4	1		7						3
Totals		36	45	6	6	8	26	12	7	19	10	

June 17

(1) Lt Helms returned from 50th MR&RS, Bielefeld, and will be assigned to 76th Inf Div.

(2) Lts Isabell and Harris departed to join 3rd Armd Div and 203rd FA Bn respectively.

(3) Lt Sharp departed to join 2nd Armd Div Arty.

(4) Lt Kershaw returned from Gütersloh and will join HQ 228th FA Gp.

June 18

(1) Lt Kershaw departed in L-4J 45-4549, instructed to turn it in at Ansbach after arriving at 228th Gp.

(2) Lt Harris returned from 203rd FA Bn and was requested to turn in L-4A 43-29130 to Ansbach and also to notify Lt Isabell, 34th Div, to turn in 43-30205 to the same place.

(3) Capt. Zicard ferried aircraft to Bielefeld.

June 20

Lt Col. Leich returned from visit to VIII Corps Arty (Bad Salzburg), VI Corps Arty (Gmund), Seventh Army (Augsburg), Third Army (Bad Tolz) and 12th Army Gp (Wiesbaden), having, together with Capts Mathews and Zicard, delivered all the gear of Capt. Scannell and Lt Capps to VI Corps airstrip.

June 22

Capts Mathews and Zicard delivered our original L-5B, 44-16731 (63-AA) 'The Skipper', to Seventh Army Arty Airstrip (Augsburg). Now we have three.

Appendix 1

Headquarters Ninth US Army – Locations, April 1944-April 1945

1944

15 April:	Activated as Eighth US Army at Fort Sam Houston, Texas.
11 May:	Advance Party of the Army Headquarters flew to the UK.
22 May:	Redesignated Ninth US Army (to avoid possible confusion with the British Eighth Army).
10 June:	Main body of the Army HQ departed Fort Sam Houston.
12 June:	Main body arrived at Camp Shanks, New York.
22 June:	Main body sailed from New York City on the *Queen Elizabeth*.
28 June:	Main body disembarked at Gourock, near Glasgow, and moved by train to Bristol to join the Advance Party.
29 June:	Army HQ (Command Post) opened at Clifton College, Bristol.
27 August:	Army HQ initiated movement from Bristol to France.
29 August:	Army Command Post (CP) opened at Saint-Sauveur-Lendelin.
30 August:	Rear echelon of Army HQ opened at Périers.
3 September:	Army CP opened at Mi-Forêt, near Rennes.
4 September:	Rear echelon of HQ opened at Mi-Forêt.
5 September:	NUSA became operational at 12 noon, taking over from the Third Army the assault on Brest and the protection of the south flank of 12th Army Group along the Loire River. Units now under command of NUSA were VIII Corps with the 2nd, 8th, 29th and 83rd Infantry Divisions and 6th Armored Division.
2 October:	Army CP opened at Arlon, Belgium.
4 October:	NUSA with VIII Corps and the 2nd and 8th Infantry Divisions took over the sector between the First and Third Armies.
14 October:	Rear echelon opened at Maastricht (Wijk), Netherlands.
22 October:	Army CP opened at Maastricht. VIII Corps, with the 2nd, 8th and 83rd Inf Divs and the 9th Armored Div, passed to control of the First Army. XIX Corps, with the 29th and 30th Inf Divs and the 2nd Armored Div, passed from the First to the Ninth Army.
8 November:	XIII Corps became operational with NUSA at 12.01 a.m., assuming command of the 84th and 102nd Infantry Divs.
20 December:	NUSA placed the under the control of British 21st Army Group.

1945

10 March:	Army CP opened at München-Gladbach.
20 March:	Rear echelon opened at Rheydt.
4 April:	NUSA reverted to US 12th Army Group. Army CP opened at Haltern.
11 April:	Hanover cleared by XIII Corps.
12 April:	Army CP opened at Gütersloh.
18 April:	Rear echelon opened at Münster.
23 April:	Army CP opened at Brunswick.

Appendix 2

The Ninth US Army – Units equipped with liaison aircraft, 12 September 1944

HQ Ninth Army, Arty HQ Air Section (unit code markings 63)
Attached to HQ NUSA: 125th LS (HQ Flight and C Flight) (no unit code markings carried)
III Corps Arty HQ
  10th Armd Div Arty HQ (unit code markings 78)
      419th Armd FA Bn
      420th Armd FA Bn
      423rd Armd FA Bn
  26th Inf Div Arty HQ (unit code markings 74)
      101st FA Bn
      102nd FA Bn
      263rd FA Bn
      180th FA Bn
  44th Inf Div Arty HQ
      156th FA Bn
      217th FA Bn
      220th FA Bn
      157th FA Bn
  95th Inf Div Arty HQ
      358th FA Bn
      359th FA Bn
      920th FA Bn
      360th FA Bn
  102nd Inf Div Arty HQ (unit code markings 76)
      379th FA Bn
      380th FA Bn
      927th FA Bn
      381st FA Bn
  104th Inf Div Arty HQ
      385th FA Bn
      386th FA Bn
      929th FA Bn
      387th FA Bn

Attached to HQ III Corps: 125th LS (one Flight) (no unit code markings carried)

VII Corps Arty HQ (unit code markings 26)

    6th Armd Div Arty HQ (unit code markings 55)

        128th Armd FA Bn

        212th Armd FA Bn

        231st Armd FA Bn

    2nd Inf Div Arty HQ (unit code markings 25)

        15th FA Bn

        37th FA Bn

        38th FA Bn

        12th FA Bn

    8th Inf Div Arty HQ (unit code markings 38)

        43rd FA Bn

        45th FA Bn

        56th FA Bn

        28th FA Bn

    29th Inf Div Arty HQ (unit code markings 43)

        110th FA Bn

        111th FA Bn

        224th FA Bn

        227th FA Bn

    83rd Inf Div Arty HQ (unit code markings 47)

        322nd FA Bn

        323rd FA Bn

        908th FA Bn

  324th FA Bn

Attached to HQ VII Corps: 125th LS (one Flight) (no unit code markings carried)

XIII Corps Arty HQ (unit code markings 68)

    9th Armd Div Arty HQ (unit code markings 67)

        3rd Armd FA Bn

        16th Armd FA Bn

        73rd Armd FA Bn

    94th Inf Div Arty HQ (unit code markings 65)

        301st FA Bn

        56th FA Bn

        919th FA Bn

        390th FA Bn

Attached to HQ XIII Corps: 125th LS (one Flight) (no unit code markings carried)

Appendix 3

50th Mobile Reclamation and Repair Squadron – Ninth US Army aircraft serviced, 6 November 1944-31 May 1945

Notes:

1. This appendix is based on the records and official history of the 50th Mobile Reclamation and Repair Squadron. As part of the 42nd Air Depot Group, IX Air Force Service Command, this unit was responsible for the major servicing, repair and salvage of liaison aircraft assigned or attached to the Ninth US Army. As in the original records, the dates given here cover the period from 1700 hours on the day indicated to 1700 hours the previous day.

2. It has not been possible to locate some of the places named in the original records and this is probably due to incorrect spelling. Prunssum, for example, should almost certainly be Brunssum, while Hunnicum, Eioich, Engleshoven and Brochelen are also suspect.

3. Some aircraft movements to and from the 50th MR&RS went unmentioned in the original records, and this is reflected here when an aircraft appears to have been received on two occasions with no interim departure. Other entries show two successive delivery flights, with no indication of the aircraft having been received between them.

4. In addition to abbreviations listed in the main text, the following are used in this appendix:

CC	Crash crew pick-up
Del	Delivered (to the unit shown)
MR	Mobile Reclamation and Repair Squadron
Rec	Received (from the unit shown)
Rpr	Repair
Salv	Salvaged
s/n	Serial number

Aircraft s/n	Type	Unit	Movement details
40-3111	L-1C	125th LS	Del 23.3.45
41-19018	L-1A	45th ADG	Rec 3.3.45; Del 4.3.45
42-15285	L-4A	45th ADG	Rec 31.3.45
42-15286	L-4A	NUSA	Del 4.5.45
42-16713*	L-5B	125th LS	Rec 5.4.45

[*This serial number, as given in unit records, is incorrect; 42-16713 was actually a Stearman PT-17. Almost certainly the correct serial number was 44-16713.]

Aircraft s/n	Type	Unit	Movement details
42-36442	L-4A	125th LS	Del 3.5.45
42-36766	L-4A	45th ADG	Rec 31.3.45; Del NUSA 10.5.45

42-98522	L-5A	32nd FA Bn	Rec 13.5.45; Del 19.5.45
42-98987	L-5	–	Rec for Rpr 30.12.44; Del 125th LS 25.5.45
42-99007	L-5	153rd LS	Rec 24.5.45
42-99052	L-5	47th TAC	Rec and Del 29.5.45
42-99114	L-5	125th LS	Rec 30.4.05; Del 10.5.45; Rec 22.5.45
42-99116	L-5	125th LS	Del 3.1.45; Rec 31.1.45; Del 1.2.45; Rec 5.4.45
42-99284	L-5	125th LS	Rec and Salv 15.1.45
42-99285	L-5	125th LS	CC from Maastricht 14.11.44; Del 1.12.44
42-99292	L-5	125th LS	Del 26.12.44
42-99301	L-5	125th LS	CC from Herrlan, France, 1.11.44
42-99303	L-5	125th LS	CC from Kornelimünster, Germany, 7.1.45; Del 4.2.45
42-99306	L-5	125th LS	Del 16.12.45
42-99311	L-5	125th LS	Rec 21.1.45; Del 31.1.45
42-99347	L-5	125th LS	Rec 1.3.45; Del 9.3.45
42-99351	L-5	125th LS	Rec 5.12.44; Del 6.12.44; Rec 6.5.45; Del 16th ADG 13.5.45
42-99355	L-5	125th LS	Rec 13.5.45; Del 28.5.45
43-701	L-4B	9th Engnr Cmd	Rec 29.3.45; Del 30.3.45; Rec 3.4.45; Del 6.4.45
43-889	L-4B	22nd Ftr Sq 36thtServ Gp	CC 12 miles from Maastricht 1.11.44
43-891	L-4B	NUSA	Del 3.5.45
43-933	L-4B	23rd MR	Rec 19.5.45; Del 10th ADG 28.5.45
43-986	L-4B	125th LS	Del 2.5.45
43-1313	L-4B	125th LS	Del 2.5.45
43-1341	L-4B	125th LS	Del 3.5.45
43-1428	L-4B	125th LS	Del 3.5.45
43-29052	L-4A	125th LS	Del 2.5.45
43-29082	L-4A	45th ADG	Rec 31.3.45; Del NUSA 4.5.45; Rec and Del 6.5.45
43-29093	L-4A	45th ADG	Rec 31.3.45; Del NUSA 4.5.45
43-29115	L-4A	45th ADG	Rec 31.3.45
43-29126	L-4A	45th ADG	Rec 31.3.45; Del NUSA 4.5.45
43-29130	L-4A	45th ADG	Rec 31.3.45; Del NUSA 19.5.45
43-29180	L-4A	45th ADG	Rec 31.3.45
43-29195	L-4A	45th ADG	Rec 31.3.45
43-29487	L-4H	23rd MR	Rec 14.3.45
43-29502	L-4H	258th FA Bn	CC from Maubach, Germany, 27.12.44; Del 3.1.45; Rec and Del 28.3.45; Rec 24.4.45; Del 26.4.45

43-29507	L-4H	2nd Armd Div	Rec 7.12.44; Del 9.12.44
43-29512	L-4H	78th FA Bn	Rec and Del 4.12.44; Rec 5.12.44; Del 6.12.44; Rec 2nd Armd Div 13.12.44; Del 20.12.44
43-29607	L-4H	78th FA Bn	Del 9.12.44
43-29622	L-4H	695th FA Bn	Rec and Salv 2.5.45
43-29629	L-4H	65th FA Gp	Rec 1.12.44; Del 8th Inf Div 26.12.44
43-29634	L-4H	774th FA Bn	Rec 14.2.45; Del 15.2.45
43-29638	L-4H	258th FA Gp	Del 7.2.45
43-29642	L-4H	2nd Armd Div	CC from Prunssum 11.11.44 (see Note 2)
43-29647	L-4H	XIX Corps	Rec 3.4.45; Del 959th FA Bn 11.5.45
43-29657	L-4H	23rd MR	Rec 19.5.45, Del 10th ADG 28.5.45
43-29662	L-4H	258th FA Gp	Rec and Del 22.12.44; Rec 7.2.45; Del 8.2.45; Rec 14.2.45; Del 15.2.45; Rec 23.3.45; Del 24.3.45; Rec and Del 6.5.45; Rec 28.5.45
43-29663	L-4H	23rd MR	Rec 19.5.45
43-29667	L-4H	78th FA Bn	Rec 5.12.44; Rec from NUSA 15.2.45; Del 16.2.45; Rec and Del 14.3.45
43-29669	L-4H	35th Inf Div	Rec 29.3.45; Rec 2.5.45; Del 125th LS 3.5.45
43-29709	L-4H	203rd FA Bn	Rec and Del 2.1.45
43-29731 (32-E)	L-4H	228th FA Gp	CC from Eioich 3.3.45 (see Note 2)
43-29756	L-4H	196th FA Gp	Rec and Del 10.1.45
43-29768	L-4H	2nd Armd Div	Rec 26.2.45; Rec from 102nd FA Bn 26.4.45; Del NUSA 10.5.45
43-29770	L-4H	203rd FA Bn	Rec and Del 9.1.45
43-29774	L-4H	25th FA Bn	Del 13.3.45; Rec from 252nd FA Gp 16.5.45; Del 29.5.45
43-29778	L-4H	23rd MR	Rec 14.3.45; Rec from 695th FA Bn and Del 26.3.45; Rec and Del 13.5.45
43-29780	L-4H	23rd MR	Rec 19.5.45; Del 10th ADG 28.5.45
43-29783	L-4H	696th FA Bn	Del 2.5.45
43-29791	L-4H	NUSA	Rec and Salv 6.3.45
43-29810	L-4H	228th FA Bn	Rec 8.12.44; Del 9.12.44; Rec 28.12.44; Del 104th Inf Div 20.1.45
43-29830	L-4H	797th FA Bn	Rec and Del 26.12.44
43-29831	L-4H	258th FA Bn	CC from Hunnicum 29.10.44 (see Note 2); Rec and Del 31.5.45
43-29845	L-4H	489th FA Bn	Rec 15.12.44; Del 16.12.44; Del 18.12.44
43-29850	L-4H	79th Inf Div	Rec 23.5.45; Del 24.5.45
43-29905	L-4H	5th Armd Div	Rec 2.5.45; Del 125th LS 2.5.45
43-29968	L-4H	793rd FA Bn	Rec 3.5.45; Del NUSA 10.5.45

43-29996	L-4H	32nd FA Bn	Rec and Del 26.5.45
43-30002	L-4H	7th Armd Div	Rec 19.5.45; Del 31.5.45
43-30004	L-4H	23rd MR	Rec 14.3.45
43-30013	L-4H	2nd Armd Div	Rec 11.3.45; Del 75th Inf Div 2.5.45
43-30018	L-4H	29th Inf Div	Rec 26.4.45; Del 30.4.45; Rec and Del 11.5.45; Rec and Del 26.5.45
43-30021	L-4H	29th Inf Div	CC from Engleshoven 18.11.44 (see Note 2)
43-30022	L-4H	23rd MR	Rec 14.3.45; Del 2nd Armd Div 3.4.45; Rec 4.5.45; Del 5.5.45
43-30027	L-4H	23rd MR	Rec 19.5.45; Del 10th ADG 28.5.45
43-30040	L-4H	29th Inf Div	Rec and Del 21.1.45; Del 5.3.45
43-30044	L-4H	NUSA	Rec and Del 15.5.45
43-30046	L-4H	202nd FA Gp	Rec 12.1.45; Del 17.1.45
43-30051	L-4H	XIX Corps	Rec 2.12.44; Del 5.12.44; Rec 26.1.45; Del 6.2.45
43-30061 (54-C)	L-4H	5th Armd Div	CC from Herrath, Germany; Rec and Del NUSA 27.4.45; Rec 2.5.45; Del 3.5.45; Rec 12.5.45
43-30066	L-4H	23rd MR	Rec 19.5.45; Del 10th ADG 28.5.45
43-30078	L-4H	29th Inf Div	Rec 19.2.45; Del 21.2.45; Rec 2.3.45
43-30086	L-4H	793rd FA Gp	Rec 6.12.44
43-30096	L-4H	793rd FA Gp	Del 8.12.44
43-30106	L-4H	29th Inf Div	Rec 5.5.45; Del 7.5.45
43-30157	L-4H	265th FA Bn	Rec 8.12.44
43-30164	L-4H	23rd MR	Rec 19.5.45; Del 16th ADG 28.5.45
43-30178	L-4H	23rd MR	Rec 19.5.45
43-30186	L-4H	83rd Inf Div	Rec 24.12.44; Del 25.12.44
43-30195	L-4H	NUSA	Rec and Del 15.5.45; Del 35th Inf Div 15.5.45; Rec 24.5.45; Del 26.5.45
43-30200	L-4H	23rd MR	Rec 14.3.45; Del 2nd Armd Div 4.4.45; Rec and Del 11.5.45
43-30205	L-4H	65th FA Bn.	Rec 26.4.45; Del 30.4.45
43-30206	L-4H	29th Inf Div	Rec 28.3.45; Rec and Del 7.5.45
43-30207	L-4H	NUSA	Del 7.12.44; Rec 20.12.44; damaged in an air raid on the 50th MR&RS airstrip 1.1.45; Del 909th FA Bn 9.3.45
43-30211	L-4H	202nd FA Gp	Rec 10.1.45; Del 12.1.45' Rec 17.1.45; Del 19.1.45; Rec 9.5.45; Del NUSA 17.5.45
43-30215	L-4H	959th FA Bn	Rec 5.3.45; Del 102nd Inf Div 24.3.45
43-30220	L-4H	30th Inf Div	Rec 1.3.45

43-30229	L-4H	2nd Armd Div	CC from Prunssum 11.11.44 (see Note 2); Del 102nd FA Gp 2.12.44
43-30235	L-4H	269th FA Bn	Rec and Del 21.1.45; Del NUSA 24.4.45
43-30236	L-4H	219th FA Bn	Rec and Del 26.3.45
43-30237	L-4H	557th FA Bn	CC from Verviers, France, 28.10.44; Rec from 753rd FA Gp 21.1.45, Del 22.1.45
43-30240	L-4H	30th Inf Div	Rec and Del 2.5.45
43-30244	L-4H	79th Inf Div	Del 28.4.45
43-30249	L-4H	5th Armd Div	Rec 13.2.45; Del 14.2.45
43-30252	L-4H	23rd MR	Rec 14.3.45; Rec from 959th FA Bn 11.5.45
43-30261	L-4H	NUSA	Rec and Del 4.2.45; Rec from 35th Inf Div 27.2.45; Del 28.2.45; Rec 31.3.45; Del 4.4.45; Rec 27.4.45; Del 2.5.45; Rec 12.5.45; Del 24.5.45; Rec 25.5.45; Del 28.5.45
43-30275	L-4H	NUSA	Rec 29.4.45; Del 79th Inf Div 2.5.45; Rec 24.5.45
43-30282	L-4H	NUSA	Del 5.4.45
43-30292	L-4H	78th Inf Div	Rec 15.1.45; Del 25.1.45
43-30296	L-4H	35th Inf Div	Rec 31.3.45; Del 4.4.45; Rec 10.5.45; Del 11.5.45
43-30298	L-4H	–	Salv 7.3.45
43-30300	L-4H	404th FA Gp	Rec 2.5.45; Del 3.5.45
43-30304	L-4H	256th FA Bn	CC from Terwinselen, Holland, 20.11.44
43-30318	L-4H	79th Inf Div	Rec 28.4.45; Del NUSA 14.5.45; Rec 17.5.45; Del 19.5.45
43-30337	L-4H	NUSA	Rec 3.2.45; Del 35th Inf Div 4.2.45; Rec 25.2.45; Del 161st Inf Div 27.2.45; Rec and Salv 14.5.45
43-30338	L-4H	NUSA	Rec 11.2.45; Del 13.2.45; Del 29th Inf Div 5.3.45; Rec and Del 9.3.45
43-30352	L-4H	7th Armd Div	CC from Asten, Holland, 1.11.44
43-30361	L-4H	83rd Inf Div	Rec 3.5.45; Del 10.5.45
43-30362	L-4H	119th FA Gp	Del 14.3.45
43-30373	L-4H	NUSA	Rec and Del 1.1.45; damaged in an air raid on the 50th MR&RS airstrip 1.1.45
43-30377	L-4H	349th FA Gp	Rec and Del 15.5.45
43-30385	L-4H	196th FA Gp	Del 25.4.45
43-30388	L-4H	83rd Inf Div	Rec 27.4.45; Del NUSA 10.5.45
43-30396	L-4H	XIII Corps	Rec and Del 2.12.44; Rec from 102nd Inf Div 11.2.45; Del 197th FA Gp 5.3.45; Salv 21.5.45

43-30401	L-4H	NUSA	Del 15.5.45
43-30406	L-4H	NUSA	Rec 3.2.45; Del 35th Inf Div 4.2.45; Rec 21.3.45; Del 23.3.45; Rec 4.4.45; Del 5.4.45
43-30407	L-4H	2nd FA Bn	Rec 15.3.45; Del 17.3.45
43-30411	L-4H	29th Inf Div	Rec and Del 9.3.45; Rec and Del 15.3.45
43-30420	L-4H	30th Inf Div	Rec and Del 10.12.44
43-30430	L-4H	30th Inf Div	Del 2.3.45
43-30444	L-4H	35th Inf Div	Rec 16.2.45; Del 161st FA Bn 21.2.45; Rec 35th Inf Div 26.4.45; Del 10.5.45
43-30454	L-4H	–	Rec and Del 7.1.45; Del 35th Inf Div 21.2.45; Rec and Del NUSA 14.3.45
43-30456	L-4H	70th FA Bn	Del 1.12.44; Rec 20.2.45; Del 774th FA Bn 23.2.45; Rec and Del 28.3.45; Rec and Del 692nd FA Bn 9.5.45
43-30464	L-4H	23rd MR	Rec 19.5.45
43-30471	L-4H	691st FA Bn	Rec 10.12.44; Del 252nd FA Bn 10.12.44; CC from 691st FA Bn (no location given) 27.12.44; Del 27.12.44; Rec 27.1.45; Del 28.1.45
43-30486	L-4H	70th FA Bn	Rec and Del 24.3.45; Rec 12.5.45; Del 13.5.45
43-30495	L-4H	2nd Armd Div	CC from Maubach, Germany, 14.11.44; Del 65th FA Gp 2.12.44
43-30497	L-4H	23rd MR	Rec 14.3.45; Del (no location given) 26.3.45
43-30499	L-4H	211th FA Bn	Rec 6.12.44; Del 8.12.44; Del 25.4.45
43-30503	L-4H	265th FA Bn	Rec and Del 14.2.45; Del 26.4.45
43-30508	L-4H	7th Armd Div	Rec 9.12.44; Del 10.12.44
43-30509	L-4H	49th FA Bn	Rec 9.12.44; Del 10.12.44
43-30523	L-4H	7th Armd Div	CC from Maastricht 1.11.44
43-30529	L-4H	196th FA Gp	Rec and Del 10.1.45; Rec and Salv 5.2.45
43-30531	L-4H	2nd FA Bn	Rec 17.2.45; Del 19.2.45
43-30538	L-4H	737th FA Gp	Rec 4.5.45; Del 737th FA Bn 6.5.45
43-30540	L-4H	211th FA Bn	Rec and Del 8.12.44; CC 15.12.44; Del 20.12.44; Del 4.2.45
43-30545	L-4H	–	Rec 18.2.45; Rec 211th FA Gp 30.1.45; Del 3.2.45
43-36407	L-4A	–	Rec for Rpr 30.12.44; damaged in an air raid on the 50th MR&RS airstrip 1.1.45; Del 2nd FA Bn 10.1.45
43-36504	L-4A	311th FA Gp	Rec 21.3.45
43-36766	L-4A	NUSA	Rec 2.5.45

43-98987	L-5	125th LS	Rec 9.5.45
44-16731	L-5B	NUSA	Rec 10.2.45; Del 9.3.45
44-17104	L-5B	125th LS	Rec 9.5.45; Del 12.5.45
44-17169	L-5B	16th ADG	Rec 27.4.45; Del 95th Inf Div 2.5.45
44-17176	L-5B	XIII Corps	Rec 10.5.45; Del 11.5.45
44-17178	L-5B	XIII Corps	Rec and Del 26.5.45
44-17182	L-5B	8th Armd Div	Rec 12.5.45
44-17189	L-5B	NUSA	Rec 24.4.45; Del 3.5.45; Rec 12.5.45; Del 13.5.45; Rec 19.5.45
44-17200	L-5B	30th Inf Div	Rec 23.5.45; Del 26.5.45
44-17202	L-5B	2nd Armd Div	Del 26.4.45; Rec and Del 2.5.45
44-17209	L-5B	404th FA Gp	Rec and Del 16.5.45
44-17325	L-5C	16th ADG	Rec 26.4.45; Del 35th Inf Div 27.4.45; Rec 35th Inf Div and Del NUSA 4.5.45; Rec NUSA and Del 35th Inf Div 9.5.45; Rec 35th Inf Div and Del NUSA 13.5.45; Rec 21.5.45; Del 35th Inf Div 26.5.45
44-17359	L-5C	16th ADG	Rec 26.4.45; Del 102nd Inf Div 27.4.45
44-17362	L-5C	16th ADG	Rec 26.4.45; Del 5th Arm Div 27.4.45; Rec and Del 7.5.45
44-17460	L-5E	NUSA	Rec and Del 15th ADG 25.4.45; Rec 27.4.45; Del NUSA 28.4.45; Rec and Del 30.4.45
44-17464	L-5E	16th ADG	Rec 27.4.45; Del 29th Inf Div 28.4.45
44-28551*	L-5B	NUSA	Rec 21.5.45; Del 22.5.45
44-70042*	L-4J	35th Inf Div	Rec 10.5.45

(*These serial numbers, as given in the original records, are incorrect; 44-28551 was reserved for a B-24J Liberator (contract cancelled) and 44-70042 was a B-29 Superfortress.)

44-77918	L-4H	516th FA Bn	Rec and Del 27.12.44
44-79545	L-4H	753rd FA Bn	CC from Hunnicum 11.11.44 (see Note 2); Del 252nd FA Bn 6.12.44; Rec and Del 10.12.44; Rec and Del 13.2.45; Rec and Del 7.3.45.
44-79546	L-4H	753rd FA Bn	Rec and Del 10.1.45
44-79547	L-4H	23rd MR	Rec 14.3.45
44-79554	L-4H	–	Rec 21.3.45; Del 95th Inf Div 28.3.45
44-79559	L-4H	XVI Corps	Del 5.12.44
44-79561	L-4H	758th FA Bn	Del 11.2.45; Rec 7.3.45; Rec and Del 11.3.45; Rec and Del 22.5.45
44-79597	L-4H	5th Armd Div	Rec 8.2.45; Del 95th FA Bn 14.2.45
44-79630	L-4H	252nd FA Bn	Rec 6.12.44; Del 472nd FA Gp 25.12.44; Rec and Del 7.1.45; Rec and Del NUSA 14.2.45; Rec and Del 10.5.45

44-79639	L-4H	84th Inf Div	Del 29.5.45
44-79644	L-4H	754th FA Gp	Rec 13.5.45; Del 750th FA Gp 14.5.45
44-79647	L-4H	691st FA Gp	Rec 21.1.45; Del NUSA 24.1.45; Rec 26.2.45; Del 691st FA Bn 24.4.45
44-79651	L-4H	755th FA Bn	Rec and Del 30.11.44; Rec 7.2.45; Del 758th FA Bn 9.2.45; Rec 27.4.45; Del 755th FA Bn 10.2.45
44-79662	L-4H	–	Rec for Rpr 30.12.45; Rec and Del NUSA 14.3.45; Rec and Del 777th FA Bn 28.3.45; Rec and Del 4.4.45; Rec 29.4.45, Del 30.4.45; Rec 19.5.45; Del NUSA 21.5.45; Rec 26.5.45; Del 777th FA Bn 29.5.45
44-79663	L-4H	777th FA Bn	Rec 4.12.44; Del 8.12.44; Rec and Del NUSA 3.1.45; Rec 29.4.45; Del 777th FA Bn 4.5.45
44-79678	L-4H	252nd FA Bn	Rec 29.3.45
44-79681	L-4H	25th FA Bn	Rec 10.12.44; Rec 78th Inf Div 22.1.45; Del 95th Inf Div 6.3.45; Rec 3.5.45; Del NUSA 10.5.45
44-79689	L-4H	XIX Corps	Del 12.2.45
44-79701	L-4H	472nd FA Gp	Rec and Del 5.12.44; Rec 14.12.44; Del 16.12.44; Rec 25.12.44; damaged in an air raid on the 50th MR&RS airstrip 1.1.45; Del 808th FA Bn Rec and Del 472nd FA Gp 20.1.45; Rec and Del 808th FA Gp 27.4.45
44-79709	L-4H	29th Inf Div	Rec and Del 8.12.44; Rec 31.5.45
44-79710	L-4H	472nd FA Gp	Rec and Del 4.12.44; Rec 25.12.44; Del 27.12.44; Rec and Del 2.1.45; Rec 24.1.45; Del 26.1.45; Rec 13.2.45; Del 14.2.45; Del 25.4.45
44-79713	L-4H	808th FA Bn	CC from Maastricht; Salv 29.12.44
44-79716	L-4H	NUSA	Del 4.5.45; Rec and Del 7.5.45
44-79718	L-4H	692nd FA Bn	Rec and Del 27.4.45; Rec and Del 14.5.45
44-79719	L-4H	692nd FA Bn	Rec 31.12.44; Del 1.1.45; Rec and Del 24.1.45
44-79723	L-4H	NUSA	Rec 1.1.45; damaged in an air raid on the 50th MR&RS airstrip 1.1.45; Del 2.1.45
44-79731	L-4H	407th FA Gp	Rec 14.2.45; Del 25th FA Bn 7.3.45
44-79737	L-4H	83rd FA Bn	Salv 9.12.44

44-79741	L-4H	349th FA Bn	Rec and Del 3.1.45; Rec 31.1.45; Del 1.2.45; Rec 11.2.45; Del NUSA 14.2.45; Rec and Del 349th FA Gp 7.5.45; Rec 15.5.45
44-79745	L-4H	401st FA Gp	Rec and Del 22.12.44
44-79765	L-4H	29th Inf Div	Rec 20.1.45; Del 22.1.45
44-79766	L-4H	NUSA	Del 4.5.45
44-79786	L-4H	349th FA Gp	Rec and Del 391st FA Bn 2.5.45
44-79788	L-4H	211th FA Gp	Rec 1.1.45; Del 78th Inf Div 21.1.45; Rec 25.1.45; Del 8.2.45
44-79890	L-4H	79th Inf Div	Rec 26.4.45; Del 28.4.45
44-79918	L-4H	615th FA Gp	Rec 10.1.45; Del 516th FA Bn 10.1.45
44-79924	L-4H	23rd MR	Rec 19.5.45; Del 16th ADG 28.5.45
44-79937	L-4H	809th FA Gp	Rec 24.12.44; Del 26.12.44
44-79938	L-4H	104th Inf Div	Rec 12.1.45; Del 690th FA Bn 31.1.45; Rec NUSA 14.2.45; Del 258th FA Gp 25.2.45; Rec 119th Inf Div 1.3.45; Del 2.3.45
44-79950	L-4H	207th FA Bn	Del 9.2.45
44-79953	L-4H	84th Inf Div	Rec 26.4.45; Del 2.5.45
44-79954	L-4H	NUSA	Rec 7.2.45; Del 584th FA Bn 19.2.45; Rec 31.5.45
44-79960	L-4H	104th Inf Div	Rec 25.1.45; Del 407th FA Gp 14.2.45; Rec and Del NUSA 23.2.45
44-79965	L-4H	516th FA Bn	Rec and Del 27.12.45
44-80013	L-4H	102nd Inf Div	Del 102nd Inf Div 1.12.44
44-80022	L-4H	NUSA	Rec 1.1.45; damaged in an air raid on the 50th MR&RS (63-C) airstrip 1.1.45; Del 3.1.45; Rec 31.3.45; Rec and Del 3.5.45; Rec 14.5.45 and 22.5.45
44-80029	L-4H	45th ADG	Rec 31.3.45
44-80035	L-4H	758th FA Bn	Rec 9.2.45; Del 10.2.45; Del 31.5.45
44-80036	L-4H	XIII Corps	Del 5.12.44; Rec 83rd Armd Div 13.1.2.44; Del 14.12.44; Rec and Del Third Army FA 1.1.45
44-80037	L-4H	–	Damaged in an air raid on the 50th MR&RS airstrip 1.1.45; Del NUSA 22.2.45
44-80042	L-4H	2nd Armd Div	Rec and Del 3.12.44; Rec 26.4.45; Del 2.5.45; Rec 25.5.45
44-80049	L-4J	102nd Inf Div	Rec 1.12.44; Del FUSA 18.12.44
44-80061	L-4J	102nd Inf Div	Rec 3.12.44; Del 24.12.44
44-80083	L-4J	102nd Inf Div	Rec and Del 9.1.45; Del 793rd FA Bn 3.5.45

44-80091	L-4J	30th Inf Div	Rec 7.2.45; Del 10.2.45
44-80095	L-4J	102nd Inf Div	Rec 3.1.45; Del 258th FA Bn 6.2.45; Rec 25th FA Bn 5.3.45
44-80107	L-4J	84th Inf Div	Rec 27.4.45; Del NUSA 10.5.45
44-80110	L-4J	23rd MR	Rec 23.3.45
44-80113	L-4J	909th FA Bn	Del 6.12.44; Rec and Del 84th Inf Div 22.12.44
44-80116	L-4J	2nd Armd Div	Rec 6.4.45
44-80120	L-4J	695th FA Bn	Del 2.5.45; Rec 28.5.45
44-80124	L-4J	102nd Inf Div	Rec and Del 22.12.44; Rec and Del XIII Corps 6.1.45; Rec 22.2.45
44-80127	L-4J	84th Inf Div	Rec and Salv 2.5.45
44-80128	L-4J	102nd Inf Div	Rec and Del 9.1.45
44-80133	L-4J	102nd Inf Div	Rec and Del 6.1.45
44-80139	L-4J	84th Inf Div	Rec and Del 6.1.45; Rec NUSA 17.5.45 and Del 19.5.45
44-80145	L-4J	–	Rec and Del 7.1.45; Rec NUSA 13.2.45; Del 102nd Inf Div 14.2.45; Rec 14.3.45; Del 2nd Armd Div 4.4.45
44-80149	L-4J	–	Rec and Del 1.1.45
44-80153	L-4J	NUSA	Del 15.5.45
44-80157	L-4J	NUSA	Rec and Salv 6.3.45
44-80161	L-4J	102nd Inf Div	Rec and Del 8.1.45; Rec 7.2.45; Del 8.2.45; Rec and Del 14.3.45
44-80162	L-4J	–	Picked up from Brussels 18.1.45; Del NUSA 19.2.45
44-80183	L-4J	325th FA Bn	Rec 6.12.44; Del 84th Inf Div 8.12.44
44-80186	L-4J	A-93 Liège	Rec 14.2.45; Del 696th FA Bn 28.2.45
44-80187	L-4J	Liège Depot	Rec 5.12.44; Del 228th FA Bn 29.12.44
44-80188	L-4J	Liège Depot	Rec 5.12.44; Del 78th Inf Div 26.12.44; Rec 13.1.45; Del 203rd FA Bn 8.2.45
44-80193	L-4J	261st FA Gp	Rec 17.1.45; Rec 25.1.45; Del NUSA 30.1.45; Rec and Del 261st FA Bn 15.3.45; Rec and Del 2.5.45
44-80200	L-4J	–	Picked up from Brussels 18.1.45; Del NUSA 5.2.45; Rec 38th Inf Div 16.5.45; Del 35th Inf Div 23.5.45
44-80201	L-4J	261st FA Bn	Rec and Del 10.1.45; Del 19.1.45; CC from Engleshoven 3.2.45 and Salv 26.3.45 (see Note 2)
44-80208	L-4J	NUSA	Rec 20.1.45; Del 407th FA Gp 1.3.45; Rec and Del 5.3.45; Rec and Del 24.3.45; Rec and Del 6.4.45; Del 26.4.45

44-80211	L-4J	Liège Depot	Rec 5.1.45; Del Arty Gp 20.1.45
44-80212	L-4J	A-93 Liège	Rec 13.2.45; Del NUSA 9.3.45; Rec 31.3.45; Rec 27.4.45; Del 28.4.45; Rec 22.5.45; Del 25.4.45
44-80215	L-4J	Liège	Rec 5.1.45; Del 104th Inf Div 24.1.45
44-80220	L-4J	A-93 Liège	Rec 26.2.45; Del NUSA 10.3.45
44-80223	L-4J	A-93 Liège	Rec 26.2.45; Del 84th Inf Div 2.3.45
44-80226	L-4J	Liège Depot	Rec 5.12.44; Del FUSA 18.12.44
44-80232	L-4J	–	Picked up from Brussels 18.1.45; Del 978th FA Bn 6.3.45; Rec 14.3.45; Del 311th FA Gp 21.3.45; Del NUSA 10.5.45
44-80233	L-4J	690th FA Bn	CC from Brochelen 3.3.45 (see Note 2); Rec Liège 5.1.45 (63-J); Del 69th FA Bn (?) 21.1.45
44-80235	L-4J	202nd FA Gp	Del 6.2.45; Rec and Del 261st FA Bn 4.3.45; Rec 25.4.45, Del 28.4.45; Rec 23.5.45; Del 24.5.45
44-80236	L-4J	Liège Depot	Rec 5.12.44
44-80239	L-4J	102nd Inf Div	Del 5.1.45; Rec XVI Corps 25.2.45; Rec NUSA 14.3.45; Del 258th FA Bn 17.3.45; Rec 258th FA Gp 2.5.45; Del 7.5.45
44-80240	L-4J	Liège	Rec 5.1.45; Rec NUSA 1.3.45 and Del 29th Inf Div; Rec 2.5.45; Del 3.5.45
44-80241	L-4J	84th Inf Div	Rec and Del 16.12.44
44-80245	L-4J	Liège Depot	Rec 5.12.44; Del Pool Delivery 30.12.44
44-80276	L-4J	75th Inf Div	Rec 3.5.45; Salv 5.5.45
44-80283	L-4J	78th Inf Div	CC from Rotgen, Germany, 24.12.44; Del 27.12.44
44-80285	L-4J	23rd MR	Rec 19.5.45; Del 16th ADG 28.5.45
44-80292	L-4J	78th Inf Div	Rec 22.1.45; Del 102nd Inf Div 27.4.45
44-80295	L-4J	78th Inf Div	CC from Rotgen, Germany, 24.12.44; Del 27.12.44
44-80298	L-4J	78th Inf Div	Rec 26.12.44; Del 78th Inf Div 25.1.45; Rec 78th Inf Div 8.2.45; Rec 959th FA Bn 7.3.45
44-80302	L-4J	309th FA Bn	Rec and Del 15.5.45
44-80330	L-4J	NUSA	Rec 22.2.45; Del 23.2.45
44-80333	L-4J	NUSA	Rec 17.5.45
44-80337	L-4J	45th Inf Div	Rec and Salv 6.4.45
44-80347	L-4J	A-93 Liège	Recd 12.2.45; Del NUSA 9.3.45; Rec and Del 5th Armd Div 2.5.45
44-80350	L-4J	119th FA Gp	Rec 26.2.45; Del 959th FA Bn 6.3.45
44-80368	L-4J	NUSA	Rec 20.12.44; Del 104th Inf Div 13.1.45

44-80386	L-4J	8th Armd Div	Rec and Del 16.5.45
44-80387	L-4J	275th FA Bn	Rec 5.3.45; Del 7.3.45; Del 25.4.45
44-80395	L-4J	196th FA Gp	Rec 31.5.45
44-80401	L-4J	NUSA	Rec and Del 9.3.45
44-80406	L-4J	349th FA Gp	Rec 26.1.45; Del 29.1.45; Rec 9.2.45; Del 10.2.45; Rec 3.5.45; Del 16.5.45
44-80449	L-4J	8th Armd Div	Rec and Del 13.2.45; Rec and Del 23.2.45
44-80472	L-4J	8th Armd Div	Del 14.5.45
44-80478	L-4J	8th Armd Div	Rec 23.5.45
44-80479	L-4J	8th Armd Div	Rec 6.4.45
44-80523	L-4J	23rd MR	Rec 19.5.45; Del 16th ADG 28.5.45
44-80525	L-4J	17th Abn Div	Rec 6.4.45
44-80535	L-4J	NUSA	Rec and Del 13.3.45; Rec and Del 102nd Inf Div 14.3.45; Rec 24.3.45; Del NUSA 15.5.45
44-80546	L-4J	8th Armd Div	Rec 13.2.45; Del NUSA 14.2.45; Rec 9.3.45; Del 422nd FA Gp 10.3.45
44-80558	L-4J	696th FA Bn	Rec 28.2.45; Del 2nd Armd Div 10.3.45; Rec 4.4.45
44-80568	L-4J	882nd FA Bn	Rec and Del 16.5.45
44-80571	L-4J	84th Inf Div	Rec and Del 2.5.45; Rec 5.5.45; Del 6.5.45; Rec and Del 16.5.45
44-80577	L-4J	102nd Inf Div	Rec 13.2.45; Del NUSA 5.3.45; Del 9.3.45; Rec 31.3.45
44-80580	L-4J	NUSA	Rec 5.4.45; Rec 2nd Armd Div 26.5.45
44-80582	L-4J	A-93 Liège	Rec 26.2.45; Del 197th FA Gp 5.3.45
44-80583	L-4J	745th FA Bn	Rec and Del 26.3.45
44-80591	L-4J	A-93 Liège	Rec 12.2.45; Del 909th FA Bn 9.3.45; Del 239th FA Gp 15.5.45; Rec NUSA 16.5.45; Del 411th FA Bn 26.5.45
44-80597	L-4J	NUSA	Rec 13.2.45; Del 228th FA Gp 25.2.45
44-80603	L-4J	A-93 Liège	Rec 14.2.45; Del 5th Armd Div 25.2.45; Del NUSA 28.2.45
44-80604	L-4J	755th FA Bn	Del 25.4.45
44-80617	L-4J	NUSA	Rec 13.2.45; Del 14.2.45
44-80629	L-4J	A-93 Liège	Rec 26.2.45; Del 95th Inf Div 6.3.45
44-80659	L-4J	763rd FA Gp	Rec and Del 2.5.45
44-80669	L-4J	A-93 Liège	Rec 26.2.45; Rec 5th Armd Div 29.5.45
44-80689	L-4J	252nd FA Gp	Rec 16.5.45
44-80745	L-4J	252nd FA Gp	Rec 14.3.45; Salv 15.3.45
45-4549	L-4J	NUSA	Del 27.4.45; Rec and Del 16.5.45

Appendix 4

The 125th Liaison Squadron

Lineage

30.7.40: Designated 125th Observation Squadron and allotted to the National Guard.
10.2.41: Activated.
15.9.41: Ordered to active service.

Redesignations

13.1.42: 125th Observation Squadron (Light).
4.7.42: 125th Observation Squadron.
2.4.43: 125th Liaison Squadron (inactivated 15.12.45)

Assignments

4.6.44: USSTAF in Europe.
7.6.44: 9th AF (attached principally to HQ Command ETO 7.6.44-17.7.44; to Ninth Army 17.7.44-15.11.44; and to XXIX TAC (Prov) 15.11.44).
1.12.44: IX Fighter Command (attached to XXIX TAC (Prov) and further attached to 12th Army Group 15.11.44-8.6.45; and principally to Sixth Army Group 8.6.45-25.7.45).

Station locations (from date shown)

Cheltenham: 8.6.44
Chedworth: 19.6.44
Erlestoke: 9.7.44 (operating from nearby New Zealand Farm airfield, with detachments in France after 23.8.44)
Saint-Sauveur-Lendelin: 1.9.44
Rennes: 3.9.44
Arlon: 1.10.44

Maastricht: 21.10.44
München-Gladbach: 9.3.45
Haltern: 4.4.45
Gütersloh: 12.4.45
Brunswick: 24.4.45
Heidelberg: 10.6.45
Frankfurt-on-Main: 25.7.45-15.12.45

125th LS non-combat losses listed in USAAF accident reports

Date	Pilot	Aircraft	Accident location
12.7.44	Quentin L. Anderson	L-5 42-99316	2 miles E of Wilton, Wiltshire
17.7.44	Donald E. Neill	L-5 42-99356	New Zealand Farm (stall)
14.9.44	Henry W. Lishaness	L-5 42-99096	Les Nevens, France
31.10.44	Eugene O'Brien	L-5 42-99301	4 miles N of Heerlen, Holland
14.11.44	John S. Wall	L-5 42-99285 (based Y-44)	Wolk, Belgium
1.12.44	Israel H. Rosner	L-5 42-99307	Maastricht (Y-44)
	Samuel D. Brose	L-5 42-99318	Maastricht (Y-44)
4.12.44	None	L-5 42-99306	Maastricht (Y-44)
5.1.45	Harry R. Eilrich	L-5 42-99303 (based Y-44)	Kornelimünster
13.1.45	Jack S. Pridgen	L-5 42-99284 (based Y-44)	Kornelimünster
19.1.45	None	L-1C 41-19006	Maastricht
	None	L-1C 41-19021	Maastricht
	None	L-5 42-99311	Maastricht
30.1.45	Philipp Kuhn (119th FA)	L-4H 43-29770	Maastricht (Y-44)
7.3.45	Charles P. McBride	L-5 42-99303 (based Y-44)	Vlyringen, Belgium
1.5.45	George E. A. Reinburg Jr	L-5 42-99305	Signy-le-Petit, France

Appendix 5

USAAF serial numbers –
Piper L-4 variants

The following list of serial numbers is intended to help identify the variant (L-4A, B, H or J) of a specific aircraft when this information is not given in the journal reports. L-4Cs, Ds, Es, Fs and Gs are not included here as they were impressed civilian Piper aircraft types not used operationally.

L-4A (including some aircraft originally designated O-59A):
42-15159 to 42-15329
42-36325 to 42-36699
42-36700 to 42-36824
42-38330 to 42-38457
43-29048 to 43-29246

L-4B:
43-491 to 43-1470

L-4H:
43-29247 to 43-30547
43-29049, -29073, -29111, -29144, -29150, -29172, -29173 and -29175
44-79545 to 44-80044

L-4J:
44-80045 to 44-80844
45-4401 to 45-5200
45-55175 to 45-55215
45-55224 to 45-55257 and 45-55259, -55260, -55263, -55264, -55267*
(*The production of some aircraft in this batch was cancelled in August 1945, while others were converted to J3C-65 Cub configuration and sold on the civil market.)

Appendix 6

Piper L-4 aircraft known to have served with the Ninth US Army

The following list (in USAAF serial number sequence) gives the dates on which references are made to specific aircraft in the NUSA Air Journal sections of the main text. Of these aircraft, those handled by the 50th Mobile Reclamation and Repair Squadron (see Appendix 3) are also indicated.

42-15233 – 28.5.45
  -15285 – 50th MR&RS
  -15286 – 15.4.45, and 50th MR&RS
  -29093 – 23.3.45
  -29126 – 23.3.45
  -36166 – 23.3.45
  -36442 – 15.4.45, 17.4.45, 2.5.45, and 50th MR&RS
  -36504 – 23.3.45
  -36766 – 50th MR&RS
43-701 – 50th MR&RS
  -889 – 50th MR&RS
  -891 – 15.4.45, 19.4.45, and 50th MR&RS
  -933 – 50th MR&RS
  -968 – 15.4.45
  -986 – 19.4.45, 30.4.45, and 50th MR&RS
  -1313 – 15 4.45, 19.4.45, and 50th MR&RS
  -1314 – 15.4.45
  -1341 – 19.4.45, 2.5.45, and 50th MR&RS
  -1428 – 15.4.45, 17.4.45, 2.5.45, and 50th MR&RS
  -1432 – 10.5.45, 14.5.45
  -2976 – 4.11.44
  -21932 – 17.4.45
  -28622 – 28.4.45
  -28706 – 24.4.45
  -28770 – 1.2.45
  -29052 – 15.4.45, 17.4.45, and MR&RS
  -29082 – 30.3.45, 15.4.45, 25.5.45

43-29095 – 30.3.45
   -29115 – 30.3.45
   -29126 – 30.3.45
   -29130 – 30.3.45, 15.4.45, 20.4.45, 18.6.45
   -29132 – 15.4.45
   -29161 – 15.4.45, 17.4.45
   -29163 – 31.5.45
   -29185 – 30.3.45
   -29187 – 2.6.45
   -29195 – 30.3.45, 13.4.45
   -29286 – 30.3.45
   -29419 – 16.4.45
   -29487 – 31.3.45, 12.4.45
   -29502 – 31.12.44
   -29503 – 10.5.44
   -29507 – 50th MR&RS
   -29512 – 11.12.44, and 50th MR&RS
   -29607 – 28.4.45, and 50th MR&RS
   -29610 – 27.12.44
   -29622 – 18.4.45, and 50th MR&RS
   -29629 – 30.11.44, 2.12.44, 28.12.44, and 50th MR&RS
   -29634 – 50th MR&RS
   -29638 – 11.3.45, and 50th MR&RS
   -29641 – 10.11.44
   -29642 – 19.11.44, and 50th MR&RS
   -29647 – 1.4.45, 15.4.45, and 50th MR&RS
   -29657 – 10.5.45, 25.5.45
   -29663 – 25.5.45
   -29667 – 17.3.45
   -29669 – 28.4.45, 2.5.45
   -29706 – 4.5.45, 5.5.45
   -29710 – 10.5.45
   -29731 – 25.2.45, 26.2.45, 28.2.45, 3.3.45
   -29739 – 31.5.45
   -29756 – 24.4.45
   -29768 – 20.9.44, 21.4.45
   -29770 – 1.2.45, 8.2.45, 20.2.45, 24.2.45
   -29776 – 2.6.45
   -29778 – 25.3.45
   -29780 – 25.5.45
   -29788 – 7.5.45
   -29791 – 4.3.45
   -29792 – 10.5.45

43-29793 – 28.5.45
  -29809 – 25.5.45
  -29810 – 12.1.45
  -29831 – 28.10.44, 31.10.44
  -29850 –10.5.45
  -29905 – 30.4.45
  -29968 – 2.5.45
  -30002 – 17.5.45
  -30004 – 2.4.45, 31.3.45
  -30010 – 13.4.45
  -30013 – 30.4.45
  -30016 – 25.2.45
  -30022 – 31.3.45
  -30027 – 10.5.45, 25.5.45
  -30040 – 17.4.45
  -30044 – 31.3.45
  -30046 – 7.3.45
  -30051 – 25.1.45, 2.2.45, 25.5.45
  -30061 – 2.3.45, 3.3.45, 17.3.45, 7.5.45
  -30066 – 10.5.45, 25.5.45
  -30078 – 28.2.45
  -30091 – 17.11.44
  -30104 – 25.2.45, 17.3.45
  -30124 – 31.5.45
  -30152 – 10.5.45
  -30164 – 10.5.45, 25.5.45
  -30178 – 10.5.45, 28.5.45
  -30200 – 13.3.45
  -30205 – 18.6.45
  -30207 – 24.4.45, 14.9.44, 17.9.44, 28.2.45
  -30215 – 28.2.45, 4.3.45, 5.3.45, 23.3.45
  -30229 – 10.11.44
  -30237 – 27.10.44, 4.11.44, 10.11.44, 13.11.44
  -30249 – 1.3.45
  -30252 – 14.4.45
  -30282 – 5.3.45, 4.4.45
  -30287 – 28.5.45, 31.5.45
  -30292 – 14.1.45, 30.1.45
  -30296 – 5.3.45, 7.3.45
  -30304 – 19.11.44
  -30310 – 20.9.44, 4.11.44
  -30332 – 12.9.44
  -30341 – 7.5.45, 9.5.45

43-30352 – 1.11.44
  -30362 – 28.2.45
  -30373 – 7.6.45
  -30385 – 4.5.45, 5.5.45
  -30388 – 26.4.45, 7.5.45
  -30396 – 10.2.45, 4.3.45
  -30401 – 13.4.45, 7.6.45, and MR&RS
  -30411 – 14.5.45
  -30446 – 10.5.45
  -30454 – 17.2.45, 20.2.45
  -30464 – 10.5.45
  -30479 – 20.5.45
  -30486 – 2.6.45
  -30495 – March-April narrative and 15.11.44, 30.11.44, 2.12.44, 12.4.45
  -30497 – 13.3.45, 25.3.45
  -30498 – 20.5.45
  -30503 – 4.6.45
  -30513 – 17.9.44, 26.9.44
  -30523 – 14.9.44, 24.10.44, 29.10.44, 31.10.44, 4.11.44, 10.11.44, 20.2.45, 31.5.45
  -30528 – 24.3.45
  -30529 – 3.2.45, 5.2.45
  -30531 – 12.9.44
  -30532 – 10.5.45
  -30540 – 14.12.44
  -30543 – 10.5.45
  -30546 – 8.3.45
  -30961 – 12.5.45
  -36229 – 2.12.44
  -36354 – 31.5.45
  -36504 – 7.6.45
  -36776 – 5.3.45
  -36787 – 28.5.45
  -38006 – 16.5.45
  -39629 – 25.12.44
  -49768 – 25.2.45
44-70042 – 50th MR&RS
  -77918 – 50th MR&RS
  -79423 – 13.6.45
  -79545 – 5.12.44, and 50th MR&RS
  -79546 – 50th MR&RS
  -79547 – 50th MR&RS
  -79548 – 13.11.44
  -79554 – 21.3.45, 5.4.45, and 50th MR&RS

44-79559 – 17.11.44, 23.11.44, 25.11.44, 30.11.44, and 50th MR&RS

-79560 – 2.11.44

-79561 – 2.11.44, and 50th MR&RS

-79597 – 50th MR&RS

-79625 – 24.10.44

-79626 – 29.10.44

-79630 – 5.12.44, 24.12.44, and 50th MR&RS

-79639 – 20.4.45, and 50th MR&RS

-79644 – 50th MR&RS

-79647 – 50th MR&RS

-79651 – 50th MR&RS

-79661 – 2.11.44

-70662 – 50th MR&RS

-79663 – 50th MR&RS

-79664 – 2.11.44

-79665 – 2.11.44, 22.12.44, 24.12.44, 31.12.44, 4.1.45, 31.1.45, 16.5.45

-79669 – 17.3.45

-79671 – 25.10.44, 1.11.44, 2.11.44

-79672 – 24.10.44, 27.10.44, 13.4.45

-79676 – 6.3.45

-79678 – 50th MR&RS

-79681 – 20.1.45, 29.1.45, 20.2.45, 6.3.45, 2.5.45, 6.5.45, 7.5.45, 9.5.45, and 50th MR&RS

-79689 – 4.2.45, 50th MR&RS

-79691 – 29.10.44

-79701 – 6.11.44, 24.12.44, 27.12.44, and 50th MR&RS

-79709 – 50th MR&RS

-79710 – 22.1.45, and 50th MR&RS

-79713 – 2.11.44, 27.12.44, and 50th MR&RS

-79716 – 16.3.45, 20.5.45, and 50th MR&RS

-79717 – 9.4.45, 10.4.45

-79718 – 50th MR&RS

-79719 – 50th MR&RS

-79723 – 50th MR&RS

-79731 – 2.11.44, 13.2.45, 3.3.45, 7.3.45, and 50th MR&RS

-79733 – 2.11.44

-79737 – 12.9.44, 5.12.44, 9.12.44, and 50th MR&RS

-79741 – 2.11.44, 13.5.45, 18.5.45, and 50th MR&RS

-79743 – 2.11.44

-79744 – 25.10.44, 10.11.44

-79745 – 50th MR&RS

-79762 – 2.11.44

-79765 – 50th MR&RS

-79766 – 50th MR&RS

44-79768 – 10.11.44

  -79774 – 13.3.45

  -79775 – 12.9.44

  -79776 – 12.9.44

  -79778 – 13.3.45

  -79781 – 17.2.45

  -79786 – 12.4.45, 2.5.45, and 50th MR&RS

  -79788 – 28.12.44, 11.1.45, 23.1.45, and 50th MR&RS

  -79789 – 2.11.44

  -79790 – 50th MR&RS

  -79793 – 12.9.44

  -79889 – 29.10.44, 10.4.45

  -79890 – 50th MR&RS

  -79904 – 29.10.44

  -79905 – 29.10.44

  -79911 – 29.1044

  -79916 – 29.10.44

  -79918 – 50th MR&RS

  -79919 – 29.10.44

  -79921 – 29.10.44

  -79924 – 10.5.45, 25.5.45, and 50th MR&RS

  -79926 – 29.10.44

  -79929 – 29.10.44

  -79933 – 24.4.45

  -79935 – 29.10.44

  -79936 – 29.10.44, 30.1.45

  -79937 – 50th MR&RS

  -79938 – 11.1.45, 21.1.45, 27.1.45, 4.2.45, 24.2.45, and 50th MR&RS

  -79939 – 29.10.44

  -79945 – 29.10.44

  -79949 – 29.10.44, 31.10.44, 31.5.45

  -79950 – 17.1.45, 3.2.45, and 50th MR&RS

  -79953 – 29.10.44, and 50th MR&RS

  -79954 – 29.10.44, 31.10.44, 31.1.45, 6.2.45, 4.5.45, 28.5.45, and 50th MR&RS

  -79960 – 23.1.45, 13.2.45, 28.2.45, 4.3.45, and 50th MR&RS

  -79965 – 50th MR&RS

  -79991 – 2.11.44

  -79999 – 2.11.44

  -80004 – 13.3.45

  -80009 – 30.3.45

  -80010 – 16.4.45

  -80013 – 17.11.44, 23.11.44, 26.11.44, and 50th MR&RS

  -80022 – 15.11.44, 13.3.45, and 50th MR&RS

44-80024 – 4.12.44

  -80027 – 8.3.45

  -80029 – 50th MR&RS

  -80030 – 17.11.44

  -80031 – 17.11.44

  -80035 – 50th MR&RS

  -80036 – 17.11.44, 23.11.44, 5.11.44, and 50th MR&RS

  -80037 – 15.11.44, 21.2.45, and 50th MR&RS

  -80042 – 15.11.44, 8.1.45, 30.4.45, and 50th MR&RS

  -80044 – 2.11.44

  -80049 – 29.10.44, 30.11.44, 18.12.44, and 50th MR&RS

  -80061 – 29.10.44, 1.12.44, 2.12.44, 24.12.44, 28.5.45, and 50th MR&RS

  -80083 – 29.10.44, 21.4.45, 2.5.45, and 50th MR&RS

  -80091 – 50th MR&RS

  -80095 – 29.10.44, 1.1.45, 20.1.45, 3.3.45, 5.3.45, 7.4.45, and 50th MR&RS

  -80102 – 6.1.45

  -80107 – 4.12.44, 24.4.45, 7.6.45, and 50th MR&RS

  -80110 – 21.3.45, 15.4.45, 17.4.45, and 50th MR&RS

  -80113 – 50th MR&RS

  -80116 – 1.4.45, and 50th MR&RS

  -80118 – 17.11.44

  -80119 – 25.11.44, 8.12.44, 9.12.44

  -80120 – 19.4.45, 28.4.45, and 50th MR&RS

  -80121 – 50th MR&RS

  -80124 – 29.10.44, 21.2.45, 16.5.45

  -80127 – 10.4.45, and 50th MR&RS

  -80128 – 29.10.44, and 50th MR&RS

  -80133 – 29.10.44

  -80138 – 50th MR&RS

  -80139 – 50th MR&RS

  -80143 – 10.2.45

  -80145 – 29.10.44, 11.3.45, 1.4.45, 7.4.45, and 50th MR&RS

  -80149 – 29.10.44, 5.5.45, 7.5.45, 9.5.45, and 50th MR&RS

  -80153 – 7.4.45, and 50th MR&RS

  -80157 – 4.3.45 and 50th MR&RS

  -80158 – 25.12.44

  -80159 – 18.5.45

  -80161 – 29.10.44, and 50th MR&RS

  -80162 – 13.1.45, 17.2.45, and 50th MR&RS

  -80163 – 10.3.45

  -80175 – 10.3.45

  -80183 – 50th MR&RS

  -80186 – 27.12.44, 29.1.45, 13.2.45, 27.2.45, and 50th MR&RS

44-80187 – 3.12.44, 27.12.44, and 50th MR&RS
  -80188 – 3.12.44, 4.12.44, 11.1.45, 1.2.45, 2.2.45, and 50th MR&RS
  -80193 – 50th MR&RS
  -80196 – 10.5.45, 14.5.45, 7.6.45
  -80198 – 10.12.44
  -80200 – 13.1.45, 29.1.45, 2.2.45, and 50th MR&RS
  -80201 – 2.2.45, 1.3.45, 24.3.45, 6.5.45, and 50th MR&RS
  -80203 – 19.2.45
  -80206 – 4.12.44, 13.1.45
  -80208 – 21.1.45, 1.3.45, and 50th MR&RS
  -80211 – 2.1.45, 4.1.45, 14.1.45, and 50th MR&RS
  -80212 – 11.2.45, 13.2.45, and 50th MR&RS
  -80215 – 2.1.45, 4.1.45, 22.1.45, 23.1.45, 14.5.45
  -80217 – 12.4.45
  -80220 – 25.2.45, 8.3.45, and 50th MR&RS
  -80223 – 25.2.45, 27.2.45, 28.2.45, and 50th MR&RS
  -80226 – 3.12.44, 4.12.44, 18.12.44, and 50th MR&RS
  -80232 – 13.1.45, 6.3.45, 23.3.45, 30.4.45, 5.5.45, and 50th MR&RS
  -80233 – 2.1.45, 4.1.45, 16.1.45, 17.1.45, 25.1.45, 25.2.45, 3.3.45, and 50th MR&RS
  -80235 – 2.1.45, 4.1.45, 29.1.45, 2.2.45, 21.4.45, and 50th MR&RS
  -80236 – 50th MR&RS
  -80238 – 25.12.44
  -80239 – 3.12.44, 4.12.44, 5.12.44, 1.1.45, 24.2.45, and 50th MR&RS
  -80240 – 2.1.45, 4.1.45, 16.1.45, 17.1.45, 4.2.45, 28.2.45, 30.4.45
  -80241 – 5.4.45, 5.5.45, 4.6.45, and 50th MR&RS
  -80245 – 3.12.44, 4.12.44, 28.12.44, and 50th MR&RS
  -80248 – 10.3.45
  -80276 – 29.4.45, 30.4.45, and 50th MR&RS
  -80283 – 23.12.44, 24.12.44, 27.12.44, and 50th MR&RS
  -80285 – 10.5.45, 25.5.45, and 50th MR&RS
  -80292 – 20.1.45, 23.1.45, 30.1.45, 24.2.45, and 50th MR&RS
  -80295 – 23.12.44, 24.12.44, 25.12.44, 27.12.44, and 50th MR&RS
  -80298 – 24.12.44, 25.12.44, 20.1.45, 21.1.45, 23.1.45, 30.1.45, 25.2.45, and 50th MR&RS
  -80302 – 50th MR&RS
  -80325 – 10.5.45
  -80330 – 50th MR&RS
  -80333 – 20.5.45 and 50th MR&RS
  -80335 – 18.3.45, 13.4.45, 16.4.45
  -80337 – 16.3.45, 25.3.45, 3.4.45, and 50th MR&RS
  -80340 – 10.3.45
  -80344 – 10.3.45
  -80345 – 4.12.44
  -80347 – 11.2.45, 18.3.45, 16.5.45, and 50th MR&RS

44-80350 – 24.2.45, 6.3.45, and 50th MR&RS

   -80358 – 4.12.44, 7.3.45

   -80368 – 3.12.44, 5.12.44, 11.1.45, and 50th MR&RS

   -80373 – 8.3.45

   -80377 – 14.4.45, 16.4.45

   -80380 – 4.12.44

   -80386 – 50th MR&RS

   -80387 – 50th MR&RS

   -80388 – 6.5.45

   -80393 – 12.4.45, 18.5.45

   -80395 – 16.3.45, 13.4.45, 31.5.45, and 50th MR&RS

   -80401 – 50th MR&RS

   -80405 – 10.3.45

   -80406 – 2.5.45, 18.5.45, and 50th MR&RS

   80449 – 7.4.45, and 50th MR&RS

   -80472 – 50th MR&RS

   -80478 – 50th MR&RS

   -80479 – 4.4.45, and MR&RS

   -80480 – 13.1.45

   -80487 – 13.3.45, 7.4.45

   -80503 – 13.4.45, 10.5.45

   -80523 – 50th MR&RS

   -80525 – 25.3.45

   -80533 – 12.5.45

   -80535 – 10.3.45, 12.3.45, 23.3.45, 15.4.45, 7.6.45, and 50th MR&RS

   -80536 – 13.4.45

   -80546 – 10.3.45, and 50th MR&RS

   -80547 – 13.3.45

   -80548 – 10.3.45, 13.6.45

   -80556 – 31.3.45

   -80558 – 25.2.45, 26.2.45, 27.2.45, and 50th MR&RS

   -80563 – 2.6.45

   -80564 – 10.3.45

   -80567 – 10.2.45

   -80568 – 50th MR&RS

   -80571 – 50th MR&RS

   -80574 – 10.5.45

   -80575 – 16.4.45

   -80577 – 11.2.45, 13.2.45, 31.3.45, 13.4.45, 16.4.45, 28.4.45, and 50th MR&RS

   -80579 – 13.4.45

   -80580 – 50th MR&RS

   -80582 – 25.2.45, 4.3.45, and 50th MR&RS

   -80583 – 16.4.45, and 50th MR&RS

44-80585 – 7.5.45

    -80591 – 11.2.45, 18.3.45, and 50th MR&RS

    -80597 – 11.2.45, 13.2.45, 25.2.45, 15.6.45, and 50th MR&RS

    -80603 – 11.2.45, 13.2.45, 25.2.45, 15.4.45, and 50th MR&RS

    -80604 – 50th MR&RS

    -80613 – 10.2.45

    -80617 – 50th MR&RS

    -80629 – 25.2.45, 6.3.45, and 50th MR&RS

    -80645 – 8.3.45

    -80659 – 50th MR&RS

    -80665 – 10.3.45

    -80669 – 25.2.45, 2.3.45, and 50th MR&RS

    -80672 – 10.2.45

    -80689 – 13.5.45, and 50th MR&RS

    -80745 – 11.3.45, and 50th MR&RS

    -80755 – 6.5.45, 7.5.45, 9.5.45

    -80774 – 28.2.45

    -80778 – 16.5.45

    -80954 – 17.2.45

45-4158 – 28.5.45

    -4520 – 31.5.45

    -4549 – 19.4.45, 18.6.45, and 50th MR&RS

    -9543 – 15.4.45